KEN DODD

MICHAEL O'MARA BOOKS LIMITED

First published in Great Britain in 2005 by
Michael O'Mara Books Limited
9 Lion Yard, Tremadoc Road
London SW4 7NQ

This paperback edition first published in 2018

A CIP catalogue record for this book is available
from the British Library

ISBN: 978-1-78929-008-0 in paperback format
ISBN: 978-1-84317-731-9 in ePub format format
ISBN: 978-1-84317-732-6 in Mobipocket format

1 3 5 7 9 10 8 6 4 2

www.mombooks.com

Designed and typeset by Martin Bristow
Printed and bound by CPI Group (UK) Ltd, Croydon, CR0 4YY

Photograph Acknowledgements

PAGE 1: Pictorial Press (*above right*), TopFoto.co.uk (*below*);
PAGE 2: PA/Empics (*above left*), Mirrorpix.com (*below*);
PAGE 3: Hulton/Getty (*above right* and *below left*), Percy Hatchman/Rex
Features (*below right*); PAGE 4: PA/Empics (*above left* and *below left*),
Hulton Getty (*below right*); PAGE 5: Harry Goodwin/Rex Features
(*above left*), Liverpool Echo (*above right*), Mirrorpix.com (*below right*);
PAGE 6: Mirrorpix.com (*all*); PAGE 7: UPPA/TopFoto.co.uk (*above left*),
Adam Butler/PA/Empics (*below*); PAGE 8: Jim Duxbury/Rex Features
(*above left*), Nils Jorgensen/Rex Features (*below right*).

Contents

For Kate. And Sheila.

Acknowledgements

IT HAS BEEN A LONG, hard slog from the broken-biscuit repair works of Knotty Ash to the finished volume you're excitedly clutching in your eager hands. There were times that I thought this book would never see the light of day, but that it has is due in part to the following individuals, who were so generous with their time: Ken Campbell, Ian Clayton, Sir Bill Cotton, Mike Craig, Michael Grade, Peter Hepple, Roy Hudd, George Melly, David Nobbs, Denis Norden, Steve Punt, Joe Riley, Arthur Smith, Alison Steadman, Professor Richard Wiseman and Victoria Wood. Special thanks also go to Jimmy Perry for contributing a perfectly splendid foreword.

I would also like to thank Clare Brotherwood, Sue Norris, Charlotte Stock, my agent Guy Rose, Alexandra Connor, and, at Michael O'Mara Books, Lindsay Davies, Helen Cumberbatch and Diana Briscoe.

In attempting to learn who's the Doddy, I've been left with many cherishable memories: such as Michael Grade, with omnipresent cigar, sitting behind a desk the size of a playing field at Pinewood Studios, telling me that he could only spare me half an hour of his time – an hour later he was performing Frank Randle's act for me; there was the early morning whisky shared with George Melly (now sadly deceased since this book was first published in 2005); the on-off flirtation with Ann Widdecombe MP over possible interview dates (which eventually came to nothing); and the hour it took to get a word in while Mike Craig was telling me how long Dodd goes on! Oh, and then there was the morning a succession of friends phoned to let me know that Dodd was appearing on *My Favourite Hymns* (so Jerry, that's what you young bucks do on a Sunday morning!). It is my hope that the resulting book goes some way to providing an answer to the question: what makes Ken Dodd tick?

Little is to be learned from merely listing his CV, however; it is far more interesting to examine the facts of his life while analysing his methods and motivations, particularly when one considers that analysis – both of his own work and of the mechanics of comedy – have been the cornerstone of Dodd's career.

It is a great pity that Dodd has never got round to removing the dust cover from his ancient Amstrad word processor and writing his own life story himself – so far, his literary output has been confined to a handful of Diddymen annuals and a book about butties. I, for one, would have been delighted to learn more about the comedy theories that he has hinted at over the years – for example, what exactly are the 'joke-creation formulas' that he mentioned at his tax trial?

It is also a shame that Dodd steadfastly ignored my numerous requests for an interview, though I derive some crumb of comfort from the fact that it was nothing personal, as he is still very much a private man these days, and only prepared to talk to a select few. Nonetheless, walking a tightrope between objectivity and admiration, I have done my best to present a fair and balanced account of one of the most unique talents this country has ever produced.

STEPHEN GRIFFIN, 2005

Foreword

IN MARCH 2004, I went to see Ken Dodd at the De Montfort Hall in Leicester. This involved a long car journey in dreadful weather, but that night is something I shall always remember as perhaps one of the few great performances of a stand-up comedian that I have ever seen.

The hall, which held over 2,000 people, was packed. Promptly on time, the lights went down and the band played 'Love Is Like A Violin'. On came Doddy, dressed in all his props and waving his tickling stick. There was a huge roar of affection from the audience and then Kenny took control.

Later I looked round. Most of the audience were in their sixties or seventies, and it was now past one o'clock in the morning. But no one had left. How they all got home, I'll never know. During those five hours, Ken Dodd had cast a magic spell over us and we didn't care about anything.

Just before the war I remember seeing the great Max Miller at the Chiswick Empire. Max was at the height of his fame. He said to the audience, 'There'll be no one to take my place after I've gone, lady.'

There'll be no one to take Ken Dodd's place after *he's* gone. But don't worry, Doddy – we're all coming with you!

JIMMY PERRY, OBE

Introduction

'It's fifteen years since I went out of my mind
– I'd never go back.'

IT'S 1980-SOMETHING on a cold, grey evening inside the now-defunct, authority-run Venue theatre in Borehamwood, where a cold, grey audience fidget uneasily on their cold, grey stack chairs. The breeze-block walls leach the place of any atmosphere – it's about as far from the lush, plush, crimson velour womb of Auntie's *The Good Old Days* as it's possible to get.

Then, from the wings explodes a vision in full-length, pillar-box-red fun fur, banging the largest drum this side of Knotty Ash. The beating is relentless. 'Do you give in?' threatens the only man in the world who can eat a tomato through a tennis racket.

We're off!

Comedian, singer and all-round entertainer, Ken Dodd has set the tone for the evening (and possibly early morning) to come. For 'relentless' is the only word to describe his act: less of a comedy set, it is more an assault on the senses, or as he puts it, 'a feast of fun and a challenge to the kidneys'. Actor Roy Barraclough has correctly observed that Dodd's is the only show during which the audience can get deep-vein thrombosis.

'This is like antibiotics,' Dodd warns the faithful – a sea of loose dentures and drying plastic pixie hoods – 'you have to finish the course!' And he's right. Once he starts he's unstoppable – like a runaway train. 'This isn't television, Missus,' he taunts, impishly fixing a gimlet eye on a suitable matron, 'you can't switch me off!'

Not even the failure of the National Grid fazes Dodd. In February 2004, when a power cut plunged the Stockport Plaza into darkness and silenced the microphones, the old trooper simply grabbed a torch, executed an impromptu tap-dance and carried on regardless. As his publicist Robert Holmes pointed out after the performance, 'The show and the audience are the most important things to Ken. The lights went out, but that doesn't stop Ken; nothing stops Ken.'

It seems churlish to complain, but this relentlessness on Dodd's part can be almost wearingly funny: the paroxysms he has been known to induce can tax his acolytes more than the Inland Revenue taxed their hero. Subjected to an average of twelve jokes a minute during a four- or five-hour gagfest, very soon members of his audience neither know what joke they are laughing at, nor do they care.

This, then, was my conversion to Ken Dodd: Hertfordshire an unlikely Damascus. Wielding his tickling stick like a wand, that evening he performed a miracle and brought some much-needed colour to Borehamwood. One has to acknowledge, however, that it is tough being a Dodd evangelist. To the ignorant – those not fortunate enough to have experienced one of his live comedy shows – Dodd is merely a purveyor of Diddymen and sugary ballads, and it is difficult to persuade them otherwise. As BBC Chairman Michael Grade, who worked with Dodd when he was a player in the variety business, operating as an agent and producer of summer seasons, remarks: 'He's so good, but the trouble is that people think, "Oh no, not Ken Dodd." Then you say, "Have you ever seen him live?" And they always say, "No, only on television." And you say, "Well, you've never seen Ken Dodd. You have not seen Ken Dodd on a Wednesday night, second house at the Opera House, Blackpool, in front of 3,200 people just wetting themselves laughing." I used to stand at the side and just watch the audience rocking . . . gales, wails of laughter . . . begging for mercy.'

Without doubt Ken Dodd is one comic that you have to see live in order to appreciate fully his wealth and depth of comedic talent. Although his television appearances helped to make him a star, the small screen generally tends to constrain and contain him, perhaps with the possible exception of *The Good Old Days* and his *An Audience With . . .* specials. He is quite simply too big for the box – he also requires the luxury of time to weave his particular kind of magic. Essentially a clown, he needs a stage and an audience in order to shine. He is the last of the dinosaurs, the last of his generation of music-hall-inspired variety comics.

Dodd is, in his own words, 'a fireworks comedian'. Not for him the slow burn; he comes on like thunder and never permits the pace to slacken for a moment. At least in the initial stages, most comedians coax and coerce their audience into mirth. Dodd is different: in his capacity as a 'catalyst for laughter' he bludgeons them into submission. Never forgetting for one minute that he was a salesman, he becomes again the barker he once was; where once he peddled ironmongery, he now trades in laughter.

The now-thinning nimbus of hair, the impossible orthodontics, the prehensile digits and the plumptious, tattifilarious vocabulary all conspire to present a man at odds with this world. He is a prime example of J. B. Priestley's assertion that the comic greats are aliens. 'Welcome to My World' is Harry

Hill's signature tune, but it would have been equally suited to Dodd if he hadn't chosen 'Happiness' for his theme music.

It has to be said that much of Dodd's material is as pensionable as his audience – curiously (and comfortingly) old-fashioned. Betraying his roots as a ventriloquist, he still trots out the monosyllabic dummy, Dickie Mint; he continues to render 'On the Road to Mandalay', bedecked with everything and the kitchen sink, in a homage to music-hall comedian Billy Bennett; and as recently as the last Gulf conflict he told us how he knew it was going to be bad when he passed Vera Lynn's dressing room and heard her gargling. Yet miraculously, age withers neither him nor his material. Just when you write him off as a tired old has-been he'll wrong-foot you and effortlessly mine a brand new seam of surrealism, bringing his set slap-bang up-to-date. 'Now for the highlight of this evening's show,' he'll suddenly announce, apropos of nothing. 'Release the goats!'

No mean comic analyst (he claims that in another life he would have liked to have been a social psychologist), and with 10,000 books on comedy and showbiz to choose from, he has read everything on the subject, from Freud to Bergson, and Twain to Leacock. He has also proposed quite seriously that there should be a chair of comedy at a university, and has suggested: 'Maybe I'll endow one before I pop off.' Over the years he has meticulously charted the varying responses to his vast repertoire of jokes across the country and cross-referenced them with a map of Britain to produce his unique 'Giggle Map', in an effort to explore which type of joke works best and where. A consequence of this painstaking attention to detail has led to him being called – less than flatteringly, perhaps – 'the slide-rule comic', as if his efforts to invest time and thought into the collective humour of the nation was a bad thing.

A fixture at venues both in Blackpool and the London

Palladium (he still holds the Palladium record for the longest-running comedy show at forty-two weeks), and a memorable Malvolio in *Twelfth Night* at the Liverpool Playhouse in 1971, Dodd has been lauded by such diverse luminaries as Kenneth Branagh, Roy 'Chubby' Brown, Alison Steadman, John Osborne, Lenny Henry and Johnny Vegas (who queued for an hour just to shake his hand). Sir Derek Jacobi, who appeared with Dodd in Branagh's film of *Hamlet*, tells me he is an enormous fan and finds him hysterically funny, and former Frankie Goes To Hollywood producer Trevor Horn has gone on record as admiring the comedian's singing voice. Even those trendy young bloods at www.chortle.co.uk have found favour with Dodd's act. 'I must admit,' Chortle's reviewer almost grudgingly volunteered, 'that I never thought I'd be quite so impressed.'

In 1990 Eric Sykes took time out of his own *This Is Your Life* programme to pay this fulsome tribute to his friend: 'I would like to say to all the young people who are young comics, who feel like they want to come up in this business, whatever you do don't watch television, because if you do you'll only get steeped in mediocrity. All you've got to do is to save up the money and go and see this fella here. Because if you think that you can do what he does then you have a place, because this man is a Chippendale in a room full of G-Plan furniture.'

When Reader's Digest polled its readers to vote for their favourite British comedian in 2004, Ken Dodd came in at a very respectable sixth position, behind Tommy Cooper, Peter Kay, Billy Connolly, Morecambe and Wise, and Bob Monkhouse respectively – not bad for a relative stranger to the cathode-ray tube in the twenty-first century. But most impressive, perhaps, is the esteem with which his peers regard him. In 1988 the *Observer* asked thirteen comedians to vote for their favourite fellow comic. No one but Dodd bagged more than one vote: he netted four – from Victoria Wood, Tom O'Connor, Bob Monkhouse and Bernard Manning. Despite Manning's apparent admiration, however, it didn't stop him delivering the following barb about his colleague: 'Ken Dodd looks like a cross between Bugs Bunny and a Brillo pad. Anybody who is so ugly abuses the privilege of belonging to the human race. If there is such a thing as reincarnation, I hope he comes back as a comic!'

Unusually, Dodd's appeal cuts across every strata of society: he has played royal Christmas parties at Windsor and working men's clubs, picking up accolades as diverse as an OBE and a nomination as one of *Loaded* magazine's Greatest Living Englishmen. His fans encompass everyone from the Queen Mother to Alf Pegg. The latter was the pensioner from Melton Mowbray who, while watching a live performance of *The Ken Dodd Show* in Leicester in 1995, laughed so much that he lost all control of his bodily functions.

'It must have happened halfway through the show,' he informed *Daily Mail* readers, 'but I was laughing so much at Doddy's jokes that I didn't realize until just before the end, when I noticed that my wife was holding her nose with a woolly shawl and pointing towards my "parking space". "Alf," she said, "I think you've crapped yourself." And I had. Now, I've seen most of England's top comedians . . . and none of them have had that effect on me, which must say something for Doddy's comic abilities.'

How many other comic acts have ever provoked such an extreme reaction among their audience? Surely there can be no higher praise.

Michael Grade regards Dodd as being the cream of the crop. 'If we're talking about what in the trade is known as a "front-cloth comic" [the original name for a stand-up comedian], he's certainly the best I ever saw,' Grade assured me. 'I did see Max Miller once, but I was very young. He didn't work on film in the same way that Ken doesn't really work on television: it's really between him and the audience . . . Max and Ken Dodd are the two all-time greats.'

His opinion is echoed by former controller of BBC One, Sir Bill Cotton. 'I think he [Dodd] is probably the foremost stand-up comedian that I've experienced,' he said. 'I always had a great affection for Max Miller [as well]. I suppose I'd mark them even.'

Meanwhile, comedy scriptwriter and broadcaster Denis Norden regards Dodd to be top of the class: 'One of the comedy elite – the dying breed that will live for ever.' And creator of *The Fall and Rise of Reginald Perrin*, David Nobbs, who in his time as a comedians' labourer provided material for the likes of Tommy Cooper, Les Dawson, Frankie Howerd, David Frost and the Two Ronnies, simply says, 'I don't know that there were any funnier than him. In the theatre, I think, he's out on his own. Ken has the stamina – he can go on for hours and hours and is hysterically funny. You know the phrase, "I laughed till my ribs ached"? I thought it was a figure of speech until I went to see Ken Dodd in Bournemouth doing a routine about a man who fell into a vat of glue at a factory in Swindon, and I laughed so much I wanted him to stop.'

Given this adulation, why does this asthmatic, arthritic man, on the cusp of his eighties, continue to roam the land plying his trade in a succession of monochrome venues more tatty than tattifilarious? After all, it is not as if he has anything to prove, and he certainly doesn't need the money. The answer is that quite simply it is his life. He is consumed by comedy; totally driven by the need to make an audience laugh (and perhaps make a few bob for his efforts). His private affairs have always played second fiddle to his professional life. Little is known, for example, about his two long-term girl-friends (never wives, mark). Consequently, the tribulations surrounding *that* court case and the unwanted attentions of a stalker were all unwelcome visitors to Planet Dodd.

Indeed it was the infamous trial in 1989 that found Dodd at his lowest ebb. For one so ferociously private, the experience of having the more intimate details of his life paraded before a panting nation was a nightmare made flesh. Not only were his finances placed under public scrutiny (when a judge asked him what thousands of pounds in a suitcase looked like, Dodd replied, 'The notes are very light,' in a tone as light as the banknotes themselves), his fiancée Anne Jones's fertility problems were also put under the spotlight, while his own insecurities were laid bare and aspects of his eccentric home life revealed. Cryptically, he told the court that he hoarded the money because to him it meant that he was a star. It was evident, therefore, that Dodd's attitude towards his finances was far from conventional.

There is clearly more to Ken Dodd than the amiable buffoon he chooses to present to the world, and though it is not likely to happen, one suspects that if he were to explore the darker side of his nature, a whole new career in drama could be his for the taking – what a chilling Archie Rice he would make. 'My life has been a series of tragedies,' he tells his audience, '. . . culminating in tonight!' Though it is a joke, he tells it with an earnestness that hints at something more.

It is not without irony that so shameless a nostalgia-mongerer should escape the post-modern analysis boom unscathed. Unlike many of his peers – Frankie Howerd, Tommy Cooper, Morecambe and Wise, Les Dawson, Bob Monkhouse, even Benny Hill and Bernard Manning – he has yet to be 'rediscovered' and therefore deconstructed, re-evaluated and reassessed. There are currently no plays about him nor recently published books, no appreciation societies, no websites specifically dedicated to him, and no BBC Four film crews have ever shadowed him. Perhaps because he has always been his own man, he has never been subjected to the vagaries of fashion; he has never experienced the seesaw career of his contemporaries, sliding into and out of favour. The words 'Doddy' and 'trendy' remain obstinately unlikely bedfellows.

Yet as poet Roger McGough pointed out in Dodd's *Heroes of Comedy* programme on Channel Four: 'I can never imagine Ken Dodd never having been there. I grew up in Liverpool and he always seemed to be around. People always talked of Ken Dodd as if he was the pier head.'

Like Corrie or sciatica, Doddy is just there: we take him for granted. Let's appreciate him while we still can . . .

I

The Missing Link of Knotty Ash

WHOLE FORESTS have been sacrificed in a bid to remind us that when it comes to comedy, the great, the good, and Cannon and Ball all hail from the north of England.

After all, George Formby senior was born in Ashton-under-Lyne; his son, along with Ted Ray and Frank Randle, was born in Wigan; Gracie Fields and her protégé Norman Evans came from Rochdale; Hylda Baker from Farnworth; Eric Sykes from Oldham; Frankie Howerd was born in York; Al Read in Salford; Les Dawson and Steve Coogan are from Manchester; Morecambe and Wise hailed from Morecambe and Leeds respectively; Tubby Turner came from Preston; Victoria Wood from Prestwich; Johnny Vegas from St Helens; and Peter Kay from Bolton. Neither should we forget Albert Modley, Dave Morris, Sandy Powell, Harry Worth, Graham Fellowes (alias John Shuttleworth), Bernard Manning, Roy 'Chubby' Brown, nor the members of the League of Gentlemen.

Liverpool alone has given us Billy Bennett, Harry Weldon, Robb Wilton, Fred Yule, Arthur Askey, Tommy Handley, Jimmy Tarbuck, Stan Boardman, Hetty King, Tom O'Connor, Bernie Clifton, Les Dennis, Leonard Rossiter, Norman Vaughan, Patricia Routledge, Alexei Sayle, Craig Charles, Paul O'Grady, Ricky Tomlinson (though he spent his first three days in Blackpool), Mike Burton, Derek Nimmo, Mike Myers's parents, Carla Lane (creator of *The Liver Birds* and *Bread*), oh, and some bloke called Ken Dodd.

But then where does that leave the likes of Marie Lloyd, Dan Leno, Sid Field, Max Miller, Norman Wisdom, Tony Hancock, Terry-Thomas, The Crazy Gang, Max Wall, Bob Monkhouse, Peter Sellers, Kenneth Williams, Benny Hill, Peter Cook, Spike Milligan, Jim Davidson, French and Saunders, Mark Lamarr, Eddie Izzard, Ricky Gervais, and Paul Merton, in the comedy landscape?

No, it is a claim that just doesn't hold water, because it is impossible to prove whether the north has produced more or fewer comics than the south. Funny is funny, regardless of geography, history, gender or background. Some folk are quite simply hilarious, others are not; some are Morecambe and Wise, others are Little and Large.

What is interesting – and this is, of course, a sweeping generalization – is how comedians from the north and south differ. In the old days of variety in particular, northern comics tended to be homely, conspiratorial gossips, who were much warmer and more vulnerable than their southern counterparts. Light years from the homespun ramblings of the very domesticated Al Read or Norman Evans, there was very little vulnerability in the quicksilver delivery of Max Miller or Tommy Trinder. These southerners had far more in common with the New York Jewish strand of comedy; they were more Catskills than Pennines.

'Northern life was different from southern life,' observes Denis Norden, 'and quite a lot of humour is a reflection of shared experience. And shared experience of life in the north was different from that in London. Scotland was another area where the audience recognized that a particular performer was part of their world. Audiences didn't go to heckle in those days, despite what you hear about the Glasgow Empire. They were there to be entertained. There was an equal amount of enjoyment gained from acrobats and tap dancers and what they called "sister acts" – it was a salad. But the comedian was the star.'

Noteworthy, however, is the disproportionate number of Liverpudlian comedians compared to the rest of the country (a study for Comic Relief revealed that Liverpool produces one comic for every 55,000 citizens, considerably more than any other town in Britain), and how they are, more often than not, exceptions to the northern rule. They may peddle domesticity, but there is precious little vulnerability in the likes of Ken Dodd or Lily Savage. Liverpool comics bear more resemblance to southerners on the whole; they are quick-talking, quick-witted aggressors, and smart arses who owe more to Phil Silvers and Zero Mostel than Albert Modley and Sandy Powell. They are talkers; their humour is, like that of the cockneys, the Irish or the Jews, primarily verbal. With his bizarre appearance and copious comic props, however, Dodd is something of an exception, but then he has always been a bit of a throwback.

Acutely aware of this north-south comic divide, Dodd was initially wary of taking on the London Palladium in 1965; the fear of being rejected, as countless northern acts had before him, weighed heavily on his mind. He needn't have worried, however, as the record-breaking forty-two-week run made him the hottest comic property in the land. As he revealed to Michael Billington in *How Tickled I Am*, the medium of television had played a vital role in paving the way for north-ern performers to be more readily accepted by a London audience: 'TV, being a great leveller, has broken down a lot of this north versus south thing. In the old days a cockney comedian would never play the north – I think only Max Miller ever got away with it – and a flat-hat, ee-bah-goom comedian couldn't go south. But the Liverpudlian is a breed on his own – we don't wear flat hats and say "Nay then, sithee" – and we have our own accents and our own culture.'

He was right to highlight the fact that television had made the wide range of British accents more accessible, and had thereby rendered regional – or indeed national – humour obsolete. For example, how many viewers know (or care) that Alexei Sayle is from Liverpool? In the past he may have weaved references to his home town into his act – 'Our estate was so boring, its twin town was Père Lachaise cemetery' – but basically he could have come from any working-class environment. And when Dodd delivers lines such as: 'We've had unleaded churches in Liverpool for years' or 'In Paris all the chairs and tables are out on the street – in Liverpool we call that eviction', it is much the same thing – it happens to be Liverpool, but it could be anywhere.

When asked what things made people laugh in the north of England, Dodd once replied, 'You have to talk about things that northerners have traditionally found comical, which is family life, domestic scenes, for instance; bath night – that is always funny for some reason or other.'

It is interesting, but not entirely surprising, to note that vintage footage of a youthful Dodd presents a much more Liverpudlian persona, and indeed, accent. It would seem that the intervening years have blunted his Scouseness. However, with Dodd, Liverpool was – and is – a mere springboard: a stargate through which he takes the unwary traveller to his own warped world. As fellow northern comedian Victoria

Wood has noticed: 'He does everything – verbal, physical. It's surreal and yet it's very much rooted in real life; very much rooted in his own childhood and words from his own childhood in Liverpool.' That said, she maintains that she doesn't think of him as a typical Scouse comic: 'He's not cocky like some Liverpool comedians.'

Quite why Liverpool should boast its own comic microclimate is open to endless conjecture. Is it the fact that life is pretty tough on the Mersey? Is it because, like London or New York, Liverpool is a heaving, bustling, bubbling stew of a city? Yes and no. After all, places like Leeds, Manchester and Birmingham are heaving, bustling cities. Life in most towns and cities can be fairly grim, and poverty is rife all over the country, but not every metropolis hosts a plethora of comic talent, so we have to look elsewhere for clues.

One reason might be because, like the cockneys of London and the Jews of New York, in Liverpool the family is paramount: witness Carla Lane's Boswell clan in the sitcom *Bread*, sitting round the kitchen table stuffing money into the ceramic chicken; it is like the Fowlers and the Beales closing ranks in *EastEnders* or the families in practically any Woody Allen or Neil Simon movie. In all these cultures there is a strong familial bond and an 'us against the world' attitude. And where this bond exists there is also a tradition of sitting down and talking to each other; there is storytelling – in many cases competitive storytelling – which is, of course, the essence of stand-up comedy.

As Ma Boswell herself, actress Jean Boht, described on Dodd's *Heroes of Comedy*: 'What happened, I suppose, in the war, is that we were all thrown back on ourselves to entertain each other a lot at home. I remember the bombing was so appalling in Liverpool and so you've got to do something to make everybody laugh. There was all this in-house entertainment, this warmth, this silliness . . . You could see that someone like Doddy would be a godsend to the entertainment of the shelter life in Liverpool. Entertaining everyone – I imagine him like that.'

Jazz singer George Melly was also born in Liverpool and is a contemporary of Dodd. He recalls a vibrant professional and amateur performing scene in the city: 'The thing about Liverpool is that (a) it's very chauvinist – everybody from Liverpool always supports everybody from Liverpool; and (b) it has a remarkable record of comedians when you think about it.'

Melly also makes the point that it wasn't just the pros on the circuit, as there were also many brilliant amateurs on the scene: 'My mother, for instance, was very good at doing sketches. They did a revue every year in the [Royal] Court or one of those big theatres to raise money for a charity. The sketches were written by a woman called Maud Button. So there was this basis of Liverpool humour both amateur and professional.'

Melly is one of the many who have attempted to pin down a reason for Liverpool's comic pre-eminence. He attributes much of it to the fact that it has strong connections to Ireland. 'It's called the capital of Ireland sometimes,' he says. 'The Irish have a very strong sense of humour – different from the English. I think that's probably where it arose from. Everybody thinks they're a comedian in Liverpool . . . and it's true in a way.'

There even appears to be a kind of competitive funniness. Eric Midwinter, author of *Make 'Em Laugh*, recalls that he once watched Ken Dodd walk across Lime Street station when 'immediately all the porters started wisecracking at him, not unlike the arrival in Dodge City of the fastest gun in the West.'

Tom O'Connor is another comedian who has tried to pinpoint his home town's comic obsession. He puts it down to hardship: 'This city has the ability to laugh at itself through adversity.' And Michael Grade agrees: 'Part of being a Scouser is being able to laugh at the world. They have a unique view of the world. There's been a lot of social deprivation and hardship in Liverpool as the docks have declined and factories have closed. They've been through an awful lot. But they have a great survival instinct in Liverpool . . . and an impish sense of humour. Humour on the terraces started in Liverpool. Remember the famous poster outside Liverpool cathedral in the sixties? "Think: what would you do if Jesus came to Liverpool?" And some Scouser scrawled underneath: "I'd move St John to inside left!" Now *that's* Liverpool. There's a Liverpool "scallywag" mentality. It's about beating authority and beating the system – just being one step ahead, always having the last word.'

But of course the famous Scouse humour is not just a product of Liverpudlian living conditions. Language also plays a part. As Denis Norden observes: 'I think it's because of the rhythm of speech. The internal rhythm of the Liverpool accent is absolutely wonderful for comedy emphasis. It's like New York. It just gets the best out of all the old comedy tricks . . . you know, like putting the funny word at the end of the line . . . The Liverpool delivery is the FedEx of comedy. When it's only faintly there, like Tommy Handley and Arthur Askey, it impels it. Ken Dodd is Liverpudlian in his rhythms, I think. In the same way that Tommy Cooper was southern in his rhythms.'

Actor Ricky Tomlinson told the *Liverpool Daily Post*: 'We have a natural wit and we don't take life too seriously. We have learned to take it in the lean years and bounce back. I wouldn't say that everyone here is a born comedian. Perhaps every other Scouser is a comedian; they're not all funny. Ken Dodd is one of the finest stand-up comedians in the world. That's an amazing achievement. Doddy is unique.'

Dodd himself tends to fall in the Melly camp. He believes it is the ethnic mix that makes Merseyside – or rather 'Mirthyside' as he waggishly dubbed it in a *Guardian* article published in June 2003 to commemorate Liverpool's becoming European City of Culture – a 'city of laughter'. 'The humour has developed because Liverpool is a melting pot of different cultures,' said Dodd. 'There has been an influx of Welsh, English, Scots and Irish people, which has given us a diverse view of life and sense of humour. It is a humour which can perceive incongruity and see oddness from a different perspective.'

It is a typical Dodd analysis, thoughtful and considered, although, given Liverpool's naval associations, perhaps he has overlooked the potential influence that a host of international visitors might have had on the city over the years.

Comedian and actor Roy Hudd thinks that the north–south divide is much less obvious than it used to be, but maintains that it still exists. He says that if you listen to Dodd you would not necessarily know that he was from Liverpool: 'That was a standard thing when Ken started in the business, but the great thing was you had to get yourself a universal accent so you could be accepted in the north or in the south or anywhere. What it did kill, which was a great tragedy, was the dialect comics. But if you think of Doddy it's not particularly Liverpool. You've got to speak in an accent that everybody can understand.'

When producer Johnny Hamp assembled *The Comedians* for Granada in the 1970s, his cocktail of comics blended hardcore, professional northerners like Bernard Manning and Charlie Williams with the likes of cockney comedian Mike Reid, but viewers probably failed to even notice.

Regional differences really only matter when you're touring, and Dodd tours . . . incessantly. It's then that his cerebral approach to laughter-making and his thorough knowledge of the local variations in the British sense of humour come to the fore; it is these crucial factors that have made such a major contribution to Dodd's continuing success. He knows more than most – perhaps more than anyone – what goes down well where, and, more importantly, what doesn't. As he is keen to observe: 'You can tell a joke in Glasgow and it'll get big laughs, but in Manchester they won't laugh.' And the reason why? 'Because they can't hear it!'

It's no secret that over the years, Dodd has painstakingly collated his famous 'Giggle Map of Britain'. Following each performance he will assiduously note the date, the season, whether first or second house, time on and time off, audience capacity, how it went, what worked, what didn't, how it could be improved, and even the weather conditions. This means that when he returns (and he always returns) he will know exactly how to pitch his act. It's the salesman in him bobbing to the surface again – always give the punters what they want. As any market analyst or ad man worth his salt will tell you, knowledge is definitely power.

When she's not playing the piano or singing, Dodd's partner Anne Jones sits out front with a stopwatch timing the laughs. At the end of the show she will present him with a breakdown of what got the longest (and shortest) laugh. Bill Cotton, for one, was astounded to learn how eagerly Dodd embraced and devoured this information. 'I thought it was just to give Anne something to do,' he said. Similarly, Dodd's unusual preoccupation with these many and varied factors has prompted comedian Steve Punt to wonder whether it's merely a type of 'displacement activity for comics'. Perhaps, but there can be no doubt that Dodd's detailed study of the nation's laughter habits has been a winning formula for him over the last few decades.

It was as a result of this analytical approach, and because Dodd does his homework, that according to Eric Midwinter he has been unfairly dubbed 'the slide-rule comic'. His detractors though, have missed the point: his genius lies not in the fact that he has taken the trouble to assemble this data, but rather in his ability to utilize and capitalize on that information. What is brilliant is his capacity for endlessly and seemingly effortlessly shifting and altering the tenet of his performance to accommodate any given situation.

On return engagements Dodd will want to know in advance the size of the auditorium and the audience, their composition and even how they will be dressed. As Eric Midwinter points out in *Make 'Em Laugh*: 'Manners maketh the man, and an audience in evening dress becomes a different proposition from the same one in lounge suits.'

Although Dodd clearly tailored his performance to the different venues where he was appearing, I would challenge the view of film director and *Yes, Minister* co-writer Jonathan Lynn that Dodd 'had a completely different act for Glasgow, Manchester, Birmingham and London'. It is impossible to imagine that even someone like Dodd, with a lifetime's worth of material, would have enough to construct a specific act for every region. Doubtless the central nub of his act remains the same, but he uses his encyclopaedic knowledge of what works better in certain areas to shape the material to his best advantage.

Dodd's friend and associate Laurie Bellew recalled the early information gathering in *Heroes of Comedy*: 'We had this ledger that was used at every performance. Every remark he made on stage was listed in the ledger and we would tick it off. A square box meant it was a great laugh, a little X meant it was only a titter, VG meant very good etc. And every performance he would study it when he came off and see where the errors were and see if we could move the material around . . . All this analytical stuff was being done in those very early days. I think before he even got his first professional engagement.'

Steve Punt toured the length and breadth of the country with his comedy partner Hugh Dennis a decade ago, and together they have hit the road again more recently. He concurs that although Dodd's Giggle Map doubtless really meant something in the early days, since then broadcasting has ironed out regional variations. In his experience, he had discovered that there was much more difference between cities and suburbs than any that existed between the north and the south: 'The big northern cities are as lively and the audiences are as "up" as you would expect, whereas the places we always found difficult were places like Guildford or Hemel Hempstead because if you start at half past seven people have only just come back from work on the train . . .'

Consequently he can clearly understand Dodd's obsession with practical details, such as where the audience is coming from, what time they return from work and how difficult it could be to park. 'We [Punt and Dennis] had a long discussion with a promoter once about whether to start at half past seven or eight o'clock. I actually think it makes an enormous difference because it's an extra half-hour of drinking time. We did comparatively little of it, but if Ken Dodd's been doing it most nights a year, every year for the last half a century, I would have thought his brain is addled with it by now.'

Dodd's Giggle Map is a unique document and an invaluable aid. What use it would be to another comic, however, is unknown. He makes no greater claim for its merits, other than it works very well for him. Here follows a brief summary of its conclusions:

Scotland – the Scots like fast-talkers and one-liners; North-East – anti-pomposity goes down well, and they like their humour dry; Yorkshire – contrary to their dour image, they tend to like friendly comics; Lancashire – warm-hearted, but harder edged than Yorkshire; Wales – wild, zany comics;

Midlands – 'singing comedians'; London and the Home Counties – they tend to make 'totems' of their comic heroes, and they also like pathos; South-West – honest, friendly comics.

For all Dodd's analysis, though, his genius lies somewhere off the map. Eric Midwinter has gone as far as to propound the theory that Ken Dodd actually invented what we think of as the Liverpool sense of humour, and by dint of his constant touring has persuaded the nation to accept that there was such a thing. He argues that this is mainly because Dodd has elected to make his home town a part of his act. Michael Grade, however, is not convinced: 'Dodd's humour draws on Liverpool, but I wouldn't say that his humour is Scouse humour . . . I've never really seen Doddy as a Scouse comedian; not like say, Jimmy Tarbuck.

'Doddy is surreal; he's off into realms of fantasy and imagination, very much in the music-hall tradition. That vocabulary, plumptiousness, tattifilarious . . . he's a man who understands the dynamics of vocabulary in a way that very few comedians can. All comedians understand emphasis – the wrong word at the wrong time and that the wrong emphasis will kill the joke. This is why people can't tell jokes, because they don't understand the construct: the funny word isn't *that* word, it's "and" – that's understanding where the joke is. But Doddy is very imaginative, he doesn't tell jokes.'

And that is why, blinking into the daylight after a five-hour Doddathon, the punter is hard-pressed to recall one line.

In his chapter on Tommy Cooper in *British Comedy Greats,* comedy writer Barry Cryer alighted on Cooper's apparent disregard for the conventions of comic delivery. He recalls that one of Cooper's favourite 'jokes' was: 'A man walked into a bar and went, "Oooooh!" It was an iron bar.' True to his singular, perhaps contrary nature, Cooper would insist on stressing the word 'bar' and not 'iron' – the complete opposite of what one might consider the norm. When Cryer pointed this out to Cooper, the lantern-jawed comic simply stared at him in disbelief and asked, 'Did they laugh?' 'Yes,' replied Cryer. 'Then shut up!' countered the great man, whereupon he dissolved into fits of laughter.

Denis Norden echoes the same point with Dodd: 'He achieves what to a comedy writer is a magical thing: he puts the emphasis on the wrong word – but it's better. Tommy Cooper is the prime example, he tells these funny, silly, little one-liners and puts the emphasis on the wrong word. Ken does the same thing – he breaks certain comedy rules. And of course that shows the extent of his talent.'

When I asked Norden why he thought that this unorthodox comic style worked so well, he replied that he simply didn't know, but that it was down to the individual magic of these brilliant comedians – their unique star quality: 'And a star is, I think almost by definition, somebody who is not like anybody else.'

The point is that it takes real genius to break 'the rules'. It is why Frankie Howerd, with his umming and ahhing, his false starts and stops, and his rambling, meandering style was a comedy great, and the more slick, polished but workmanlike gagtellers – for example, Ted Bovis, the archetypal, ventripotent, has-been comic from the BBC sitcom *Hi-De-Hi!* – stubbornly remain on the foothills of comedy.

From an early age Dodd knew that the key to success was originality; it was a lesson he learned at his father's knee. 'My father gave me one piece of very good advice when I was starting in show business,' he told presenter and artist Alexandra Connor, on the pilot TV programme *Personal Portrait*. 'He said you must always be original. There's only room for one. Find something that you can do better than anyone else. Even if it's "By Jove, Missus!"'

As if to prove the point, Dodd's first business card read: 'Ken Dodd. The comedian who is Different. Knotty Ash, Liverpool 14' – the word 'Different' was printed upside down. Typical of Dodd the self-publicist, he then drove around in a car furnished in the same livery.

Perhaps his greatest contribution to Liverpool mythology is his lionization of his home town of Knotty Ash. For reasons that nobody can fully appreciate, the words 'Knotty Ash' are amusing. Like Littlehampton or Roger Moore (for aficionados of the *Carry On* films), it is a funny name.

After coming to terms with the fact that our parents had heartlessly misled us over the existence of Father Christmas, the Tooth Fairy and the Hundred Acre Wood, it is comforting to learn that Knotty Ash is a real place. Although a search for the jam-butty mines might be in every sense a fruitless one, rest assured that despite the inevitable encroachment of Liverpool's urban sprawl, Knotty Ash remains a pleasant leafy suburb some five miles south of the city. Named Ask until the eighteenth century, it takes its name from an ash tree which stood outside the pub that was once a landmark along the Liverpool to Prescot turnpike. The word Knotty or 'gnarled' was added later.

Dodd waxed lyrical about his home town to author John Hind for his 1991 book *The Comic Inquisition*: 'The people of Knotty Ash are a cross between Liverpudlians and Lancastrians. Knotty Ash has two churches. It also has . . . four pubs, a chiropodist, a post office and a newsagent called Bobby Basket. We used to have a milkman, but he's gone now. Down the road, where there's a garage, there used to be a smithy.'

George Melly, on the other hand, has a somewhat less romantic view of Knotty Ash, regarding it as a less than distinguished, respectable lower-middle class suburb. He acknowledges that it is the name that appeals to Dodd – and he just happens to have been born there.

On *Desert Island Discs* Dodd went to great pains to inform presenter Sue Lawley that although he loved the capital with its shops and theatres, as far as he was concerned 'the north is the north': 'I'm proud to live in Knotty Ash. I love the people, you see. The people of Merseyside are absolutely wonderful. There's a tremendous sense of humour, and we're always laughing, everything's a joke. In Liverpool they're supreme optimists; they see humour and laughter in every situation. There was a German executive at Ford who once came over to get some work experience at Halewood, and he was told always to wear his badge. They said, "You see, Herr Schmidt, they've got to know who you are at all times – they're very funny people." So he's going round the factory floor and he comes to two fellas and he says to one, "Now sir, do you know who I am?" And he said, "Eh, Charlie, come over here – there's a fella over here doesn't know who he is!" That's the sort of thing that happens all the time.'

Clearly, despite such examples of flagrant brown-nosing, what makes Dodd such a Liverpool icon is his loyalty. Although he has been at the top of his profession for half a century, he has never been seduced into buying a gated executive home in Esher and a villa in Marbella. He still lives in his childhood home – an abode that estate agents might call a spacious, period residence – where he returns most evenings. To the people of Liverpool, this kind of faithfulness to his origins makes him not just the squire of Knotty Ash, but almost a deity. Woe betide the interloper foolish enough to bad-mouth Dodd on his home patch, or the juror anxious to convict 'our Doddy'.

As John Fisher points out in his seminal exploration of British comedians, *A Funny Way To Be A Hero*, such allegiance pays further dividends: whether Dodd is aware of it or not, it is a reciprocal arrangement: 'Dodd remains the one great Liverpool comedian of his day who actually clings to his native roots. In return he maintains an objective view of life as lived by the people he has to entertain, namely the masses.'

Such unstinting loyalty brings its own rewards. In 2003 his fellow Liverpudlians voted Dodd the Greatest Merseysider of all time – nudging John Lennon and Paul McCartney into joint second position. But perhaps Eric Sykes sums up his friend best of all: 'His feet are firmly planted in Knotty Ash: same house, same Liverpool skyline, and as long as I've known him, same suit.'

So much for geography. But if we are to understand fully what has made Dodd what he is, we need to take a brief look at the history of stand-up comedy.

Rather like television, stand-up comedy has become such a familiar art form it is difficult to believe that it is really only about seven decades old – about as old as Dodd himself in fact. Stand-up grew out of variety, which in turn grew out of music hall. To those weaned on BBC TV's *The Good Old Days*, music hall comprised comedians, singers and novelty acts strutting their stuff before an audience of well-behaved toffs, sporting a range of bizarre outfits and iffy mutton-chop whiskers. But of course this is a rose-tinted, highly sanitized vision. In truth, music hall was a seething cauldron of alcohol-fuelled raucousness and impropriety, a working-class den of drunken debauchery, and a hot bed of vice and prostitution – a hot bed of hot beds, no less. The real entertainment on offer in the early days was far removed from the well-ordered fare introduced by the extravagantly verbose, flamboyantly garbed, hanky-waving Leonard Sachs.

As the term 'music hall' might suggest, the emphasis was very much on the music. The comic song held sway; there was little in the way of patter. Offerings such as Marie Lloyd's 'The Cock Linnet Song' (better known as 'My Old Man Said Follow the Van') and Gus Elen's 'It's A Great Big Shame' were the standards of the day in the early twentieth century. As anyone who has listened to those early crackly recordings of the likes of Dan Leno or Harry Lauder will tell you, though, time has not been kind to these legends of the music hall. Comedy is as susceptible to the vagaries of fashion as anything else. But to the keen comic student, it is fascinating to hear these old recordings; to listen to Harry Lauder break off between verses and start to gabble, seemingly incoherently. To the modern ear, this 'patter' is more perplexing than amusing. It seems a long, long way from these primitive ramblings to the slick observations uttered at the Comedy Store, but it is embryonic stand-up all the same.

It has been claimed by those who should know better that Frankie Howerd would have been a great music-hall comedian, but they are confusing real music hall with the simulated brand featured in *The Good Old Days*. In Victorian music hall, where subtlety, moderation and sophistication were never prerequisites, Howerd would not have stood a chance. Among an inebriated rabble he was too long-winded and too subtle to compete against the ale. As Dodd – perhaps the only contemporary entertainer who might have made a fist of it – has discovered, in order to survive in a pitiless, hostile environment, you really can't beat a good drum.

Strictly speaking though, no modern-day comic (not even the visually eccentric Vic and Bob or Rik Mayall and Ade Edmondson) would have cut the mustard in music hall – and why should they? That particular strand of entertainment is dead in the water, and quite right too: all things must change and evolve. No, what we are really talking about when we refer to Howerd, Cooper and Morecambe and Wise is 'variety' – or what the Americans call 'vaudeville'. Variety embraced the advent of real stand-up comedy, and through radio, film and especially television, enjoyed great longevity – right up until the early 1960s, in fact, when the circuits collapsed.

In Britain the music halls themselves had slowly developed from shabby, men-only, back rooms of taverns to far grander efforts, with names to match. In a bid for respectability, they were called such things as the Coliseum, the Palace and the Empire. At the beginning of the twentieth century they eventually got their act together – alcohol and prostitutes gave way to a far more structured regime. After the first Royal Variety Show in 1912, it was suddenly all right for decent, middle-class folk to attend such performances.

Some of the variety acts were just downright bizarre: along with the usual tumblers, acrobats, fire-eaters, jugglers, ventriloquists, dog acts, contortionists and conjurors, there was, for example, a man who appeared on stage dressed in a voluminous coat, within which was concealed virtually any train ticket or card that anyone could name; his whole act was based on audience members calling out the most obscure journey they could imagine, and in response he would produce an appropriate ticket, or they would name an equally esoteric club and he would show them a membership card. Despite their inventiveness, however, the speciality acts always seemed to play second fiddle to the singers and the comedians, who were by far the most popular turns among all the entertainment on offer.

As Peter Hepple, consulting editor for *The Stage* newspaper, remembers: 'Variety was very strictly controlled by the management. It used to follow a pattern of about five or six acts in the first half and about three or four in the second to allow the top of the bill to have twice as long as anybody else.' It was all choreographed to the nth degree. But then it was, as Hepple notes, another age: 'Those were the days when people used to go to bed at ten o'clock. It was a different time, a different economy, a different way of life.'

There were also different ranks of comedians. There were the stars at the top and a whole coterie of lesser mortals, and so those bobbing along at the bottom and middle of the bill tended to be workmanlike gagmen. 'A variety bill depended on you being able to bring on four lower-order comics who would do six or seven minutes,' explains Steve Punt. 'If you're only doing six or seven minutes you've got to do jokes because you can't explain to the audience who you are or what you do and get your personality across in that amount of time. So at that level you'd now be doing open spots and short first-half acts on the pub circuit.'

Inevitably the fledgling comic these days will be lured towards the box. He might be flattered by the blandishments of a hungry TV executive, but if he had any sense he would resist burning his act on television. As Steve Punt tellingly reveals: 'In the late eighties or early nineties, in the wake of *Saturday Night Live,* there were several television shows where they would put three or four comics on the bill – just a compere and a few comics. But after a while people get a bit wary of them. They know that what they're essentially doing is coming to your show, and nicking your best five minutes. So the best bit of your act goes out to two million people, and then the next time you do a gig someone shouts "Seen it", and ruins the whole thing.'

Like many others, Denis Norden mourns the passing of the variety circuits and has his own personal theory for their disappearance. The current generation, he thinks, is one that is no longer entertained by entertainment: 'To some extent – but it's an oversimplification – we used to go and see people doing things that we knew we couldn't do and were impressed by it. Now we go to see people doing things that we realize we could do if somebody would give us the opportunity. Those in that first category were displaying a certain skill that they honed over years in some cases. But now there isn't time to spend honing those skills – you've got to make it immediately.

'Dancing, singing, playing instruments – to some extent again, a gross over-generalization – every variety comedian could sing, dance or play an instrument. It was part of his equipment. It was like a bus driver knowing the rules of the road. When you think of Morecambe and Wise, and Mike and Bernie Winters, they could do all those physical things. They weren't confined to verbal humour.'

Gradually, however, comedy patter became king, although song and dance continued to play a part. The old comics adhered to musical numbers or musical instruments with all the tenacity of a limpet to a rock. If the laughs didn't come, they'd comfort themselves with the fact that at least with a song or a tune they could leave the stage with a modicum of dignity. Then, as now, there was nothing more ignominious than coming off to total silence.

Although often lumped together with the likes of Howerd, Cooper, and Morecambe and Wise, Ken Dodd is different. With varying degrees of success, his contemporaries adapted to the small screen, but Dodd didn't. He had his moments on the box, certainly, but when television work dried up he sought sanctuary in what undoubtedly is his element – he concentrated on touring the halls, vowing to play every live venue in the country. Like the old, pre-TV, music-hall stars of yesteryear, he lives on the road. Not having squandered his act on television – and having acquired fifty years' worth of material – he is free to perform much the same stuff for months on end, honing, polishing and perfecting it as he goes, so that by the time he returns to a particular theatre there's an audience anxious to hear a spin on the same stories. It is a lifestyle more akin to Robb Wilton, Norman Evans, and Wilson, Keppel and Betty, than Ricky Gervais or Johnny Vegas. As such, Dodd represents a unique link to our comic heritage – he is living archaeology. Forget about an over-exuberant Tony Robinson and his team of florid yokels in unfortunate knitwear – if you want to bring the past to life, go to see a live Ken Dodd show. To enjoy the comedian in full flow is to appreciate the type of comedy that our grandparents and great grandparents would have enjoyed in years gone by.

What is surprising, however, is that despite this, Dodd remains as refreshingly funny and relevant (or irrelevant) today as he would have been during the Victorian era. His singularity and determination to plough his own furrow may have rendered him fashion-proof and earned him a fortune in the process, but has it shunted him into the sidings in terms of critical acclaim? Kenneth Williams was right when he wrote in his infamous diaries in 1985: 'It's weird how this country rewards the mediocre & ignores excellence. Alan Badel is a case in point (straight actor) & there are others in variety – Ken Dodd – who have to steer a lonely path.'

Of course this path has only become a lonely one in recent years. In many ways Dodd is a man out of his time. It is difficult to sell him to those who think of him as a bog-standard, gag-telling club comic. As Denis Norden says, 'His style – remember, he tells jokes, he does one-liners, he doesn't do "Have you noticed that . . . ?" and he always finishes with singing – his style has been superseded, but not his energy and the way he uses his body and his eyes.'

It could be argued that he has sacrificed cult status (something in which, I suspect, he has no interest) on the altar of his association with Dickie Mint and 'Tears', and that his unwavering intention to become a family entertainer has probably robbed him – for the time being, at least – of general approbation and adulation. David Nobbs has ascribed this to the dominance of TV: 'I think on television there was always a slight childish element to Ken Dodd. It was in the theatre, over the longer haul, where his mastery was revealed. Nonetheless, he's a very successful man.'

Victoria Wood also blames the box. 'He doesn't work so well on television,' she replies, when asked why Dodd wasn't a cult figure, '. . . and he doesn't appeal to gay men.'

Ken Campbell, himself something of a theatrical outsider, is another avowed Dodd fan. The maverick comedy actor and writer tries to catch Dodd's show at least once a year, and confesses to occasionally borrowing those famous Dodd rhythms: 'I've got a way of doing that sometimes. You wouldn't realize that that's actually what I'm doing, but it is.'

Campbell remains unstinting in his praise for Dodd: 'I think he's the best, really. He seems to be the absolute top,' and such is his dedication to him that when he somewhat facetiously applied to run the National Theatre in 2001, he suggested that part of the theatre's remit should be to host a Ken Dodd show on Sundays at the Olivier. Campbell later turned this 'job application' into a one-man show – *If I Ruled the National Theatre* – at the Institute of Contemporary Arts (ICA), and found at least one ally in his worthy proposal, in *Guardian* critic Michael Billington.

'He's dead right that great comics deserve their place on the National stage,' wrote Billington in October 2001. 'Having failed to bring us Morecambe and Wise, Tommy Cooper or Max Wall during their lifetimes, the National should play host to Ken Dodd, still the greatest solo performer in Britain.'

He'd have found further support from Michael Grade: 'I would love to see Doddy come to London one more time and do a one-man show. Forget all the variety acts and all that – just come on and be rediscovered by the intelligentsia and the establishment. I'd love to see him do that . . .'

2

When Doddy Was Diddy

IN THE WORLD of show business it is almost accepted beyond question that comics become comics because they either led a childhood filled with misery, deprivation and/or violence, perhaps subjected to continual parental rejection and cast aside like the salad in a kebab; or they were bullied at school (except for Alexei Sayle, that is, who claims to have been the clown *and* the bully). In either case, they used humour as a defence mechanism, preferring to be laughed *with* rather than laughed *at*, and hoping that if they made the bullies laugh they would avoid getting beaten up.

As ever though, Dodd flies in the face of the accepted norm. In Michael Billington's *How Tickled I Am*, the comedian disclosed that although his family were far from well-off, his frugal upbringing hadn't affected him adversely: 'Entertainers do their best to tell you a hard-luck story of a childhood spent with tattered, threadbare clothes and the behind hanging out of their trousers. I can't tell you that. I suppose we were poor in a way, but we didn't make a career out of it.'

He reiterated the point to Alexandra Connor in the television programme *Personal Portrait*: 'I had a very, very happy childhood. A lot of people say comics have miserable, poverty-stricken childhoods, but I didn't. I had a wonderful childhood. I had a marvellous mother and father, a lovely brother and sister, and we were a very, very happy family. I was very lucky because my father was the funniest man I ever knew. My mother was wonderful: a great optimist. She always said to us: "You can do anything you want to do, you can be anybody you want to be, as long as you want to enough." She used to say to me: "Kenny, I don't care where you go as long as you wear a clean shirt."' Rather like the word 'diddy', perhaps the phrase, 'Where's me shirt?' was also a well-trodden Dodd family term.

Kenneth Arthur Dodd was born at Liverpool Maternity Hospital on 8 November 1927 – not 1931, as claimed in his *Who's Who* entry. Despite numerous requests for his correct birthdate from the *Who's Who* compilers, he has always opted to ignore them. Claiming to feel thirty-five, he has said, 'I don't want to be thought of as a veteran.'

Thus he is a Scorpio, which, according to *Parkers' Astrology*, indicates a character that is determined and magnetic on the plus side, and obsessive and obstinate on the negative; there is also a connection with a strong desire for financial security, which is undoubtedly an issue for further discussion. His mother Sarah (née Gray) and father Arthur produced three children: Ken was the middle child, his brother Bill is two years older, his sister June is three years younger.

Situated in the rural environs of Knotty Ash, the Dodd family home in Thomas Lane, which was bought by his grandfather, was built around 1740. It is a former farmhouse with a large garden and is a fairly impressive affair; a big, well-proportioned, double-fronted period property, light years away from what we might consider to be the home of a 'poor' family. Doddy Towers, as Dodd came to christen it, has become a haven, a refuge from the slings and arrows of outrageous curiosity. It comes as no surprise that few journalists have been invited to step across the threshold. Puzzlingly, although Dodd has always claimed to have lived in this house from birth, it was later mentioned in his 1989 trial that he and his family had moved to Thomas Lane when he was five years old. Furthermore his birth certificate clearly indicates that his home address at birth was 76 Empire Street, a road that no longer exists following its demolition in the 1960s.

Living in the same house for much of his life, he says, has given him a strong sense of perspective: 'To live – or be based – in a place where you've always been, that is very important in humour.' On the face of it the use of the term 'based in' might seem curious, but given that Dodd spends most of his waking hours either on the road or on the stage, it is no doubt accurate. Over the years, Dodd says he has 'rebuilt and refurbished' the house, and although many have advised him to move, he never has. But whether it is because he is genuinely devoted to the people of Knotty Ash or because 'I don't like being in slow traffic' is anyone's guess.

According to their famous son, who has likened his parents to 'Peter Pan and Wendy', Arthur and Sarah Dodd were devoted to one another, though his father's gambling habit and the consequential visits from the bailiffs must surely have created certain tensions between the couple. Dodd's mother understandably took hold of the purse strings and ran a frugal home. Her 'careful' attitude to money is pivotal in attempting to understand Dodd's singular take on the subject. One of his friends was of the strong opinion that her beliefs instilled in him an obsession with money, a distrust of banks and the mindset that everyone was out to get you.

Ken Dodd

In *Desert Island Discs*, when Sue Lawley touched on the question of his father's love of 'a flutter on the horses', Dodd set out to clarify matters. 'Oh yes,' he acknowledged, 'he was a punter. He wasn't a gambler, there's a difference, you see. A gambler . . . is one of those people who goes into the betting shop and puts fifty quid on a horse – that's crazy.' He was later a little nonplussed when she asked if it was fair to say that his father was anything like Albert Tatlock, the irascible and cantankerous curmudgeon from *Coronation Street*, as had been reported.

Of his mother, he spoke in loving terms: 'My mum was a lovely lady – she was quite small, she was a mini-mum. She gave us the most precious thing I think any parent can give any child: she spoke to us, she talked to us. We used to spend hours and hours just talking to my mum. We'd talk about her childhood and her schooling – she was quite a brainy lady. She just talked to us. I think that's why we were so happy.'

If everything he tells us is true, young Ken's childhood seems to mirror that of the American comedian and writer Mel Brooks, who claimed that he was always being thrown in the air by a variety of adoring relatives: 'I was fifteen before my feet touched the ground.'

Dodd's recollections of his early childhood reveal a life of freedom and domestic bliss: 'I am told that at the age of two I walked into the living room and told my mother, "I've made you a nice new draining board," having smeared a half-inch layer of cocoa all over it, and smoothed it down so it was a nice brown wood.' In one of Dodd's very early memories, he recollects crossing a busy road intent on buying a kite from a local shop at the tender age of three. Even when he was little he had a natural eye for a bargain, and rather than spend more money on a brand-new toy, he opted to buy two damaged kites for a penny. 'I thought it was better to have two broken ones for a ha'penny each, than a proper one for threepence. This confirms what everyone says: I'm a marvellous businessman!'

As to the young Dodd's personality, he has described himself as an unassuming youngster: 'I wasn't in the least an entertainer. I was shy and modest – as I still am!' Indeed, he claims that he was 'still rather shy' when he became a professional entertainer.

Regarding his youthful pastimes, Dodd painted a picture of typical outdoor pursuits with friends, comparing their boyhood games to the antics he used to read about in the *Just William* books: 'I had my gang with the Smith twins and Dave Corrie – we ran wild round the fields round Knotty Ash. My hobbies seemed to be digging holes, lighting fires, burning my coat and falling out of trees. A most wonderful childhood.'

Yet as the late Bob Monkhouse pointed out in his excellent *Behind the Laughter* specials for the BBC, although Dodd apparently had a pleasant home-life with loving parents, one is 'always aware of the fact that he is of another species. The way he's lived his life is extremely unusual.'

Dodd's father was a full-time coal merchant and part-time saxophonist and clarinetist, though during a downturn in the coal business in the 1920s, he also played professionally, including summers on the Isle of Man. His mother, whom he described as stern but fair, played the piano. Accordingly, music was an abiding feature chez Dodd. His grandmother brought up sixteen children and each was taught to play at least two instruments. Described by her admiring grandson as 'a remarkable woman', she went on to become Liverpool's first woman magistrate. One can't help but wonder what she would have made of her grandson's later court appearance . . .

Arthur Dodd was also keen that his son should take up music, with the result that Ken learned the cornet, accordion and piano. It was not long before he became a choirboy at St John's Church in Knotty Ash, which he has since described as his 'first attempt at being in any kind of show business'. From about the age of nine Dodd would sing with the choir twice on Sundays and receive sixpence for each service, though by his own admission, he and his fellow choirboys were anything but cherubic, for they 'used to flick paper pellets across the chancel and whisper terrible things . . . and wink at all the girls in the congregation'. Nevertheless, the young Dodd gained considerable musical experience from his days at St John's: 'I loved all that church music. You could sing out, let it rip. It's great music to sing. Furthermore, I learned something about the theory of music in the choir.'

The choir, and indeed, religion – his mother was devoutly religious – was another formative influence on the young Dodd. In interviews he recalls his days with the choir with regularity. As he told John Stapleton in the TV programme, *My Favourite Hymns*: 'I was in the choir for many years . . . until they found out where the noise was coming from. When I was a choirboy we used to indulge in all sorts of religious pursuits, like finding out the price of the bridegroom's shoes. When the bride and groom kneel in the chancel to take their vows, you can always see the bottom of their shoes, and the bridegroom always had new shoes and he always left the label on. So it was the first one to spot it . . . ah, forty-nine and eleven! Happy days in the choir with the Smith twins and Mr Balshaw the choirmaster.'

Dodd's father had just as much influence on his son as his mother: 'My father was the funniest man I ever knew because he spoke very graphically,' recalls Dodd. 'When he spoke – and he did it naturally – everything came out as a picture.'

Many years later, the cartoonist Bill Tidy recognized much the same in Dodd's act: 'He's a kind of vocal cartoonist because he paints a picture leading you somewhere and then gets out right at the end, leaving you to finish the thing yourself. I think the best example of that is his observation that it's fatal for a man over fifty-five years of age to wear light grey trousers!'

It is more than likely that Dodd's father was responsible for bringing creativity and colour into his son's Roald Dahl-like vocabulary. 'He played around with names a lot,' Dodd has said, which must surely have had a profound influence on the comedian's choice of unique adjectives and character names. For example, whenever Dodd was ill as a boy, his father would offer to call in 'Doctor Chuckabutty', and years later came the birth of 'Professor Yaffle Chuckabutty (or sometimes Rufus Chucklebutty), Operatic Tenor and Sausage Knotter'.

Dodd's parents worked extremely hard to earn an honest crust, and displayed an admirable work ethic that clearly rubbed off on their youngest son in later life. At Christmas time in particular, when the children were in bed, his father would still be out working after midnight, trying to sell his stocks of coal. Equally his mother, who was responsible for collecting the coal money, would also have to work long into the night from Thursday to Saturday to ensure that the family received proper payment for every coal delivery that was made during the week. Not only was it immensely tiring having to walk for miles on foot, but Dodd recalled that the job carried risks as well: 'It was dangerous carrying money in a handbag, and once she was set upon and robbed by four men. Mum was five feet one inch tall.'

His mother – 'I was a bit of a mummy's boy, which I wasn't proud of, but am now' – kept tight reins on the household finances, and she never really got out of the habit; years later she was to become Dodd's first bookkeeper, storing his wages in shoe boxes.

At the age of five Dodd embarked upon his academic career. He attended Knotty Ash Infant School where the headmistress, Miss Hill, he remembered, had 'a magnificently genteel habit of wandering round the classroom. She would sniff the air, and then announce, "Someone does not smell sweet in this room." Whoever it happened to be had to leave in disgrace.'

Though he claimed to be a shy pupil, he was often in trouble, mainly due to his propensity for chattering when he should have been working, but he was an intelligent boy, nevertheless, and was able to learn things without too much difficulty. It is tempting to promulgate the theory that Dodd's subsequent glee in making prisoners of the audiences at his shows is a type of retribution – some form of perverted detention, perhaps.

Although he was mischievous, he has revealed that he was never bored simply because there were so many things to keep him occupied. The fact that he was always able to fill his time with a range of different pastimes meant that he kept out of trouble, and never had to suffer the ignominy of a trip to the police station for any minor crimes: 'I broke a few windows in my time, but I hadn't the slightest desire to steal anything because I had a very good family life, and I didn't need to.'

At Knotty Ash Junior School he won a scholarship to Holt High School where life was very different: 'Suddenly I was thrown into this clinical, disinfectant-smelling establishment where everybody, all the teachers, look just like the man you see when you go to pay your rates – stern, forbidding, and not wanting to know.'

His father's dedication to work was another early influence on young Ken. And just like his dad, Dodd had always balked at the idea of rest. For many years he refused to take a vacation, claiming that they were merely 'compulsory leisure'. Only quite recently has he taken to the notion of enjoying time off work, and with hindsight has said, 'I wish I'd known at eighteen the thrill and excitement of travelling. I think everybody should travel. I think it should be compulsory. It's only when you go abroad you realize what a wonderful country this is.' The lack of holidays as a child, however, was due to the fact that the coal trade was a competitive one. If you failed to deliver the goods, there was always some customer-hungry whippersnapper lying in wait to poach your trade. It is a bit like show business – there is always some new talent ready to take your spot; spend too long out of the lime-light and people will forget who you are.

Apart from the inevitable Saturday morning trip to the pictures to take in the latest Larry 'Buster' Crabbe *Flash Gordon* adventure, the best the family could hope for was a day out at the seaside on a Sunday. 'Southport was like going abroad; and going to Scarborough was the equivalent today of going to Australia,' recalls Dodd. In these days of car-choked motorways and escalating fuel prices, it is hard to believe that not so long ago the Sunday afternoon drive was a mainstay of the British way of life. The Dodds were no exception: each Sunday, Arthur Dodd would load up the Riley and drive his brood to nearby North Wales.

Dodd had fond memories of his father's generosity, and his caring attitude towards his children. Recalling how his father used to keep the family entertained and amused by wearing silly hats, pulling faces, telling jokes and singing funny songs, Dodd described him as 'my favourite comedian'. Clearly Arthur Dodd was very close to his children, and like any good father would do his utmost to keep them happy. On one occasion, when the young Ken described a story from *The Wizard* comic book, about a boy who was able to fly on his bicycle, his father spent a whole Sunday building a pair of wings for his youngest son's push-bike, in an effort to keep him entertained and to fuel his fertile imagination: 'I pedalled furiously on it up and down the yard, and roared down a field trying to take off on this bike!'

Perhaps Arthur Dodd's greatest influence on his son, however, was their habitual visits to Liverpool's many variety houses: the Olympia, the Empire, the Royal Court, the Pavilion and the Shakespeare, which provided him with 'an early and regular taste of the lovely fruity pit orchestra, of the smell of cigar smoke and orange peel. The lovely magical world of live variety theatre – a huge, illustrious world.' Given the family traits – the work ethic, the yearn to earn, the love of music and language, and above all, the passionate interest in all things theatrical – it is little wonder that the youthful Dodd soon had a show-business career in his sights, albeit a part-time one initially.

After his father had planted the seeds of showbiz in his young son's mind, Dodd started to acquire comic heroes such as Arthur Askey and 'Stinker' Murdoch from listening to the wireless: 'When you saw Arthur work it was like watching a firework display go off – there was so much energy. He was a wonderful, wonderful little man.' Another of Dodd's favourites was Ted Ray, whom he has described as 'probably the greatest stand-up comedian of them all: suave, sophisticated, beautifully dressed and impeccable timing'. Other comic heroes, whom Dodd looked up to as role models included Tommy Handley, who featured in *ITMA* [*It's That Man Again*], and Will Hay, star of numerous comedy films such as *Oh, Mr Porter!* and *Good Morning, Boys*. Of these comic luminaries, and others, Dodd has since remarked, 'If I thought there was a little of Will Hay, Arthur Askey, Ted Ray, Robb Wilton, Frankie Howerd . . . in me I would be very proud.'

It must have been particularly gratifying, therefore, for Dodd to learn many years later that he had become one of Askey's own favourite comedians. The diminutive comic was even known to promote Dodd's act to people who had been less than impressed with Dodd's television appearances, by saying to such doubters, 'Have you seen him in a theatre? He is a genius.'

Dodd was also fond of Sid Field and Nat Jackley: 'I once laughed so much at Nat in the back row of the gallery at the Liverpool Empire, that I fell forward a couple of rows!' As for women, he regarded Lucille Ball as the queen, but has also expressed an admiration over the years for the likes of Joan Davies, Hylda Baker and Marti Caine.

The gift of a Punch and Judy set from his parents on his eighth birthday triggered an intense interest in entertainment for the young Ken, who 'practised like mad, built a stage out of orange boxes and organized concerts in a hen coop in the yard'.

A keen reader of boys' magazines, such as *The Wizard*, *The Rover* and *The Hotspur*, Dodd has described himself as 'a very mischievous little boy', particularly in regard to his interest in the stink-bomb and itching-powder advertisements that he eagerly read in the back pages of *The Wizard*.

Another ad in *The Wizard* was to change Dodd's life – it is a story he is particularly fond of recounting. The advert read: 'Amaze your friends! Fool your teachers! Send sixpence in stamps.' In exchange for his pocket money, little Ken received a leatherette Swiss bird warbler and a booklet entitled 'How to Become a Ventriloquist'.

During his interview with Alexandra Connor, he explained that the correct term for the 'dummy' was a 'ventriloquial figure': 'My father bought me one for a birthday present and, like an idiot, I called him Charlie Brown . . . [but] a ventriloquist can't say the letter "b" – you say "gread and gutter" and a "gottle of gear" . . . As a boy I was sort of half amazed by the magic of ventriloquism, and then half entertained and amused by the comical side of it.'

Following the propitious birthday gift of the ventriloquist's doll, and a few extra-curricular lessons from an old pro 'vent', at the age of eight Doddy was in a position to launch himself on an unsuspecting world, or at least St Edward's orphanage in Knotty Ash. Armed with Charlie Brown and a script written by his dad ('And very good it was, too'), the diddy Doddy stormed the audience with his patter, a little tap-dancing and a musical interlude. He was a success, received payment of 2s 6d and soon found himself in demand at charity functions and Scout gang shows. The die was cast.

He recalled his early successes to Connor: 'At the end of the show the Father Superior took me to his office and gave me half a crown. About three months later, [at] Knotty Ash School (where I went to school), I did the headmaster's parent-teachers' dance. And the headmaster took me to his office and gave me a shilling. You see, very early on in my career in show business I had to learn a very important fact: how to take a cut gracefully.'

Performing was now in his blood, and he embraced any opportunity to present his act to a willing audience, travelling the length and breadth of Merseyside with his suitcase full of props to do so: 'The case was bigger than me and I used to lug it all over the place by bus . . . I did a show at the Scala in Widnes at the age of ten and I played the [Liverpool] Philharmonic Hall when I was twelve.'

Given his individuality, it is difficult to pin down who or what Dodd looked to for guidance when developing his on-stage personality. There is, perhaps, the eccentricity of Billy Bennett, the brashness of Max Miller, the irrepressible cheerfulness of Arthur Askey, but for the most part Dodd is clearly his own man: 'My father's advice was that you must be original, you must have your own style, and I have always tried to do that.'

'Like all great comedians – I don't know who influenced

him,' says Michael Grade. 'But whoever influenced him, in the end he's come out with a highly original persona; a highly original view of the world.' Michael Billington, however, can discern a surrealist bent to his style: 'There's a tradition of English nonsense, which is semi-surreal, that goes back to Edward Lear and Lewis Carroll, and I think that filters into Dodd. He works through a succession of odd surrealist images.'

But perhaps comedy writer and ex-BBC producer Mike Craig has the right answer. He believes that Dodd's main influence was Billy Bennett, the dinner-jacket-clad, walrus-moustached, music-hall comedian, who specialized in parodies of Victorian and Edwardian monologues, and who was most famous for his eccentric version of 'On the Road to Mandalay'. 'When he started,' said Craig, 'he wore a Billy Bennett outfit: the tuxedo that was too small for him, the trousers that were too long, the hobnail boots, the knapsack . . . He's a wonderful throwback to circus really. It's overloaded with all this paraphernalia. It's a bit of Max Miller, a bit of everything all rolled into one.'

'He's always said openly that he learned a lot from Robb Wilton and Ted Ray, Arthur Askey and people like that,' observes the *Liverpool Echo*'s arts editor, Joe Riley. 'He's generous in attributing people he admired. Although if you actually look at his act, he has more to do with Max Miller than any of those.'

Peter Hepple of *The Stage* notes that there is no one who works at quite the speed he does: 'I would have thought he was a great fan of Robb Wilton, but he's nothing like Wilton. It was not the custom for performers at variety venues to work at the speed that Ken Dodd does. He would tell forty gags where somebody else would tell ten. I personally have never seen anyone who can work at that speed and switch effortlessly from one thing to another.'

Roy Hudd, meanwhile, can see that in the thinking of the patter of the routines there is a dash of the Goons as well as Lewis Carroll and Stephen Leacock: 'A lot of it is Spike's old theory: start at A, go towards Z, but just before you get there, go off. Don't take the direct route. I'm sure there's a lot of it there.'

For the most part, however, Hudd is convinced that Dodd has always allowed himself to be guided by the people who pay his wages when it comes to deciding how to keep them entertained: 'Basically, Ken's whole persona and style of his jokes has been dictated by his audience. And that is a great servant of the public and that is a great comedian. What did Leno and all those people say at the end of the Drury Lane pantomime? "I remain your obedient servant." And I think Ken's the same. He used to keep all the graphs and things – every comic does it – but I'm sure there are things in there that he doesn't think are the slightest bit funny, but it might have come out of an ad lib one night and the audience laughed and he thought, "Christ, I'll keep that in." So I don't know what Ken thinks is particularly funny and what his audience thinks is funny. If they're exactly the same, well, my God, you've got a brilliant man . . . Ken, to me, thinks like the punters. And it's got to be for real because he's ninety-eight per cent correct all the time.'

Whoever or whatever influenced him, Dodd has never lost the child in him, but he nonetheless mourns its passing in others: 'I think everyone is born with a chuckle muscle; that is to say that everyone is born with a sense of fun, a sense of playfulness. If you're lucky your sense of humour stays with you all your life. But sometimes, I suppose, due to stress or pressure or worry or troubles, some people's chuckle muscle dries up and drops off. They lose the playfulness of life.'

Professionally, at least, that is something Dodd has never had to worry about. Fellow Liverpudlian Jean Boht recognized that trait in him: 'He's such a child. Like all great clowns he's a baby, isn't he? He's never grown up.'

As with most children, animals played a large part in Dodd's early life. The large stable building on Thomas Lane accommodated a host of horses, cats, canaries and dogs, and provided the local kids with many opportunities to play and enjoy hours of fun. To this day Dodd is still very much a pet person, and throughout the 1980s his large, black poodle, Doodle, travelled the country with him in his Ford Granada estate. But it was the memory of a childhood visit to Wrexham horse sales with his father, where they bought a carthorse called Duke, that has stayed with him over the years. He used to love watching the horses being put through their paces on the hard and soft ground before a sale was made, and savoured the sight of men completing a deal when a horse was bought: 'They spat on their hands, and they were fine handclasps. Then the man who sold the horse would give a bit of money back to the buyer, usually a silver coin. They called that "luck money". Visiting horse sales gave me a great insight into animals and human nature.'

Whether he was aware of it or not, the young Dodd was already learning by stealth many of the life skills necessary to become both an amateur psychologist and a professional comedian. He acquired his trademark gnashers in the same serendipitous fashion. As if constantly testing the ground, as a boy he was always keen to 'do things differently'. Consequently he often injured himself when engaged in risky activities, such as walking backwards to school when he managed to hit the back of his head on lampposts. It was while attempting a similarly dangerous feat that he ended up with his trademark teeth: 'I tried to ride my bike with my eyes shut, which is something you should never do, because ultimately you hit the kerb. I did, and I sailed over the handlebars and landed smack on my choppers, and that jutted them out.'

According to Dominic Shelmerdine's book *My Original Ambition*, Dodd was initially eager to follow in his father's footsteps and become a saxophonist, but his accident put paid to that notion. 'Unfortunately my sticky-out teeth were not in tune with this wish, and I kept biting the end off!'

He later observed: 'As a child I always wanted curly hair. I'd loved to have had straight teeth and curly hair – I got them the other way round!' Though he's made light of it since, at the time the effects of the accident left him in terrible pain – 'I cried for days,' he remembers. Now, however, those prized gnashers, which, like his rather distinctive mole he has steadfastly retained, are reportedly insured for £4 million.

Dodd's first experience of professional show business came when he was twelve. He saw an advertisement in the *Liverpool Post* – 'Dancers wanted for pantomime' – and he went along to audition. Unfortunately for the aspiring young entertainer, it transpired that the ad had been intended to attract only girls, but as a compromise he was offered the role of props boy instead for four weeks of the school holiday in a production of *Cinderella*. Despite it being a backstage job, there was one notable occasion when he managed to get caught on stage during a performance, when he wasn't quick enough to remove a rat trap and pumpkin from the stage when the lights were low, just as the Fairy Godmother had granted Cinderella her wish: 'I think I must have been a bit slow getting off, and when the light came up I was still there. So that was how I made one of my first appearances, and got one of my first laughs – standing on a stage with a rat trap in one hand and a pumpkin in the other. And the coach and ponies galloping towards me!'

His love of music-hall turns had been inspired by his parents' interest in variety shows, which contained an eclectic mix of performers, from acrobats and jugglers, to ventriloquists, comedians and singers. It soon became clear to Dodd that the performer wielding the power at these shows, whom Dodd has called 'the engine driver', was the comedian. With this in mind he asked his father one day, 'Dad, how do you "comede"?' and Arthur Dodd helped him to learn how to tell jokes.

Away from the glitz and glamour of the stage he joined his brother and father in the family coal-merchant business. Occasionally they would even let him drive the lorry – until he backed it down a 15-foot hole, that is – and he didn't drive again until he got his licence at the age of seventeen. All the exercise he got from carrying heavy sacks of coal back and forth made Dodd an athletic youngster. In fact, in one of his rare moments of leisure time, he and some friends cycled from Liverpool over the Welsh border to Betws-y-Coed.

In reflective mood, many years later, Dodd told TV reporter John Stapleton, 'Many times in your life – particularly when you're a teenager – you feel as if you are in a forest; a dark, gloomy land, everything is crowding you and it's all puzzling and weird. And then someone comes along, perhaps a good person who knows what they're doing, and says, "No, no – this is the way." And he'll show you the way. And life becomes so much more enjoyable when someone shows you the way.'

Dodd the angst-ridden teenager is hard to picture. As a member of a singing group called The Crows, which he formed with six of his friends, he seems to have had rather a good time in his adolescence. One therefore wonders whether he was speaking from personal experience in that instance – and if he was, who was his guide? It is difficult to believe that he had any time for anxiety, as he was far too busy entertaining and nurturing an interest in comedy with performances at 'Boy Scouts' concerts, boilermakers' hot-pots, dockers' soirées, and masonics'.

As war raged and Nazi bombs rained down on Liverpool, the fifteen-year-old Dodd spotted another newspaper advert – this one asking for performers to entertain the Forces. He went along to Priory Road School in Anfield where he did his ventriloquist's act for the Air Training Corps Cadets in a concert party called The Spitfires. Although the young Dodd was terrified, the audition did wonders to boost his confidence. After the show, a man who called himself Billy Caton, approached the fledgling entertainer and said he was an agent. Because Dodd had only encountered agents in books, this introduction thrilled him no end: 'I thought, "Blimey! This is it! Stardom at last."'

But another backstage visitor had far more of an effect on him. Not only was Hilda Fallon an attractive young woman, but she also ran a juvenile concert party called The Mersey Mites. She invited Dodd to join and, excitedly, he agreed. He remains unstinting in his praise for Hilda Fallon, whose other 'discoveries' include Freddie Starr, and former actor and now producer Bill Kenwright. 'She had the gift of motivation – she made you feel ten foot high,' Dodd was to later remark. 'There are certain people like circus trainers who have a psychic ability to communicate in some way with animals and train them. In exactly the same way, Hilda Fallon is one of them. She could train people to be entertainers. She could take a girl or boy and mould them into a smashing little artiste.'

One of Dodd's first engagements under Hilda Fallon's umbrella was at a nightclub. Bearing in mind that he had only ever seen nightclubs in Hollywood musicals, where everyone wore glamorous clothes and drank copious amounts of champagne while huge orchestras played in the background, his knowledge of such venues in Liverpool was limited, if not non-existent, and so the hard reality came as a bit of a shock. After the group of Mersey Mites boarded the Birkenhead ferry, caught the Crosville bus to Ellesmere Port, and finally arrived at the 'nightclub', the venue turned out to be Flatt Lane Labour Club; a place sadly lacking in either glitz or glamour. On entering the building, he was faced with 'a lot of people sitting round in flat hats, sipping pints. The ladies all seemed to have Guinnesses in front of them – and meat pies.' Needless to say it immediately became apparent to the young performer that this venue was no Hollywood nightclub. Despite his initial disappointment, he was paid 1s 9d for performing his vent act and telling a handful of jokes.

Dodd left Holt High School at fourteen and in doing so bade farewell to formal education. Unsurprisingly, he went to work in the family business, helping his father during the day and entertaining as a sideline. The day-to-day work, which he enjoyed, kept him trim and healthy: 'I had a body like Tarzan and muscles like Samson then.'

He started working in the office, and after the incident with the 15-foot hole was well and truly behind him, he was later trusted enough to drive the lorries. Making coal deliveries was hard work, particularly as it was necessary to be out in all weathers, come rain or shine. Each night he would return home in a blackened filthy state from head to foot. Looking back on this grimy time of his life, he later remarked that 'a bit of coal dust never hurt anybody', which was not without irony, given that both his father and he were to be plagued with emphysema.

There were compensations, however, as, with his brother Billy, he loved to chat up the ladies of Liverpool, which would provide yet more grist to his comedy mill. This period was to colour his whole view of life, and in particular, his art. Clearly he revelled in this rosy, cosy, smokeless-coal-fuelled post-war Britain. It was a world of nutty slack and black-leaded grates; of Hudsons washing powder and Playtex girdles. A world, indeed, of feather dusters. This gloriously parochial view of little Britain became the lifeblood of his act, and – incredibly, since those who share his memories are now an endangered species – remains so to this day.

It soon became evident that our Ken was never going to be content as a mere drudge. In an amazing example of youthful entrepreneurship, at the tender age of nineteen he decided to branch out by himself and become a self-employed salesman of pots, pans and polishes; a peripatetic tinker. From the back of an old furniture van, which had been converted by a carpenter friend named Fatty Oldham, he flogged what he called 'Kaydee' products to the good ladies of Liverpool, knocking on doors and saying to his prospective customers: 'Good morning, madam. Can I interest you in a brush or a bar of soap?' From these humble beginnings he worked hard and eventually moved on to opening a couple of shops, as well as producing his own disinfectants.

'I always wanted to be a success, so I realized that I'd have to strike out on my own,' he later told John Stapleton. The fact that he had to knock on countless doors boosted his confidence in dealing with people, and, as he himself has admitted, the experience also helped him to conquer his nerves as a comedian on stage.

At that point in his life he had become self-employed for the first time – indeed, he has never been anything else since – but more importantly he was learning what working-class humour was: the language that real people used. Customers loved his jokes and his cheering banter, particularly on wet and windy days when there was little to be happy about. He claims that it was from those days that he first coined the phrase 'Missus', another mainstay of his stage act. All comedians, he says, are a double act: the comic and the audience. 'Missus' is a useful cipher, a neat means by which to connect the comedian to those out front. Max Miller knew it, as did Frankie Howerd. And Doddy knew it too.

As Michael Billington has noted, 'I think he brings the salesman's art to comedy. He knows that laughs don't just happen; laughs have to be earned and laughs have to be acquired and projected, and there's a value to be placed on them. So I think there's an extraordinary range of things that work from this wild brain and wild imagination that he's got to his purely commercial salesman's instincts.'

Dodd's enterprise proved a formative lesson on a political level, too. He has become a vociferous advocate of self-reliance and enterprise: to whatever he turned his hand, it was obvious that Ken was always going to be a success . . . and never short of a few bob. If he had been born fifty years later, it is not inconceivable that he would have been a dot.com millionaire. This advocacy of all things enterprising, in turn, led to his much-publicized admiration for the work of Margaret Thatcher in the 1970s. Like many comics of the old school he admired the way she put Britain back on the map and instilled a sense of patriotism – let's not forget that even his tickling stick is red, white and blue. Thatcher reciprocated, going on record as saying that Dodd was her favourite comedian.

Over the years he has retained a tycoon mentality and still regards himself as a businessman. 'I believe that individual endeavour, providing it's legal, and giving service to one's fellow human beings, is entitled to be rewarded,' as he commented in Billington's *How Tickled I Am*. 'All men, I think, take to competitive games, and in a way business is like a competitive game, therefore the manliness and masculinity in you comes out strongly. To take a beating from another businessman is tantamount to being given a good hiding. So it's a matter of pride you run your business as competently and competitively as possible.'

It could have been the Divine Margaret herself speaking.

This attitude could apply to Kaydee pots and pans as much as KD tickles and titters. A businessman is a businessman, whatever his line of work. Dodd brought that hard-edged business ethic from the back of his van and deposited it in the dressing room. Few comics have quite the same focus or drive, however: most are motivated only by laughs, many have no interest in money, make lousy businessmen, and are often taken for a ride by unscrupulous agents and producers. Benny Hill, for example, would only cash cheques when a pile of them dislodged an ornament on his mantelpiece. But right from the start, Dodd's performing career was instigated primarily with a view to swelling his coffers. All the money he earned as a part-time entertainer went into his business. Like all would-be entrepreneurs, he appreciated that he needed capital to expand. Tinkering door-to-door by day, he would tinker with his act by night. He has insisted that it was never his intention to embark upon a career as a professional comedian; it was simply a means of subsidizing his Kaydee empire. However, when it became clear that he could earn even more money by becoming a full-time entertainer, only then did he think it prudent to spend less time building up his sales business and more on developing his comedy act.

While he had no desire to change his amateur status, his mother was disappointed, and thought that professionalism was clearly the next step. It was she who initially recognized his comic gifts and encouraged him to add more comedy to his vent act. In spite of his mother's resolute faith in his comedic talents, however, cautious Ken thought he was too young to be a comic. Perhaps he felt that despite having youth on his side, and being possessed of a young man's natural stamina, energy and enthusiasm, he was still missing such vital elements as experience, knowledge and gravitas, which he thought were needed to make a successful comedian. Until he acquired these essential extras, and achieved the necessary balance that was crucial to his act, it is possible that he imagined he wouldn't be properly equipped to launch a professional career in comedy.

It seems inconceivable: Doddy the reluctant comic. It is as if – at that period in his life, at least – the decision to become a comedian came as much from the head as from the heart. But thus was born 'Professor Yaffle Chuckabutty, Operatic Tenor and Sausage Knotter', and how apt that the man who once flogged feather dusters would eventually make his name by waving one around on stage.

Those early days saw Dodd booked for some bizarre engagements. For example, there was the time he performed at a funeral directors' annual dinner held at a Bradford hotel. He and four other entertainers were informed, 'If you don't go on, you don't get paid'. The speeches were lengthy, and a jobsworth licensee said the event would have to finish at 11 p.m. on the dot come what may. At 10.45 p.m. he announced, 'OK, and now for the show.' All the acts stood around looking bemused, wondering which of them would get the chance to do their routine. Then it dawned on them that if they all did two-and-a-half minutes each they would all receive their money. 'We were laughing more than the audience,' Dodd explained. 'Each one went on, told one-and-a-half jokes and was practically yanked off by the next artist waiting to go on and collect £1.'

It was all a steep learning curve for the young Dodd as he played some pretty grotty dates, like the supposedly upmarket affair at the Sandon Hotel in Liverpool. It turned out to be a beer-and-stout bottlers outing. Dodd arrived at 10 p.m. and before he could begin his act he had to crunch his way through the masses of broken glass that littered the floor, evidence that a good time had already been had by all. Then there was his first all-male stag dinner. He asked amateur tenor Ernest Reynolds – by day, a detective superintendent – if he should 'mix it a little', to which the policeman replied: 'Look son, these are intelligent men and you can tell any sort of joke, white or blue, as long as it's clever and doesn't insult their intelligence. That's all you have to remember at stag shows.'

Even though he was finding entertaining more lucrative than selling wares, he was still reluctant to turn pro, which his mother attributed to her son's love of home. However, Dodd soon progressed to becoming a regular on the after-dinner circuit in hotels all over Liverpool and Birkenhead. Often he did two or three in one night. Oddly, it was Dodd's original intention to become a visual comedian – he didn't want to tell jokes, but gradually he realized that he loved words. He then started building up joke files and developing his spoken act, with a view to getting into radio.

He also used to work a lot with a tenor called Ken Pike. Together they decided to cast their net a little wider than Liverpool and opted to try Manchester, which would prove to be an important step forwards in the development of Dodd's career in entertainment because his appearances in Manchester introduced him to a number of prominent Jewish people connected to the show-business world: 'From one particular show I got five offers from London agents like Bernard Delfont, Lew Grade and others. I was tickled by the interest in me.' Consequently this made Dodd think long and hard about whether it was now the right time to cross over to the professional side of show business.

Then, in the spring of 1954, twenty-seven-year-old Dodd received a letter that would change his mind . . . and his life. It was from David Forrester, a London agent, who, like Delfont and Grade, had learned of Dodd's act from the favourable reviews that had followed his numerous appearances in Manchester. An introductory meeting was soon arranged, and it was during afternoon tea at the Adelphi Hotel in Liverpool that the two became acquainted. Despite the comedian's initial misgivings about the idea of having an agent, it soon transpired that the husky-voiced, fiftysomething clearly knew his stuff.

In an interview with *Liverpool Post* reporter Philip Key,

Dodd recalled that Forrester had ordered tea and cakes for them both, but that Dodd had had to pay for them. Consequently, it became clear to Dodd that the agent obviously had some worth if he could manage his clients' money as well as he could take care of his own. Describing the meeting in Billington's *How Tickled I Am*, Dodd revealed why he decided to engage Forrester's services as his agent: 'I chose him not because he was a good agent – in the conversation, in fact, he appeared to be a terrible agent – but he looked like my dad: roughly the same height and had a head shaped like an egg. He looked like my dad, so I trusted him.'

Dodd quickly realized that David Forrester was not the usual brash kind of cove; he was more of a gent. Thus, after signing up with him (or rather *not* signing up – they didn't have a contract for nineteen years), and with his new agent's backing, he was prepared to take a leap into the unknown and, to the delight of his parents, make the decision to turn pro.

Having abandoned all thoughts of expanding his business empire in order to concentrate his efforts on developing a career in the world of entertainment, therefore, when Dodd took his first tentative steps as a fledgling showbiz professional, it was an altogether different kind of empire that he sought desperately to conquer . . .

3

Sharpening the Acts

THE EMPIRE THEATRE, Nottingham has the distinction
of being the venue for Ken Dodd's professional debut.
The date was 27 September 1954. Many years later he was
to be instrumental in saving the theatre from closure (indeed,
as a tireless campaigner of live theatre, he has since helped to
save many others, including the Manchester Palace, the
Blackpool Grand and the Morecambe Winter Gardens), but
back in 1954 the Empire was where he first saw his name in
print . . . just. 'I was a small name on the bill,' he later said.
'Not as big as the printer's.'

Though Dodd's name might have been writ small, David
Forrester had been working hard on behalf of his new client,
and it had only taken him a matter of weeks to arrange this
initial engagement. Sharing a bill with a singer called Tony
Brent, jazz trumpeter Kenny Baker, a group of singers called
The Kordites, three strongmen and 'one or two strong girls',
Dodd recalled: 'It was my first week as a pro – a brand new
stick of greasepaint, a few new gags, six clean shirts and a
soul full of hope!'

Fifty years on, Kenny Baker still remembers Dodd's act. He recollects that Dodd wore a hat with corks on it – the kind normally associated with Australians – except that his hat had been adapted into one that sported ping-pong balls. Part of his act consisted of him miming to noises emanating from the orchestra – for example, using his teeth to mimic castanets. 'It was marvellous how he had worked out how he could do things with the use of the orchestra,' said Baker, who thought it was very clever and well thought out. 'You could tell that he'd studied his business.'

And he certainly had. It was during his first professional performances that Dodd began his legendary post-show analysis, when, after each show he would buy himself a pie and a coffee, then retire to his hotel to go through his act, gag by gag, to work out which jokes had been successful, and which jokes had failed to pass muster. As far as Dodd was concerned, 'It seemed only common sense to me to go over what one had done, and try and refine and improve it.'

It is odd how quite often familiarity breeds not contempt, but contentment; how the more we know something the more we like it. For example, how many times have you listened to an unfamiliar track on an album, not really liked or indeed even remembered it, only to start enjoying it after repeated playings? It is the same with a new comic. It is common for the majority of people to take an immediate dislike to an unknown quantity. We gaze at them defiantly, our impassive expressions screaming: 'Go on – make me laugh, then.' It is only when we have warmed to the personality behind the microphone that we accept them as a friend. Then the mask begins to crack and we start to laugh.

Having said that, the Great British audience is an incredibly loyal one; once they have accepted a comedian, they take them to their bosom and will forgive them practically anything – a case in point being Tony Hancock, a man who at the peak of his career abandoned everything the public loved about him – his Railway Cuttings-based character in particular – dispensed with his best writers, and embarked on a series of ultimately disastrous film, TV and stand-up projects in a futile attempt to look for something new. It is also true that very occasionally the heart-felt admiration we have for a comic topples over into the realms of love, which is why the death of a comedian hits us far more than the passing of a tragedian – for example, what are the odds that few of us can remember where we were when we heard of the death of John Gielgud, but that many still feel the sense of loss when they first became aware of Eric Morecambe's demise? Actors are aloof; comedians are of the people. Actors talk to each other; comedians talk to us.

We are now so familiar with the accoutrements and idiosyncrasies of Dodd's act that it is difficult to imagine what that first Nottingham audience witnessed. What were they to make of this weird, garishly-attired apparition, given to performing unique renditions of 'The Floral Dance' and 'On the Road to Mandalay'? It is one thing leaning on a mike, dripping in gold jewellery and trotting out a few gags, but when you are presenting something completely fresh to an initially bewildered public, you are really flying by the seat of your pants. There is, after all, a very thin line between inspired surrealism and plain silliness. Dodd, however, remembers that his professional debut went reasonably well – he didn't storm 'em, but neither did he embarrass himself.

Jazz singer and fellow Liverpudlian George Melly first heard of Dodd in the 1950s. 'The band leader I was with through the fifties, Mick Mulligan, came on a train from the north and he said to me: "I sat next to a guy who's apparently a comedian called Ken Dodd. And he had me in fits until we got to Euston." And that was the first time I'd ever heard of him.'

But Dodd's anonymity was not going to last for long; he was on the way up. The downside to his new circumstances on the road, however, was that he soon discovered it wasn't much fun spending time away from home and living in digs. And thanks to David Forrester's endeavours, that is exactly what he found himself doing – drinking in the delights of Leeds, Sunderland, Blackpool and Manchester. The then *Manchester Guardian* noted: 'The trammels of gentility still cling to the splendid down-at-heel madness as portrayed by Mr Ken Dodd at the Hippodrome last evening.'

The rise of 'The Unpredictable Ken Dodd', as he was then billed, was fairly meteoric. In 1955 he played his first summer season at the Central Pier, Blackpool, on a bill headed by Kenny Baker, which also included Morecambe and Wise and Jimmy Clitheroe; within a year of his professional debut in Nottingham, Dodd topped his first bill at the Royal Court, Warrington. ('It's now a supermarket, I think,' the comedian has since commented.) In 1956 he returned to the Central Pier with Jimmy James, Jimmy Clitheroe once again, and Roy Castle, and by 1958, it was Dodd who was topping the bill in Blackpool. A year later he had his first TV series.

Looking back, it is hard to appreciate how unimportant television was considered in the 1950s. Radio still ruled, while the huge wooden box in the corner of the room with its curious valves and tiny grey screen was perceived as something of a novelty; in the early 1950s, because only a limited number of households could afford such a luxury item, there were still fewer than two million homes which had access to a TV set that was capable of receiving a signal.

Still, when BBC producer Barney Colehan expressed an interest in seeing Dodd with the possibility of putting him on his show, *The Good Old Days*, Dodd was cautiously interested – after all, the music-hall-inspired programme that was broadcast from Leeds City Varieties could not have been a more perfect vehicle for him. The opportunity arose after Colehan bumped into Jess Yates while staying at a hotel in Llandudno in August 1954. Yates, the former photographer-turned film-maker, had suggested to the producer that it might be worth his while to nip over to Colwyn Bay to catch this bright young comic from Liverpool, where he was appearing in a summer-season bill.

They drove over to see the show and Colehan was indeed impressed. 'Ken Dodd had immediate rapport with the audience,' he recalled. 'He looked funny and his humour was original, and his warm, infectious personality captivated everyone.' Realizing that his comedic style was ideal for *The Good Old Days*, he offered him a spot on his TV programme there and then. Dodd did not feel quite ready, however, and it wasn't until the following year, on 11 March 1955, that he made his first appearance on the show, for which he was paid the grand sum of £32. 9s. 4d. Colehan was justifiably proud of his discovery, later remarking of the outstandingly talented Dodd: 'His patter was quick and topical and his face was his fortune. The audience laughed at him before he spoke a word.'

Radio work beckoned for Dodd at roughly the same time. He made his debut on *Workers' Playtime* – an incredibly popular programme that took various variety turns round the country performing to factories and businesses – although his tendency to do another twenty minutes after his eight-minute act hardly endeared him to the bosses. It was later, while appearing at the Sunderland Empire with Jimmy James in 1955, that Dodd got to know James's son (and stooge), Jim Casey. Casey, who was later to become a BBC radio producer, was at that time writing scripts for the Corporation, and was to become instrumental in promoting Dodd's talent. Like Colehan, he was impressed by Dodd, and was greatly amused by his act when he saw it for the first time. He was particularly struck by Dodd's visual attributes as a comedian, and felt that there was a certain star quality about him. Even his discerning father was in agreement.

Not long after Casey had joined the BBC, he recommended Dodd to the then head of light entertainment in Manchester, Ronnie Taylor. Despite being an hour late for the proposed meeting (his lack of punctuality would become a recurring theme throughout his professional career), Dodd was offered his first radio series. He duly accepted the proposal, and in September 1958 began work on *It's Great To Be Young,* alongside a cast that included impressionist Peter Goodwright and Judith Chalmers. Recorded at the Manchester Playhouse on Sunday afternoons, the programme was co-written by Jim Casey and Frank Roscoe, and was also produced by the former.

Things were starting to move along swiftly for Dodd, but it was not all plain sailing. In *Personal Portrait*, he told Alexandra Connor about his debut as a young comic at the 'house of terror', the Glasgow Empire, a venue notorious for its dislike of English comedians. 'On the Monday morning the manager said, "Right, who are the comedians?" And three of us stepped forward. And he said, "No football gags – cos we need the seats – and Friday night all English comedians get the bird" (a slow hand clap).' Dodd also went on to reveal that he and his fellow comics were also told to expect such taunts as 'Away hay an' boil yer head!'

'So on the Friday I tottered on to the stage with my shirt hanging out and my hair all over the place, and this man uncoiled himself from the second row, looked up and said, "Cripes! What a horrible sight!" And that was my first laugh in Glasgow.'

Of course, his first line, borrowed from an American comic and later used by comedian Ted Ray when he was surprised by his appearance on *This Is Your Life*, didn't help;

'I suppose you're all wondering why I sent for you' was hardly likely to go down a storm with the working men of Glasgow.

What is odd – possibly unique, even – is how Dodd's act seems to have sprung from the womb more or less fully formed. It did not appear to take him years of trial and error to develop into the manic Doddy we recognize today. Although his act is in a perpetual state of flux ('I've never done the same show twice in all the fifty years I've been in show business, because every audience is different'), the basic ingredients were there right from the beginning.

As Bob Monkhouse observed in *Behind the Laughter*: 'I find it quite extraordinary that certain comedians seem to burst into bloom overnight. They might have been quite ordinary entertainers – even second or third raters – and then suddenly they have this wonderful period of creative strength. And with Doddy it all seemed to happen within twelve months. He seemed to know how to say "tattifilarious" and "plumptious" and go "nikky nokky noo" . . . and the Diddymen and the jam-butty mines and the little old grand-dads rolling out on a sea of marmalade to dive for oranges . . . It all was there, and somehow it never needed to change after that because all the creativity had happened. He had his great burst – it was like the universe had been created, but it was that his was comedy.'

It should not be forgotten, of course, that although his professional career was in its infancy by the late 1950s, he had already clocked up almost twenty years' experience as an amateur. As Kenny Baker had acknowledged, he had certainly done his homework. And perhaps because he was not offering orthodox stand-up comedy fare, Dodd appears to have given the theory of comedy a lot more thought than most.

'It's very psychological, laughter,' he told Alexandra Connor. 'Laughter comes from the back of your mind . . . or rather jokes come from the back of your mind, not the front. Laughter is the outward display of pleasure – feeling good all over. And it is a wonderful thing. Men and women are the only animal that laughs . . . or needs to, or cries, I think, as well. People say the hyena laughs but that's a bark. God has given us this wonderful gift of laughter, which is a balm to a mind that is hurting. It is a soothing influence; it is a release, a relaxation. A wonderful feeling, effervescent – that's a place in Wales!'

In attempting to explain his many humour theories, he has described them in a highly visual sense on numerous occasions, using a scale of colours to convey his views. 'There's a rainbow of laughter,' Dodd has often said. 'Right at the very top there's the white laughter, the laughter of pure joy, and you can hear that any time you want for free if you're passing any children's playground or schoolyard, and you can see little children jumping up and down for sheer joy of being alive. And as you go through the spectrum of the rainbow there are different colours; there's red, yellow, blue. And near the bottom are the dark colours of sarcasm, irony, satire and insult.'

Here is a sharp mind at work, and not just a clever comic mind, but one with an inherent intelligence. But as comedian Steve Punt has said, he can't imagine why anyone would think that any comedian wasn't intelligent, particularly when it would be impossible to write about anything without having a well-informed interest in the world. The creation of jokes requires a certain intellect because it is primarily about drawing ideas together that wouldn't necessarily go together naturally. Comics tend to be trivia fans who acquire a lot of knowledge, although not in a traditionally academic way. Indeed, often they're the bright ones who have slipped through the system. 'I've generally found over the years that almost all comedians are quite bright, albeit often in the sort of teachers-didn't-know-how-to-deal-with-it-kind of way,' says Punt. All of which could possibly account for Dodd's mischievous streak at school.

When a young Barry Norman was sent to interview Dodd the day before his first run at the London Palladium came to a close in the mid-1960s, he asked the comic if he was surprised by the fact that he'd attracted the attention of the intelligentsia. Dodd replied that he wasn't, and made the point that their enjoyment was related to the sheer originality of his act. For those people willing to dismiss him merely as a 'stand-up patter man', he issued an outright denial of such an ignorant suggestion: 'I'm not. I do visuals, a bit of wit, a bit of satire, political lampoons, a lot of way-out stuff – the full kaleidoscope of comedy.'

Even with his genius and supreme confidence, and despite being armed with an act prepared with the utmost meticulousness, it comes as something of a surprise to learn that unlike his hero Arthur Askey, who claimed never to have suffered from nerves in his life, Dodd was – and indeed still is – always petrified on stage. His friends and colleagues will attest to this; it is no affectation. Mike Craig, for one, cannot understand why Dodd should be nervous, given his popularity and years of experience. But psychologist Professor Richard Wiseman, who has witnessed Dodd backstage at close hand, is not so sure it is nerves: 'What a lot of charismatics do is create a sense of chaos around them, and he does that. They don't want certainty – certainty's boring. It's all a bit mad. It's about transgressing boundaries, as indeed humour is, as indeed his act is. It's all about saying, here's normality and I'm bigger than that. And here are the boundaries and these are things you shouldn't really say and I'm going to say them.'

Whether that theory is correct or not, Dodd sees it simply as nerves . . . and it goes without saying that in those early days it was even worse. 'When I first started in the business,' he later explained to Alexandra Connor, 'I used to get terrible nerves – dreadful stage fright. You reason it out: everybody's afraid of what they don't understand.'

Concluding that his stage fright was down to ignorance, he set about conquering it by trying to understand what makes a comic work. To that end, if you're going to make a stab at putting a comedy act together, he reasoned, you're going to need certain ingredients. With his love of music, Dodd quickly hit on the idea of incorporating that into his act: 'Mimicry is very important and in those days there were all sorts of baritone singers singing things like "The Floral Dance". I thought this was a good thing to burlesque, to exaggerate. So I used to appear as Professor Rufus Chucklebutty, Operatic Tenor and Sausage Knotter, and I used to come on in an old tailcoat.' This early costume, coupled with the sticky-up hair, was all about anarchy. It was, he says, his 'gesture of defiance'. As any self-respecting punk will admit, hair is a highly visible sign of iconoclasm. It is also a useful method for Dodd to signal his mood: in tattifilarious mode on stage it is all over the place, reminiscent of a windswept haystack; when he wants to be taken seriously (i.e., in Shakespearean roles or in a court of law) it is tamed, plastered down like a tailor's dummy.

Then, he thought, what about a few comedy props? Dodd used them initially as a means of controlling his nerves: 'Props are an extension of a comedian or an actor's personality. I first started carrying a big, battered, old euphonium to stop me waving my hands around. When you first go on the stage, anybody who's not used to it waves their hands round like a windmill, they're all over the place. It's nervousness, I think, or maybe trying to exaggerate things more than they should be. So you need something to anchor you down.' He told Michael Billington that he opted for the euphonium because to him it epitomized music, and was an apt musical symbol: 'I hadn't realized it then, but it was also very phallic.' In that simpler, more innocent age the joke was that although Dodd would always lug the huge great musical instrument on to the stage, ultimately he never played it.

Approximately two years after making his professional debut, he converted an ordinary feather duster into the 'tickling stick', which had the advantage of being another phallic symbol, and was an effect that became instantly synonymous with his comedy act. He has compared it to the type of prop that a jester would have used at court – 'The jester of old used to have all these various props; he had a slapstick, which is two pieces of wood that makes a slapping sound. He had a fool's licence: he was able to do and say things that nobody else dare.' It is true to say that there has always been something of the risqué, something of the seaside postcard about Dodd, which has sometimes proved to be infectious: in the 1960s many a school playground rung to the sound of schoolboys' crude usurpation of Dodd's signature tune – 'A pe-nis, a pe-nis, the greatest gift that I possess. I thank the Lord that I've been blessed with more than my share of a pe-nis' – though somehow one suspects that Dodd would not have approved.

Next, he turned his attention towards thinking up a suitable catchphrase. Most comedians' catchphrases just seem to come into being; in some cases the audience beats the performer to recognizing one. True to form though, Dodd gave his considerable thought. 'I wanted a catchphrase that would stand the test of time – that you could permutate. So I'd say, "How tickled I am" and then you could put another bit on to it – "How tickled I am under the circumstances. Have you ever been tickled under the circumstances, Missus? How tickled I am by all this good will. Have you ever been tickled by Good Will, Missus? Good old Willie." See, you can permutate it.'

Finally, if you're going to be a family entertainer – and that was always Dodd's intention – you need to provide some kind of distraction for the younger members of your audience. Thus were born the Diddymen: 'We had a family word in our house and that was "diddy" – anything that was small, quaint, whimsical and lovable.' From an early age he was always making doodles of these rotund, diminutive characters. He reckons his Great Uncle Jack, who always wore a bowler hat and loved his pint, was the inspiration for them, although as writer John Fisher notes, they also owe a little to Lord Snooty and his Pals in *The Beano*.

But Dodd did not have the monopoly on Diddymen – Arthur Askey, for one, told jokes about them, and also jambutty mines and treacle factories. An explanation as to their origins comes from Arthur Askey, who revealed that they were simply a common local joke in the Liverpool area at that time. 'I was a diddy man. My Uncle Arthur, who was five feet three inches like me, he was a diddy man,' said Askey. 'Everybody used to crack jokes about the treacle mines at Oglett and the jam-butty mines at Otterspool.' Similarly, jam butties, or jam sandwiches, had their origins in being part of the staple diet of the poor in Liverpool in the 1920s and 1930s – the combination of cheap bread and sugary jam gave those who were desperate some much-needed energy food. 'The jam butty was what you got for being good in Liverpool in the Depression,' according to the *Liverpool Echo*'s Joe Riley. 'A jam butty was a big treat in Liverpool in Ken Dodd's youth, and it's just become a rather nonsense thing now, but again it comes from reality.'

Riley maintains that a lot of Dodd's act was very localized, and 'more derivative than people think'; all that mythology and folklore of jam-butty mines and Diddymen, he says, was not based on Liverpool humour, but it related to a very small area of the city: 'The whole idea of the

Diddymen came from Arthur Askey and Ted Ray. They went around calling themselves "diddy men" because it was a Liverpool phrase. If you were smaller than most people you were the "diddy man" in the family.'

But whereas the likes of Askey dropped these parochial references as they migrated south, Dodd stood by them, and was rewarded for his perseverance in retaining his quirky northern terms by becoming a national treasure.

Joe Riley notes that like many comedians of that era – including Frankie Howerd, Tommy Cooper, Morecambe and Wise – Ken Dodd never managed to export himself to America: 'A lot of American comics came this way – Jack Benny, Danny Kaye, Bob Hope – but he never managed to sell himself as a British act abroad because his act was about stealing the lead off roofs, having a bath in a tin bath, falls of soot, and Dickie Mint. It was very parochial in a way. In fact it's a wonder he managed to export himself to London, quite frankly.'

Armed with all this comic ammunition, nature gifted Dodd the rest. As Barney Colehan observed, his face was his fortune. Indeed Dodd's whole appearance proved a bonus: 'I started using my hair, my teeth, of course, which I've made a lot of – "By Jove, Missus! I'm the only one in our house who can kiss a girl and nibble her ear at the same time!" And my fingers – I don't know how they got like that – I'm not double-jointed. So you make the most of what you've got. Your body becomes a prop.'

He has also said that he was lucky to have such unique teeth, eyes and hair, because, as far as he was concerned, 'you can't be frightened of anyone like that, can you?' On the face of it, 'frightened' is perhaps an odd word to use, but Dodd himself confessed to John Hind that as a youngster he didn't like Laurel and Hardy because he found them 'threatening' – a criticism, ironically, some have levelled at Dodd. A few people I have spoken to confessed to me that they thought there was something slightly sinister about Dodd; they find him unsettling, in the same way they find clowns disturbing. Of course, the faithful cannot see that at all, and it is clear that right from the start Dodd was anxious to be perceived as a non-threatening, family-oriented entertainer.

Slowly but surely, like Frankenstein's monster, Dodd was acquiring all the attributes he deemed necessary to become a successful comedian and expertly moulding them together. But in the same way that an average chef and a talented chef might take identical ingredients and produce wildly varying dishes, so a competent comic and a brilliant comic will come up with acts of contrasting quality. As cartoonist Bill Tidy has said: 'Comedians with check suits and propellers on their hats have always left me cold. They've got to have more than that. Doddy only uses that as a trapeze – he's off . . . whizz. I think he could come on dressed as a bear and they'd know it was Doddy straight away.'

The thought that went into his act was, and is, impressive. 'It looks like it's three-and-a-half hours or five hours or seven hours of anarchy,' says Michael Billington. 'But it's not. It's carefully calibrated, carefully structured. And it's this combination, I think, of apparent wild spontaneity with an act that is most beautifully structured and organized that makes him unique among working comedians.'

Michael Grade reiterates the point: 'All his entrances are calculated. What suit will he wear, and when. It's all worked out, nothing's left to chance. And all the gags are written on the hands – all the routines to remind him. His hands are covered in Biro and if you watch, you'll see him.'

Indeed, I was told by someone who was once backstage with Dodd's later partner, Anne Jones, that when asked how long he would be, Anne stopped to catch a snatch of his act and said, 'About twenty minutes.' Sure enough, he finished exactly twenty minutes later.

Denis Norden is very much in awe of Dodd's retrieval system: 'What he has is this enormous library inside his head – something he shares with Bob Monkhouse. He had this quite exceptional memory; if it was a physical characteristic he'd be a freak. But it's no good having that unless you have powers of instant retrieval. And both of them have it – it comes up the chute from the recesses of the subconscious.'

Nicholas Parsons has also noted this aspect of Dodd. 'Ken Dodd's brain is like a comic computer,' he said. 'You can throw anything at him and he will immediately come back with a joke – or even a series of jokes – on that subject.' Similarly, Victoria Wood has remarked: 'It doesn't seem to be a set routine. He seems to be bringing in chunks of jokes as they appear appropriate as he goes along. He must have such a sort of encyclopaedia in his head of stuff that he can call on.'

When explaining the skills required to become a comic to Alexandra Connor, Dodd revealed that a comedian is part orator. 'You have to harangue an audience. You have to play an audience, the different parts of an audience. You have to be an actor because you have to act the jokes. You have to be an observer because you have to take little pieces, slices of life, people's characterizations. A poet, a singer, dancer, mime . . . all these things come together to make what we call a solo comedian.'

Once the would-be comic has acquired these skills and some material, it is then that the problems really start. Where does he or she go from there? According to Dodd, the first thing to do is to establish a rapport with the audience, in the same way that actors do: 'I call it building a bridge. Your first words are very important when you go on stage because you have to try to make them like you, try to make them love you.' This is a point he stressed again during his *Desert Island Discs* broadcast with Sue Lawley: 'An audience's relationship with an artist is absolutely wonderful. Gracie Fields used to say it was like a silver thread between the performer and the audience.'

Having built that bridge it is then necessary to retain contact with the audience, by first avoiding the temptation to play to the first two or three rows. Instead, it is better to concentrate on the audience in the seats upstairs: 'You've got to make them feel that they're part of the show – you have to try to hug them all and bring them all to you.' According to Dodd, it is possible to do this by trying to talk to each member of the audience on a one-to-one basis. 'You do as far as you can see, which is about twelve rows back, you speak to the people. I get most of my act from the audience. I've always done a double act. Like you have Laurel and Hardy, there's always been myself and the audience. Every audience is different because it's a permutation of different people, of different personalities.'

Possibly taking his cue from his hero Arthur Askey, Dodd is one of the few celebratory comedians who prefers not to rely on negative criticism to generate his humour, as Victoria Wood points out: 'Whereas most comedians come on and say, "You know, I've had a terrible day" or "I'll tell you something awful that's happened," Ken comes on and says, "What a beautiful day . . ." I can't think of anyone else who starts in that way, who manages to get jokes out of something positive.'

As ever with Dodd, the optimism is as calculated as everything else about his act: 'I do optimistic comedy – "What a beautiful day!" I'm as good as saying, "Trust me with your chuckle muscle, trust me with your sense of humour. Trust me – let me tickle your mind because I'm harmless and all I want is to make you laugh and to love you."'

The word 'love' seems to crop up quite often when Dodd talks about his motivation in wooing the viewing public, and gaining their confidence, but ultimately it is a question of his dominating them. 'I think you have to make the audience trust you,' says Dodd. 'For a time it's a partnership, but gradually you get the upper hand.'

It is, of course, a power thing, and Dodd has made no secret of the sense of the feeling of empowerment that performing gives him: 'To go out to a giant audience is a wonderful feeling when you've "got them". There comes a time when you go on stage and you do all the nonsense – "Hello, folks! Please, please love me; please, please love me" – and then suddenly you tell one or two really good ones and that's it! Got 'em! Got 'em! And then you can relax, you can do any sort of joke you like.'

Power and love – they seem to go hand in hand. These are the gifts audiences bestow on Dodd. Here – along with a certain amount of financial remuneration – is his raison d'être. He would be the first to admit that he has been particularly fortunate in being able to combine the two so successfully.

There appears to be no end to Dodd's analysis – he has even given thought to the issue of tense, by clarifying the difference between 'is' and 'was' comedy. As he described in *Behind the Laughter*: '"Is" comedy happens now, and if you make it look like an ad lib, as if you are making it up on the spur of the moment, it's very, very appealing. "Was" comedy is "There was this fellah . . ." – you're relating an anecdote that happened. But if you actually perform the anecdote or make it look like it's happening now, it has ten times the effect. You have to use your body language, any acting ability you have, any impressions – it all helps to make that straight line believable so that when the tag comes in it's very, very potent.'

Dodd claims there are two ways to perform, either *with* an audience or *at* them. Whereas a singer performs *at* an audience, and either people did or didn't like the song, a comedian has to work at building each and every line *with* an audience, not unlike building a house. Thus, if a couple of lines fall flat, the house will collapse and the audience is completely lost; according to Dodd, a good comedian tries to make sure that never happens.

As for material, he believes that it is crucial to talk about the most important thing in an audience's life – themselves: 'Strangely enough, people love to be joshed, kidded, just teased. People love to hear the place got at, slagged: "By Jove! What beautiful architecture here. This is what they call early Portakabin with a hint of mock Wimpey." They love to hear that.' Then, after members of the audience have tentatively taken the bait, Dodd's next step is to reel them in by piling on the jokes: 'I think I try to get as many gags in and as many bits in as I can. Probably sometimes I overdo it. But I try to work on five t.p.m. and when I'm on a roll seven t.p.m. – titters per minute.'

This is a point not lost on Nicholas Parsons: 'The pace of his delivery, the style of his delivery keeps him going, and once he's got you laughing he keeps you laughing at sometimes quite simple and inane things.' As Dodd told Monkhouse, it was imperative that once the momentum had been built up sufficiently, a comedian should never let an audience rest: 'No, you keep them on a roll if you can. When you get an audience on a roll, that's it.'

It all sounds quite simple when put like that, but embryonic comedians may derive some crumb of comfort from the fact that even for Dodd, there have been times when it has all gone horribly wrong. Hard though it may be to believe, even Doddy has died on stage in front of less receptive audiences: 'Sometimes an audience doesn't give you what you want because of various reasons. Sometimes the weather can affect people. I've actually stood on the stage at Blackpool Opera House and among 3,500 people on a wet day I've seen a cloud hovering about 15 feet above the audience. Honestly. Steam coming off the audience.

'When the laughs aren't coming, perhaps when you're trying new material out and it isn't happening, then your top lip sticks to your teeth and you get "flop sweat". And then you've got to get out of it as best you can.'

It is at such difficult times that Dodd has had to rely on quick-thinking and the sudden inspiration of an ad lib: 'An ad lib is the most wonderful thing. It's miraculous. When you've been in love with comedy a long, long time and when you've performed comedy a long, long time you learn to trust your brain.'

When the old comic John Gay got a bolt-from-the-blue brainwave, he used to say that he was getting a spirit message from Dan Leno; Dodd wholeheartedly agrees. He claims that a good 75 per cent of his current act was ad-libbed at some point or another, and that whenever he gets a good response to a particular off-the-cuff joke, then it usually stays in his act for ever. He even goes as far as to furnish the boys in the band with notebooks, so that if inspiration should strike and he thinks an ad lib is worth remembering, he gives them the nod and they write it down.

The combination of theory and analysis is one thing; inspiration and experience is another matter entirely. 'You're able to call upon a little imp inside you,' explains Dodd. 'I don't know what you'd call it, a crazy spirit, that tells you instinctively what to do. That if you're doing an explorer bit or a soldier that you've got to wear long, khaki shorts – there's no other way of doing it.' Something with which the late Eric Morecambe would doubtless concur.

Even when an act is going well, and the audience seems to be lapping up joke after joke, there is still the fear that everything might fall flat, even for confident performers like Dodd. He himself has said that there is an element of insecurity within all comics, based on the belief that you are only as good as your last laugh: 'All comedians are conscious of the fact that you're walking a tightrope all the time. A joke is like a watch mechanism: there can't be one word too many or one word too few. It's all a rhythm – each word has to be a very special word in a very special place with a very special rhythm.'

Putting his various thoughts and theories into practice, Dodd had carefully assembled an act that, although might have nodded at others, turned out to be entirely unique; a delicious, delirious blend of the old and the new, the familiar and the traditional coupled with the fresh and innovative. In short, he had adhered to his father's advice and using his family, his background, his instincts and his intelligence in equal dollops had mined a seam of comedy that was totally his own. What is more, due to his naturally restless spirit, it is one that has stood him in good stead. He has always known that in order to keep himself from going stale and to retain the public's interest it was necessary to ring certain changes in his act, but none that would erode the crucial bond of familiarity that he had built up between him and his audience.

So it was that Ken Dodd found himself steadily climbing the showbiz ladder. Dave Forrester was coming up with the goods and the comedian soon realized his diary was filling up fast.

In those halcyon, pre-package-tour days, the summer season in Blackpool – a comic's shop window, according to Forrester – was crucial. In its heyday the town had about eleven theatres, including the Winter Gardens, the Grand, the Royal Pavilion, the Queen's, Feldman's, the Opera House and those on the three piers. Dodd went down extremely well with Blackpool's holidaymakers, who lapped him up to such an extent that it became increasingly difficult to lure him off stage.

By August 1955 Dodd had acquired both a strong following and a second-hand Jag. In November, impresario Peter Webster dangled a contract for the next Blackpool summer season before him: it was for a three-figure salary. That Christmas it was off to Sheffield for his pantomime debut as Jolly Jenkins in *Red Riding Hood*. Dodd loved it – he particularly liked the fact that it afforded him the opportunity to perform to children.

In May 1956 he topped the bill on his homeground, at the 2,400-seater Liverpool Empire. Both his parents and his then fiancée, Anita, were in the audience. Things were on the up for Dodd as he began to make a name for himself on the variety circuit. He found that being a good rookie comic, it was much easier to make an impact and steal the show, because he had the element of surprise in his favour. So, when Dodd appeared at the Coventry Hippodrome later that year he was able, as an unknown, to make an impression on the expectant audience. He and an equally youthful Tommy Cooper found themselves on a bill headed by Jimmy Jewel and his cousin Ben Warriss.

Initially, Dodd was given a spot immediately after Cooper's act, which he thought was disastrous, as the two performers were quite similar in many ways. Fortunately, sanity prevailed, and he was told to follow a piece of Jewel and Warriss slapstick that acted almost like a warm-up for him. He recalled the comic duo with affection and gratitude, remembering how they had both given him invaluable help: Jewel with advice and material; Warriss with introductions to influential showbiz contacts.

In the same way that Dodd's encounter with Dave Forrester had proved to be a lucky break, in the mid-1950s he was also fortunate to meet Eddie Braben, a writer whose style meshed so well with his own. The young Braben had always been obsessed with variety and comics. At the age of nine or ten he would leave his home in the Dingle, a poor part of Liverpool, and walk about three miles to the Pavilion Theatre alone in order to collect autographs. He soon became a fixture at Liverpool theatres: the Royal Court, the Shakespeare, the Pavilion and the biggest, the Empire, where all the big American names appeared. But amid these entertainment heavyweights came the up-and-coming new turns, the likes of Morecambe and Wise . . . and Ken Dodd.

After Braben had completed his National Service, his father, a butcher, bought him a fruit and veg stall in Liverpool's St John's market (the same place where Anne Robinson's glamorous mother sold poultry). By Braben's own admission, however, it was not a huge success. The pitch was in a bad position, and to compound the problem he confesses to having been paralysed by shyness: 'I found it difficult to go over to people and say, "Can I help you?" I used to stand there writing jokes on the back of bags while the fruit was going rotten.' In his spare time he continued to go and see every act in town, and eventually overcame his shyness enough to send them his jokes: 'This was something I felt I could do and I wasn't unhappy doing it. I was enthusiastic. I had to do it.' The first to buy – for 2s 6d – was Charlie Chester.

One day he became acquainted with Ken Dodd. The comedian was on the same bill as the Beverley Sisters, though much lower down. The two men found that they were both in the same boat; that is, keen to make a name for themselves in the world of entertainment. 'It was a good launch pad for both of us,' remarked Braben. 'We were both young, both enthusiastic and both had the same quirky sense of humour.'

In the end they worked closely together for fourteen years, with Braben providing material for both Dodd's stage and radio appearances. Though the writer found the pressure he was under intense, the time he spent writing for Dodd provided him with essential experience: 'The ratio of jokes was seven a minute. So if you were doing a ten-minute spot on radio that was seventy jokes. It was pretty fierce, but it was a very good training ground.'

Braben and Dodd had found in each other the ideal vehicle for each other's talents. As the *Independent*'s Paul Taylor noted in 2001: 'He made his first sale to Charlie Chester with a gag that went: "When Hopalong Cassidy was a baby, his mother knew that he was going to be a cowboy because he always wore a ten-gallon nappy." The rhythm is crucial as he illustrates with another three-step gag he penned as Ken Dodd's scriptwriter, marking the phases like the separate lines of a song: "When I was at school / I used to be teacher's pet. / I sat in a cage at the back of the class." True, these early efforts are some way from the surreal, wrong-footing riffs he would create for Morecambe and Wise, but you can admire the skill with which, say, each unit of the joke lands cleanly on a picture noun.'

Despite Dodd's early recognition of Eddie Braben's writing talents, it would appear that their partnership was somewhat one-sided. Former controller of BBC One Sir Bill Cotton often observed their curious relationship, of which Dodd was clearly the boss, and has commented that it always reminded him of the way a budgie treats its toy at the bottom of a cage. The fact was that Braben had always been in awe of Dodd. As Bobby Jaye, radio producer of *The Ken Dodd Show*, told author Gus Smith in *Ken Dodd: Laughter and Tears*: 'Eddie regarded Ken as a genius because of the way he worked his material. Some people would go so far as to say that he became his god.'

It could be argued that Dodd never fully appreciated the contribution that Braben made to the partnership – after all, just as he did later with Eric and particularly Ernie, Braben had helped to create a kind of persona for Dodd, which was crucial on radio and television.

In his autobiography, *The Book What I Wrote,* Braben recalled Dodd at his peak: 'Time and time again I've watched a Doddy audience collapse into total exhaustion under a comedy onslaught that has to be seen to be believed. Red-faced ladies of all ages, clutching the seats in front of them with both hands and gasping, "Oh my God! I'll have to go to the toilet."'

He also remembered the time a man in the audience laughed so much at the Opera House in Manchester that he cracked a rib, and how Eric Morecambe had once told him, 'I'll tell you something. We would never follow Ken Dodd.' If Morecambe and Wise could not follow him, Braben concluded, no one could. In his opinion, there was no question as to who was the funniest stand-up comedian of all time – it was Dodd.

'There's the world we live in,' Braben noted, 'and there's the very secret world Doddy inhabits. I shared it with him for fourteen years. It's the planet frenzy at a thousand miles an hour.' All in all, though, he thought it was an experience for which it was worth getting an ulcer. Besides, if he hadn't worked with Dodd he might never have met his wife Deidree, for it was Dodd who introduced them.

As Dave Forrester represented both Dodd and Braben, the inevitable split in 1969 was a slightly messy one, but eventually they went their separate ways – Braben to *The Morecambe and Wise Show* thanks to Bill Cotton, and Dodd to the Palladium. Officially they had decided to part company because Braben had wanted to do more television work than Dodd was prepared to accept, but the truth, according to both Bill Cotton and Michael Grade, was rather different. Not surprisingly it was due to a disagreement over money.

In addition to his perfect delivery of cleverly written comedy gags, Dodd, like most comedians of the time, always finished his act with a comic song. One day in the late 1950s, however, after listening to the likes of the then popular crooner David Whitfield, he thought that perhaps he could sing a ballad instead. 'So I came up to London and I saw a wonderful man called Jimmy Phillips [the boss of Keith Prowse Music],' he later told Sue Lawley, during his *Desert Island Discs* interview. 'And I said, "I want to make a record." He said, "What sort of a song?" and I said, "Well, I like 'Granada'." He said, "No, I don't think that's pop material – listen to this." And he played a melody which was called "Mon Coeur Et Un Vie". I said, "That's beautiful." There were two lyrics: one was "Violets and Violins" – Bing Crosby recorded that – and another one called "Love Is Like A Violin".'

So it was that Dodd took the opportunity to stretch his many talents yet further, and while continuing his work on the comedy circuit, he launched a second career as a singer of popular ballads. His debut recording of 'Love Is Like A Violin' was released in July 1960, and reached number eight in the charts. Follow-up records, including 'Once in Every Lifetime' and 'Pianissimo', were issued one every year until 1964, when Dodd released a bumper crop of three singles, including his signature theme 'Happiness'.

Though it hadn't taken long for Dodd to be proclaimed 'Cock of the North', he had yet to conquer the south – he was, in the main, a complete stranger to most Fleet Street showbiz reporters. An exception was the *Daily Express*'s John Barber, who took the trouble to catch Dodd's act in Bristol. 'Dancing on to the stage, he resembles a tailor's dummy escaped from Bedlam,' he wrote. 'Hair like a frightened haystack. White cuffs exploding from his dress-coat. What made me sit up was his happiness. His hopping vitality. His pace. And his instant grip of music-hall essentials.' Barber noted that in the first minute Dodd's scattergun delivery of jokes had covered a wide range of topics from marriage and sex to self-degradation and the Oedipus complex. He returned to London an avowed Dodd fan.

It is difficult these days to appreciate how huge a comic could be in the north and yet remain relatively unknown in the south. However, in order to succeed northern acts had no choice but to head down the M1 and make for London, mainly because that was where all the so-called prestige venues and the major TV and radio companies were based. In Dodd's case, however, London came to him in the form of theatrical impresario Bernard Delfont.

News of Dodd's talent had spread far and wide, and Delfont had caught wind of the fact that the comedian was well worth seeing. He came, he saw and he was conquered by Dodd. He told him to bring his show south and advised him not to change a thing. Even at that early stage the word 'Palladium' was being whispered, but Delfont was not the only impresario showing an interest, as Val Parnell, the Palladium boss, had also approached Dodd, seemingly impressed with his show. He offered Dodd various deals, but Dave Forrester wasn't convinced that the time or the opportunity was right for his client. Such was Dodd's faith in his agent's judgement, that he was prepared to take his advice without question, and wait until Forrester deemed that the time was right.

Forrester did not believe in rushing young talent. Be patient, he would urge, there is plenty of time. Never one to make rash promises he could not keep, when he told Dodd that he thought he had what it took, Dodd believed him. Dodd was fortunate in securing the services of a shrewd, sharp, but above all, honest agent. Not that he was impatient himself. In the same way that he took his time to decide to turn professional, he was in no hurry to take the next step up the career ladder. He was getting regular work throughout the year on the comedy circuit, particularly during the summer season and in panto, and by 1962 he was raking in a cool £1,000 a week – why should he be hasty? Besides, he admitted, he was nervous. Although he wanted to see his name up in lights down south, he was also scared by the bright lights of the West End. 'Everybody's so reserved and tight-lipped,' he said. 'They always remind me of those characters in a bad gangster film who all hate each other. It's different back in Liverpool.' To a certain extent he still feels that way to this day, according to Eric Sykes: 'Like most northerners, he's wary of the south. I can understand his unease.'

And so it was that in December 1963 Dodd was preparing for a new show at the Royal Court Theatre in Liverpool and not the Palladium in London. Undeniably the top of the heap in the north, the sell-out show netted him £11,000 (before tax!).

4

Sex and the Single Diddyman

'I'M A BRITISH COMEDIAN,' Dodd exclaimed in an interview in 1959, 'and my ambitions are to come to London with a review and also to make the first comedy-film musical.'

Clearly, by this time, a decidedly confident Ken Dodd was eager to shed the northern comic label that he had acquired since turning professional. Though obviously ambitious, his film aspirations were perhaps a little misguided, given that the comedy-musical genre had already been established in the world of film. A few years later, however, the big screen was still proving to be a lure. In what would have doubtless been an intriguing pairing, he went on record as saying that he wanted notoriously mercurial Peter Sellers to direct him. 'Filming would be a new, exciting experience,' he said, 'but I'm not going to rush into a scrappy little job that would simply be cashing in on what little name I might have made.'

Dodd's comic tastes are catholic – although the highly theatrical as embodied by the music hall and variety appealed, he also appreciated the subtleties of comic actors: the likes of Alastair Sim, Cary Grant and Will Hay. It is therefore not surprising that he harboured a desire to make movies. Yet paradoxically, Dodd is one of the few British comedians not to be offered a film vehicle. It is probably for the best – one cannot help but think it would have been a disaster and would have done his reputation no good at all. Television does him little enough justice, and so unless he could have found an entirely new form of presentation, his gaudy, grandiose appearance and theatrical gurning would have been grotesque beyond measure on the big screen.

As many have found to their cost, film and theatre are very different animals. Not that that ever stopped home-grown comics from trying their luck on film, although, with the exception of George Formby, Will Hay, Gracie Fields and later, Norman Wisdom, nearly all came a cropper. Morecambe and Wise, Tony Hancock, Frankie Howerd, Charlie Drake, Dick Emery, Stanley Baxter, even Tommy Cooper, all had a stab at a movie career – tellingly, it was their film fixation and the promise of a movie deal, and not necessarily more money, that allowed ITV to poach Eric and Ern from the BBC – but none of them fared particularly well. Even today, the likes of Steve Coogan and Harry Enfield, essentially comic actors, have found cinema a tough nut to crack. Films are really made in the cutting room; they're basically a director's medium. It is why the best movie comics (Charlie Chaplin, Buster Keaton, Jacques Tati, Woody Allen, Mel Brooks) have all directed themselves. When the comic relinquishes his timing to either his director or the editor, even the great Max Miller or Sid Field can come across as gauche, stifled and stiff. Dodd would have stood no chance.

Happily, his agent Dave Forrester seems to have had a more realistic grasp on the reins of his career. After years of waiting for the right deal – unbelievably, by 1964, Dodd had twice declined an invitation to appear on *Sunday Night at the London Palladium*, arguably the most prestigious television variety show at the time – Forrester informed Dodd that he should now set his compass for Argyll Street, WC1. It was time for the big one.

Timing is everything, and having watched younger, less experienced comics like Jimmy Tarbuck enjoy considerable success, Dodd must have been getting desperate to try his hand. He was later to tell John Stapleton in *My Favourite Hymns*, 'I think everyone wants to be a star. Everyone wants to be up there with the best. It seemed a long time to me, but it was only ten years. Ten years from me playing over the road here [at Knotty Ash] and topping the bill, to having my own show at the London Palladium.'

Nineteen sixty-five was undoubtedly the year of the Scouser. Entertainers hailing from Liverpool were on the rise . . . and on the march down south, headed, of course, by John, Paul, George and Ringo. Even the cautious, home-loving Dodd realized that there was never a better time to crack the south. He was particularly fortunate to have the London-based Forrester batting for him, as he had not only booked Dodd for the Palladium, but had guaranteed that his client would top the bill in his own show, *Doddy's Here!* Supported by the Kaye Sisters, Clifford Guest the ventriloquist, the Carmenas and the Ross Taylor Dancers, it was to be a slick, glitzy affair, and would prove to be the turning point for Dodd. It was the moment when he became a comic superstar. At the time, however, it was an enormous leap of faith for him, because, despite the success he'd enjoyed in the rest of the country, he was headed for a place where many northern comedians had come unstuck over the years. He cited the example of Frank Randle, who had played in suburban southern halls without encountering any difficulties – when he hit the West End, however, the critics 'assassinated him'.

Even now, *The Stage*'s Peter Hepple notes, there are acts that only work in the north. Though Britain may be small, it has very distinctive regional variations. There is a diversity not just in the north and south, but even in various towns in the same area. 'Liverpool, for instance, is really quite different from Manchester – it's as different from Manchester as Birmingham is from London – despite the fact that they're only thirty to forty miles apart,' he says.

In spite of slight reservations that southerners would not understand what a 'butty' was, Dodd was determined not to change his act too much for his new audience. He also revealed to the press that he was playing the Palladium despite being offered more lucrative work up north, and informed them that he had been 'waiting for the right show, at the right theatre, and the right money.'

So it was that just after 6 p.m. on Saturday 17 April 1965, Ken Dodd burst on to the stage at the London Palladium before a sell-out crowd. As he emerged from the wings, the coach parties of fellow Scousers let out a cry of 'Up the 'Pool', which could have hardly endeared him to the home crowd. Indeed, it was rather slow going in the beginning, as the packed house took a while to warm up; after all, sophisticated London audiences had never seen anything like it. Initially, Dodd must have thought that all his doubts about winning over a London audience had been perfectly justified, but slowly his magic seemed to work. He soon realized that southerners weren't so different after all. As he told *Desert Island Discs* listeners many years later: 'The greatest thing that ever happened for comedians was *Coronation Street* . . . the southerners didn't mind – in fact, not didn't mind, they adored – the terrace houses and the Lancashire accents.'

It is true that the first-night audience at the Palladium was a stranger to Diddymen and jam-butty mines, and the realm of the seaside landlady was another country to them, but nonetheless, Dodd's relentless barrage of material gradually loosened their stays and won them over.

It wasn't easy, however, as the old enemy – nerves – raised their ugly head once again. Dodd later confessed to Sue Lawley that he was extremely anxious on that auspicious night: 'On the big Palladium jobs, you get very nervous. The first time I played the Palladium I remember sitting in this yellow Rolls-Royce and I was on the revolve. It appears to drive in, so I had to be in the Rolls before the curtain went up. And the first time I was so terrified when I got out . . . but the wall of applause – because the people who were rooting for me from all over the country had turned up.

'People say when you get on, you feel better – you don't! Your top lip goes stiff and sticks to your teeth and you find yourself talking all sorts of rubbish. But when it's good there's no sensation, no ecstasy, like standing on a stage and seeing an audience rock with laughter.'

By the end of the show the audience refused to let him leave the stage, and the second house was due to start five minutes before the first had even finished – this was to be another recurring theme! Such were the chaotic scenes that night – 2,500 people trying to enter the theatre as 2,500 were trying to exit – that police had to close off Argyll Street altogether. The Palladium had not seen anything like it since the days of the big American stars. Certainly no home-grown comic had had anything like this kind of impact for decades. Beatlemania? Pah!

The second house overran by forty minutes, and after greeting the inevitable crowd of fans at the stage door, a delighted Dodd, armed with 700 good-luck telegrams, made off for a champagne party. It was 12.45 a.m.

Leslie McDonnell, the Palladium boss, was a relieved man. He'd been persuaded to invest money in Dodd's show to the tune of £80,000 by, among others, London agent Bernard

Delfont. McDonnell was wary, as Dodd had been, of how well a northern comic would be received in the south. He too had witnessed the unfortunate demise of northern entertainers on a West End stage, and wasn't at all convinced that regional differences could be overcome, but this time it was different, much to his relief. Doubtless he was very happy with the advanced bookings that Dodd's presence had generated, and would later be amazed by the fact that the show would go on to break every record for the theatre. During that first season at the Palladium, Ken Dodd occupied the theatre's window-less number-one dressing room (so memorably described by Eric Morecambe as 'Hitler's bunker') for just over forty-two weeks – a record that still holds to this day.

The Palladium show made Ken Dodd not only one of the most fashionable comics in the country, but one of the most bankable. As Michael Grade notes: 'There's a lot of talk about Tommy Cooper, but Tommy Cooper in his heyday was never really a draw. You didn't really top the bill with him. He was a risk. He wasn't the Tommy Cooper that we remember – it's a myth. I'm not saying he wasn't a funny man – he was a genius – but he was never up there with Ken Dodd or Morecambe and Wise or Frankie Howerd. Nowhere near in terms of box office. I mean, Ken Dodd packed the Palladium eighteen to twenty weeks, thirteen shows a week at top West End prices. Tommy Cooper never did that.'

At last, after a decade of traipsing round masonic halls and social clubs, after ten years of perfecting his talent, Dodd was a bona fide star and, unusually, like Eddie Izzard in more recent times, he'd managed to achieve it without fully utiliz-ing the power of television. And it wasn't just the audience telling him he was a star, it was also the press. The next morning theatre critics were tripping over themselves to lay plaudits at his feet – although whether such critics, more used to analysing Beckett and Chekhov than wallowing in a world of snuff mines and broken-biscuit repair works, were the right people to send to see the show is a moot point. These days, comedy shows tend to be reviewed by dedicated comedy critics, both on the fringe and in the West End, but in the 1960s heavyweight critics were wheeled out to review every first night, whether it was a serious play, a musical or a comedy performance such as Dodd's. Nowadays it is hard to imagine the *Daily Telegraph* dispatching its notable critic Charles Spencer to review a Johnny Vegas comedy show.

Nevertheless, that did not stop the *Observer*'s Penelope Gilliatt enthusiastically describing Dodd's Palladium debut thus: 'The patter is as blue as Max Miller's, and the puns come thick and fast. Like Max, Ken Dodd has a trick of innocently just missing a filthy meaning that stares everyone else in the face, like a baby behind the wheel of a sports car careering at a brick wall and swerving at the last moment.'

It was Michael Billington, then on the theatre magazine *Plays and Players*, now with the *Guardian*, who among the national critics perhaps appreciated Dodd the most – indeed, he went on to write a short celebration of the comedian in 1977, entitled *How Tickled I Am*. In *Plays and Players* he wrote: 'Mr Dodd fires at his willing audience an apparently inexhaustible stream of patter that is just shocking enough to make them glow with guilty pleasure.'

Both back in Liverpool and nationally, Dodd was met with almost universal praise from the critics. Only the *New Statesman*'s Jonathan Miller didn't quite see the joke, comparing Dodd to Archie Rice, the tired old musical-hall monster in John Osborne's play, *The Entertainer*. Billington leaped to Dodd's defence, however, pointing out that although Archie Rice and Ken Dodd may have used the same time-honoured music-hall tricks – like chatting up the audience in the front row, and teasing the conductor – they were worlds apart. In *How Tickled I Am*, Billington argued that whereas Archie Rice threw out his jokes 'like a desperate, bereft trawlerman hoping for a miniscule catch, Dodd is a pagan, festive celebrant who has the knack of establishing an almost mystic rapport with 2,000 people at once'. In other words, where Rice was a failure, Dodd is a success.

Miller's piece was tempered, however, with an almost begrudging appreciation of Dodd's technique: 'Artists like Dodd, whose work seems to reflect no personal view, run on a magnificent display of comic legerdemain. He is never still for a moment, fluttering like a conjuror with all sorts of disarming accessory mannerisms. He capers and skips, giggles, goggles and splutters with his upper front teeth. He delivers his most outrageous gags with a shrill, puerile sweetness and then opens his eyes wide in amazement at his own daring.'

He went on: 'And then there's that wild shampooed fright of hair which he whisks up into a Struwelpeter quiff. Everything he does is rehearsed down to the smallest detail. Nothing seems to have moved out of place in the six months since I first saw him at the Palladium. Every trip, pause, break-up and syncopation still comes exactly as it did. An iridescent show of artful dodging.'

Miller (who once confessed that he never liked 'star' performers) seems to criticize the polish of Dodd's show as if it was something negative. Surely the art of a performance such as Dodd's is to make it look as if it's a freewheeling, extemporaneous rollercoaster of a ride, when in reality the only thing rollercoaster-like about it is that it sticks to well-trammelled tracks.

How Dodd, who had always enjoyed the attentions of the quality press, must have enjoyed the cut and thrust of that particular argument. He'd always lapped up the adulation and adoration of intellectuals and so he must have derived great pleasure from the knowledge that Osborne, then directing a Charles Wood play at the Royal Court, took his cast to see this 'real comic artist at work' at the Palladium on a number of occasions.

'I would imagine John Osborne took his actors along for several reasons,' says actress and self-confessed Dodd fan, Alison Steadman. 'First of all, it's always good for a company of actors to bond very quickly. It creates a good working atmosphere and relaxes the actors allowing their best work to come through. What better fun than everyone laughing their heads off together, sharing a fun night. Also, Ken has great timing and never lets his audience off the hook. Once he's got them, he keeps them there. The sheer joy of performing comes across. Also there's his love of his audience and understanding of the human condition; what makes us all tick and what our frailties are.'

Certainly the playwright and his team of actors loved Dodd's show. Impressed by his boundless energy and excited by the unique entertainment on offer, the experience was quite unlike anything they had seen before. 'Ken Dodd says that there are some people who cannot take part in this very English form of evening,' Osborne later remarked. 'It is not a question of jokes. It is a fantasy and high-flying exuberance. Some people don't respond. They're born like that. They're cold. Bawdy is as meaningless to them as the loneliness of men's legs, kilted tables and sleeping on the right-hand side of the bed in the comic market.'

How fascinating it would have been had Dodd ever played Archie Rice. After all, in the 1960 film version of *The Entertainer* even the great Laurence Olivier, technically slick and adroit as ever, came a bit of a cropper when it came to the hoary old comedy routines. He captured the deadness behind the eyes well enough, but could never quite muster the brashness of the true vaudevillian. The character may have been past his sell-by date, but one can never quite believe that Olivier's Rice could ever have made it in the first place. A gift of a part for any comedian who is interested in the legitimate theatre, Archie Rice is invariably played by straight actors interested in variety. It is a pity that Dodd never had a stab at the role, but perhaps portraying a character who had sacrificed his family and his personal life for the sake of his career would have been a little too close to home.

Like many bright, intelligent people denied a formal education, Dodd appears to have a hankering for intellectual approval, and although he was wise enough to stay strictly within his field of interest – i.e., comedy – he could be said to have scholarly ambitions himself. Although it has obviously helped him with his work, the endless comedy analysis could be seen as a symptom of those intellectual aspirations. After his Palladium triumph, it was clear that he had developed considerable self-confidence in his knowledge of all things laughter-inducing. Indeed he even declared himself 'as informed on humour as an Oxford don', and suggested that his London audience were perfect for his research, being as they were 'so sophisticated' that he had free rein to try anything out on them.

Research? Good old Doddy, as even Londoners now referred to him, had clearly never lost his comic curiosity. He was never going to be happy standing still.

Denis Norden recalls seeing him at the Palladium, and tells a familiar tale: 'When he was at the Palladium I took two people who were with me for the day and the evening and they didn't want to go. They didn't like him. I said, "Have you ever seen him [live] before?" and they said no, but we've heard him on the radio and seen him on the television. But this was the kind of seven or eight minutes that they allotted to comedians. So I said, "Well, come and see." And they sat there stony-faced. Well, Ken did the long-haul and gradually the stone cracked, and they were laughing uproariously.'

In addition to the adulation of the press and the analytical interest in his techniques, however, Dodd would soon learn that there was a flipside to his new-found national celebrity, for the flinty, prying, hungry Fleet Street hacks were light years from the kindly scribes who worked on the *Liverpool Post*. Even in those days, Dodd was never one to talk about his private life. He would talk about his career and the mechanics of comedy until the cows came home, but the moment anyone broached the subject of his private life, Doddy Towers's drawbridge slammed firmly shut.

For example, when the *Daily Express* asked Dodd why he did not care for status symbols, he was happy to tell them: 'I don't want a gleaming new Bentley, or to eat in smart restaurants. I want to stay just where I am. I never forget that it's the audience, those ordinary folk, who have put me where I am, and I mean to stay one of them myself.' But when they asked why he had not married his then fiancée, Anita Boutin, he threw them off with a joke and a curt, 'I have just not got round to it.' This was to be a recurrent theme throughout his life – he was, he always maintained, too busy to marry. But then his relationship with his girlfriends is just one of the many enigmas that surround his persona.

Throughout his adult life, Dodd has had long-term romantic attachments to two particular women – Anita Boutin and Anne Jones. Despite the fact that he has worn a wedding ring for years, and his old friend Eric Sykes has referred to Anne as Dodd's 'wife', he has remained a bachelor.

Anita Boutin, who came from a French-Canadian family, was twenty-four when she gave up her nursing career to become Dodd's secretary. Her brother Billy recalled that she was a probationer nurse when she first became acquainted with Dodd at Liverpool's Vaudeville Club in the early 1950s. Though she later became a State Registered Nurse, he remembered that 'she had no hesitation in giving it all up for

Ken.' In fact, Billy Boutin believes that it was his sister who talked Dodd into becoming a professional entertainer: 'He was able to make her laugh and she knew he could make others laugh.'

Dodd had needed to engage an assistant in order to deal with his growing correspondence. He had, he told her, 300 fan letters to reply to and they were growing at a rate of fifty a week. He signed all the replies personally, but it was Anita who waded through them. Still, after six years as a nurse, her new showbiz life was both exciting and glamorous. 'I moved from the sad side of life,' she later said, 'to Ken's mad, zany world – and I loved it.'

Unbelievably, early on in their relationship, a somewhat confused Dodd once told his new girlfriend that it was his ambition to become an opera singer. It was she who convinced him that – partly due to his somewhat unconventional dental arrangements – his future lay in comedy. Of course, he realized the truth in what she said, and so for a while put his singing career on hold. 'I was once asked how I decided to become a funny man,' he later commented. 'The answer is that with a face like mine, the decision was made for you.'

Gradually, too, the secretarial relationship blossomed into love. By all accounts Anita got on well with Dodd's parents and it was inevitable that thoughts of marriage popped into her head. Unfortunately for her, though, they never seemed to enter into Dodd's. One of the many contradictions in his life is that such a conventional man who was heavily influenced by his mother's religious leanings, should so readily dismiss the idea of wedlock – 'I'm not married, Missus,' he still jokes, 'I'm naturally round-shouldered.' But then it could be argued that both of his long-term relationships have been with women whose roles were those of surrogate mothers. It is reasonable to conclude, therefore, that there is a selfish, immature side to Dodd, although his immaturity could be mistaken for a child-like characteristic, the very quality extolled as a virtue for a comedian. However one looks at it, here is a man who is used to getting his own way, a man who was protected and to a certain extent, spoilt, by his mother. By his own admission, he had 'a very short fuse and flew off the handle quite easily'.

As with most couples, there were plenty of tiffs – one of the worst resulted in Anita initially refusing to attend Dodd's debut at the Palladium. Thankfully for Dodd it was resolved and she was there as usual, taking notes during the performances as well as looking after the house he had rented in Kensington for their stay in the capital.

It was apparent to everyone that Anita was devoted to Dodd; she accompanied him to each engagement and it was mainly she who compiled the information for the Giggle Map, eventually completing over one hundred notebooks. Yet despite discussing the possibility of tying the knot (he was always too busy; there would always be time later) she began to realize that, despite being given an engagement ring, it wasn't going to happen.

There is, however, a further contradiction concerning his marital status and family life. Dodd often admitted to friends that he would dearly love children – some have gone so far as to suggest that the Diddymen and Doodle the poodle were child substitutes. For a long time, he comforted himself with the knowledge that 'Chaplin had his first child very late . . . so there's still hope' and as was later learned from the 1989 court case, having a child was still on the agenda when he was with his second long-term partner, Anne Jones. From the affectionate way he talks about his own childhood, and especially the way he speaks about his father, it is clear that Doddy the daddy would have been a great success. Perhaps because of his own immaturity, he seems to have an innate ability to connect with children. He loves them and they love him. It could be argued that having children of his own would have changed Dodd's view of the world and given him far more personal fulfilment than that provided through his appreciative audiences.

There are those who, after seeing the poignant, touching way in which he sings 'Sonny Boy' to his ventriloquial figure Dickie Mint, have also implied some kind of son substitute. But having heard about the way the doll is decapitated in the wings, the head plunged unceremoniously into a waiting carrier bag, it would seem unlikely. Dodd renders 'Sonny Boy' simply because he is a Jolson fan.

One can't get away from the conclusion that work has now become a substitute; the audience has become his family. In Dodd's life there appear to be two very distinct parts: in Doddyland, where everything is plumptious and tattifilarious, he is still thirty and all is love and laughter; in real life, where the tax man lurks, it is clear that career (and money) are given top priority.

Rumours of an engagement continued to titillate the matrons of Knotty Ash, however, and Dodd did little to quell them, but, as ever, when it came to naming the day, he fell uncharacteristically silent. As for poor Anita, when a *Liverpool Post* reporter enquired about marriage plans, all she could say was: 'It's up to Ken.'

The route to a man's heart may be through his stomach, but the key to a woman's heart is often to be located via her funny bone. For that reason – along with, perhaps, the attraction of status, celebrity, money and power – many comics enjoy success with the ladies. Indeed, the most unlikely, unprepossessing comedians – Frank Randle, Rod Hull, Dick Emery – proved to be veritable babe magnets. I had a female friend – poor deluded soul – who even confessed to a soft spot for Frankie Howerd. Dodd was certainly no fool when it came to the attraction of humour. 'I know ladies love to laugh,' he has remarked. 'Ladies have a marvellous sense of humour probably because they are more emotional than men.' He never saw any harm in indulging in mild flirtation and did little to stop female fans making a bee-line for his dressing room. It was perhaps fortunate that Anita was not the jealous type.

Michael Billington has noted that the atmosphere at any Ken Dodd performance he had been to was 'orgiastic', and has remarked, quite seriously, on the fact that as far as some of his female audience members are concerned, 'there's something quite sexual about a Ken Dodd evening.' On *Heroes of Comedy* he tried to explain Dodd's appeal to women. 'Mature women seem to enjoy Ken's act as much as anyone, and I think it's because he's egging them on and he's daring them to think about sex and talk about sex maybe at a time when it might not be the main feature of their lives.'

Victoria Wood, too, noted that his act celebrates the fun of sex between a man and a woman. 'But he always seems very pro women; his act is not about putting down women, but just about the ridiculousness of two people in a bed.' While his former radio co-star Judith Chalmers has confessed to thinking that he has tremendous sex appeal: 'It's hard to explain why. I don't know if it's the way he looks at you, but he includes you with him somehow. You think, "Oooh! He's looking at me."'

Dodd was aware of all this as he watched his Palladium show become the season's hot ticket. This was Dodd's golden period; as the country's most fashionable funny man he could do no wrong. In a weird way he became a banana-skin version of Peter Cook . . . although Cook never had his teeth insured for £10,000 in the 1960s. Whereas Cook had been packing in the intelligentsia at his achingly trendy satirical Establishment club, Dodd, bizarrely, ended up luring many of the very same audience into the more traditional

Palladium. Like Cook, Dodd was ubiquitous: he was a regular on TV in such programmes as *The Good Old Days* and his own series *The Ken Dodd Show* (he also launched BBC Two in the north); he was the subject of endless intellectual analysis; a constant stream of celebrities – Bing Crosby, Bob Hope, Prime Minister Harold Wilson – beat a path to his Palladium dressing room; he was voted Show Business Personality of the Year by the Variety Club of Great Britain in 1965.

This astounding period of success also saw him preparing for his first Royal Variety Performance, which took place on his thirty-eighth birthday in November. Backstage he mingled with the likes of Tony Bennett, Dudley Moore, Peter Sellers, Shirley Bassey, Max Bygraves and Spike Milligan; out front was his monarch . . . and delighted parents Arthur and Sarah Dodd.

After the show he took Anita and his family out to celebrate his birthday at a restaurant in Kensington. His mother told the press how proud they were of him. 'Ken never forgets us,' she said. 'He's a good son.'

It was around this time, too, that his first best-selling record usurped the success of fellow Scousers the Beatles in 1965, which allowed him to bask in the glory of having released the best charting song of the year. Dodd had recorded two songs in 1965: 'Tears' and 'The River'. His record company initially wanted to issue 'Tears' on the B-side of 'The River', but Dodd insisted they went out separately – he knew that B-sides were never played. His instincts were spot on, as both were a huge success. 'Tears' entered the charts on 2 September 1965, and improbable though it might sound, Dodd's ballad hit the top of the charts a month later and occupied the number-one position for five weeks before being displaced by the Rolling Stones's 'Get Off My Cloud'.

He soon found himself in the unlikely position of appearing on *Top of the Pops*. Looking back on those bemusing times, he described to Alexandra Connor how extraordinary the experience was for him: 'It felt wonderful to be a pop star – all these girls throwing themselves . . . the other way. I had some big ones [hits, presumably, not girls]. "Tears" did two million – two golden discs. Lovely songs like "Happiness" – which is my favourite – "Remember I Love You", "Eight By Ten". I've been very lucky because in those days I was able to choose the songs I recorded. Not all artists were as lucky as that because they were told which ones to sing . . . but I was able to choose.'

'Tears' stayed in the chart for six months, and proved to be such a success that it was subsequently listed number thirty-four in the top one hundred singles of all time.

Clearly a singing career provided him with almost as much satisfaction as his comedy, and he took it quite seriously. 'I'm very proud that I had six lessons from Heddle Nash. He told me I was a tenor; I always thought I was a baritone.'

Dodd certainly brings a musician's ear to his comedy. In fact, that splendid Welsh actor Kenneth Griffith once told the comedian that he doesn't tell jokes, he sings them; and Dodd agrees. 'Delivering a line, a gag, is similar to singing,' he has said. 'It is about weight, intonation, meaning. Listen to Sinatra. Similarly, you can play an audience like an instrument. If they are a slow audience, you have to be gentle. You have to coax them.' You only have to watch Dodd in action to appreciate what he means. It is not just the intonation of single jokes either, because he constructs his entire act as if it were a song: there are natural peaks and troughs, crescendos and pauses (although remarkably little of the latter). Also, just as a singer mixes old standards and newer numbers, Dodd deftly juggles old and new material. 'You've been very patient,' he informs the faithful, 'waiting for the new joke.'

Nowadays, his act still features what he calls a 'tearful ear-ful' in the form of romantic ballads, which simply provide a brief, but well-deserved, rest from 'exercise of the chuckle muscles', and help to change the pace of the show. He sings them, he says, to give the show more heart. 'I know a tear-jerker when I hear one – if you want an audience on their feet you have to make them cry first.'

The *Liverpool Echo*'s Joe Riley makes a fascinating obser-vation about Dodd's sideline profession as a singer: 'He'd have been a millionaire based on his singing career. People forget that. He had a bigger hit than the Beatles. If he'd done nothing else other than sing "Tears" and "Happiness" he'd still be a very wealthy man.'

Dodd himself, however, considers his Palladium appear-ances as the apogee of his many achievements. When Alexandra Connor asked him about whether he'd reached the pinnacle of his career, Dodd replied: 'I don't think I've reached my peak yet, I'm still climbing. But I suppose really playing the Palladium – I did it for forty-odd weeks in 1965 and then again in 1967. The Palladium is the temple of show business, the temple of variety. To stand on that stage where Danny Kaye stood . . . Bob Hope and Judy Garland, they've all worked on that very spot and now you're there! And in the audience one night there is Bing Crosby. I played to Bob Hope one night – and in the box, Danny La Rue!'

Clearly Dodd had begun to revel in his new-found fame, fortune and fashionability, to the extent that it was becoming increasingly more difficult to coax him off stage. As Dodd himself says: 'When I first started touring on the big theatres I was given, say twelve minutes. Twelve minutes was a good time. Now I do a little bit longer than that.'

He certainly has a flair for understatement, our Ken.

5

Going Home
in the Light

Last night at a show by Ken Dodd,
The usherette said, 'Oh my God!
He'll go on for years.
He's bound to sing "Tears".
When he finishes, give us a prod.'

THAT CHARMING LITTLE VERSE, which was created by
the cast of the BBC Radio Four series *I'm Sorry I Haven't
A Clue* during a recording in Liverpool in 1996, somehow
sums it all up. Freed from the shackles of a strong producer
or the need to accommodate a second house, if he is on a roll
and in the mood, a Ken Dodd stage show can now run in
excess of five hours. Technically, of course, it is not classed as
'overrunning' any more because it's become the norm. In fact,
not only would loyal audiences feel somehow shortchanged if
he offered less, he would find himself robbed of much of his
material – a good deal of his act now revolves around refer-

ences to the length of the performance. Besides, as he half-jokingly says: 'I've got a reputation to maintain.'

Stories of Dodd's overrunning are legion. Roy Hudd recalls the famous theatre director Dickie Hurran being asked by a stage manager: 'We've got Ken Dodd on next week. Can I have some timesheets?' [which are used to note down the running order of the show and the time allocated to each act]. The laid-back Hurran answered: 'You won't need a timesheet – you'll need a diary!' While in *British Comedy Greats*, Barry Cryer recalls a lovely story about Dodd and Eric Sykes (who is registered blind and deaf) that the former had shared with him: 'I stood with Eric in the wings and he said to me, "We're a lovely couple. I don't know when to go on and you don't know when to come off!"'

As Dodd himself is keen on telling his audiences: 'One thing about my show is that you always go home in the light . . .'; 'The usherettes will be round soon to take your breakfast orders . . .'; 'I've seen children grow out of their trousers while I've been on . . .'; 'Under your seat you'll find a will form . . .'; 'You think you can get away, but you can't. I'll follow you home and I'll shout jokes through your letter-box!'

According to Michael Grade, unlike the perfection of his comic timing, Dodd has never had any understanding of real time. It is odd that so consummate a professional should continually ignore pleas to adhere to schedules. 'It was chaotic,' recalls Grade of the old days. 'He had no sense of time. It was absolutely true that at one of the revues that we did at the Palladium there was a night when the stage manager did actually set the finale behind him and throw the keys on. He was just hopeless. You couldn't tell him – it was just a quirk with him.

'At times it was very counterproductive, because on a rainy night at the Palladium you'd have the first house inside, the second house queuing outside – 6.15 and 8.45 are the times of the shows – and it would be pissing with rain outside and they'd get there 8.15–8.30 and they didn't get in till 9.15. Very, very naughty – but that'd be my only criticism of him.'

The pleas by the management would occasionally boil over into full-scale rows. Grade remembers going into Dodd's dressing room one time and seeing his uncle, Bernard Delfont, giving Dodd 'a bollocking' for staying on and costing them a fortune in overtime: 'The musicians were getting into uranium time! Bernie was beside himself; he'd had enough. Bernie was nose-to-nose with Ken. "You cannot do this, Ken. You cannot. It's costing us a fortune. You should be more responsible. I'm sick of this!"

'He just stood there looking at Bernie and I thought he's either going to deck him or I don't know what's going to happen. And all he did was he stood there and said, "Yes, guv'nor. You've made your point. Don't keep going on about it." But it went on and on and he just stood there and took it. But it went straight over his head and the next night he did another twenty minutes. Ken Dodd and the timesheet – they've never met.'

The comedian Arthur Smith thinks that Dodd is simply a performance junkie. He recalls that in the 1980s, electrical retailers Comet used to throw hospitality days for its employees. Often they would book a couple of comedians to entertain and one year it was Smith and Dodd. Smith did his twenty minutes or so and then Dodd went on . . . and on and on. The company's MD eventually asked the younger comedian to intervene and get him off. Smith replied that as a fellow comic he could do no such thing. He remembers that Dodd went well for about forty minutes, before the audience began to get a bit restive: 'They really wanted to go for a piss or lust after the hospitality girls.' Dodd carried on regardless, however, seemingly unaware of the comparative loss of interest. 'He was still telling good gags,' says Smith.

But most comics, he thinks, know instinctively when to stop – he was surprised that Dodd apparently did not. Smith confesses that, ultimately, he would have been disappointed by the audience's response if it had been him.

Ken Campbell has a different take on the reason for the length of Dodd's performance. 'I think he's interested in people laughing at laughing,' says Campbell. 'The laughter itself has got to establish itself and then he kind of plays the laughter like it's an actual instrument. He'll come out and he'll try out some gags, and I think what he's really doing then is he's listening out in case there are any peculiar laughs, eccentric laughs – like old-lady laughs or "yak" laughs or whatever. He's spotting where they are in the auditorium, then he'll react to those laughs when they crop up. With any luck he can get one laugh that will laugh at the other laugh, so you get laughter at laughter. I think that's why he goes on so long because it doesn't feel finished for him unless he's got to that point.'

It has often been said that Dodd is very much his own man – he doesn't like being told what to do. Many an impresario and both his girlfriends could vouch for that. You could argue that when he is overrunning he is being almost deliberately contrary – after all, when he is out front, he is the boss. No one can touch him until he gets off. On the other hand, it is just possible that he is giving his audience what it wants.

He might have an impeccable sense of his own performance, but he is not so good at taking an overview. In the valued opinion of Mike Craig, who as either writer or producer has worked with just about everyone in the comedy business – from Morecambe and Wise and Harry Worth to Al Read and Mike Yarwood – and who also produced many of Dodd's radio shows, the comedian proved to be a terrible editor . . . even of his own material. Lumbered with his value-for-money work ethic, Dodd was resolute in his view that because all the jokes were there, ready and waiting, each and every one of them, therefore, should be used. Craig recollects one particular occasion in which producer and comedian thrashed out their differences: 'We've had him here for dinner and had rows across the table. "What? You can't stop me getting involved in editing!" "I can," I said, "You've done your job. Now I'll do mine and make the show funny." "Oh all right, then."'

Although he found the experience of producing a Dodd show to be frustrating, Craig also found that it could be rewarding . . . eventually; especially after he had finally edited the material down to the right length, having got rid of 'a lot of dross', and knowing that despite everything he had 'got the best out of him'. Nonetheless, he said, you couldn't let Dodd anywhere near the editing suite: 'He wouldn't understand what it was all about. He has no idea about the balance of a show – he'd want to put another song in!'

Michael Grade remembers similar problems on stage in the 1960s. He recalls that it wasn't just Dodd's act that over-ran. 'He would insist with those shows of packing them with more acts than he could possibly fit in, knowing full well that he was going to overrun. And you knew that if he said he was going to do forty minutes for his last spot, you knew it was an hour and ten. But he would insist on having seven or eight acts on the bill.'

Roy Hudd has a similar tale to tell about a Palladium boss who tried in vain to get Dodd to appreciate the importance of keeping to schedules. 'We're having to pay taxis for all the band to take them home at night you go on so long. You'll have to cut down,' the manager explained, but his request was met by a sarcastic response from Dodd: 'Oh dear, oh dear. That's terrible. Is there anybody in?'

Of course the place was bursting at the seams, and so as far as Dodd was concerned, the point being made wasn't justified. Perhaps if someone had been bold enough to suggest that the comedian should be made responsible for covering overtime expenses every time his show overran, it might have elicited a quite different reaction.

On this particular occasion, although Hudd was amused by Dodd's reply, he wasn't in full agreement with his methods: 'A wonderful line – you couldn't get near the joint, so what are they complaining about? But from a personal point of view I think he does too long – it spoils it for me. I still stick to the old thing – always leave them wanting. But you talk about value for money . . .'

It may seem churlish to complain, but is it really value for money? After all, as anyone who has been to an all-you-can-eat restaurant will tell you, gorging oneself is not necessarily a good thing. Comedian Steve Punt notes that there comes a point where it is not a question of raw value for money; in fact there is often more merit in a performance that is the right length, which doesn't just go on and on and on: 'I always found this business of finishing after midnight rather off-putting. You know when you go to the cinema it's annoying coming out and thinking "I'd have enjoyed it more if it was half an hour shorter."'

And he is not alone in that opinion: as well as Roy Hudd, both Mike Craig and *The Stage*'s Peter Hepple are in agreement. Indeed, as Hepple points out, even Max Miller never did more than half an hour. In fact, when it comes to overrunning, Dodd is the absolute opposite of the Cheeky Chappie. When Miller performed in London, he was known to leap from the stage towards the end of his act and dash up the aisle in order to catch the train back home to Brighton.

Even Dodd's admiring fans have found an evening in his company a rather gruelling affair. Following a marathon five-and-a-quarter hours of gags, punters at the first night of his sell-out *Happiness Show* at Birmingham's Hippodrome

Theatre in 2004 found it a tiring business. The local paper rounded up a few audience members as they made a break for it during the interval. Roy Pritchard, an eighty-eight-year-old retired Cadbury's worker from Bournville, was one of those who found Dodd's marathon effort a double-edged sword: 'It was a great laugh, but he went on a bit too long. You certainly get value for money though.' Another punter, fifty-five-year-old Kidderminster housewife Ruth Smith said, 'I left early because it is just too much to stay for five hours. But he is a very funny man and it's great that he makes people laugh without being smutty.' Fellow housewife Jan Smith from Sutton Coldfield, was in agreement: 'I think he's brilliant, but we need to go. It seems awful to leave before the end, but it has been almost five hours.' She is right – the rictus grin one is left with by the end of the evening is small compensation for the toll it has taken on one's seating arrangements.

Roy Hudd recalls the time Mike Craig went to see Dodd in pantomime in Manchester: 'It was just the same as his variety act – he won't come off. So Mike goes back and sees the show the next night because there were one or two people in the cast he knew. So he went backstage to see them and they'd all taken up hobbies! Painting by numbers and sewing and all that. They said, "Oh yes, we have hours off and then at the end we all come together for the walk down", or what Eric Morecambe used to call the "Who's best?" One old pro said of Dodd's show that it wasn't so much a "Who's best?" but more like a "Do you remember me?"'

Once, when he was producing Dodd's radio show, Mike Craig actually stopped recording after a while, when he knew he had enough material. He put on his hat and coat, picked up his briefcase and went out front telling him, 'Right, Ken, I'm off,' while Dodd was still holding court. The comedian was stunned, and said, 'What! You mean you're not recording this?' To Dodd's surprise the producer replied, 'No, I stopped half an hour ago.'

There are countless theories as to why Dodd is reluctant to come off stage, but Victoria Wood thinks it is because he can't bear to leave. As she observed on *Heroes of Comedy*: 'If Ken was in the theatre and one person wasn't laughing he would stay on stage until that person was. And that devotion to the job – that's what people need to learn.' She is right, of course, it could be seen as a good thing, but it is also true to say that it's an unusual kind of professionalism. It is not a characteristic she shares, as Wood herself admits that she wouldn't dream of doing more than two hours: 'I don't like it as much as he does.'

David Nobbs, too, is perplexed by this trait in Dodd: 'He thinks of it as a virtue and he's giving fantastic value for money, but by the time he finishes his audience has been locked out of their B&B or whatever. I think he would peak earlier on in the act, but that's the nature of the beast. He can't leave it alone.'

Dodd's old radio sparring partner Judith Chalmers remembers seeing him at the Palladium. 'He just went on and on and on. Captivating. Fascinating. Wonderful. Aching with laughter, hurting with laughter we were when we left. But it was so late. And people were sneaking out – they didn't want to, but they had to get their last Tube or their last bus. They had to get home and Ken was still performing.'

Indeed, many a Ken Dodd patron has missed his last train home – not for nothing has the prolific comedian been dubbed the patron saint of taxi drivers.

The ever-reliable Bob Monkhouse made the following observation: 'We've had our share of eccentrics in the business. And generally speaking, if you adopt Groucho Marx's idea that there's never more than a hundred top-flight comedians on the planet, you've got to allow for the fact that at least ninety of those are going to be a bit quaint. These are very odd people, whether they were comedians or not they'd be pretty odd. And Doddy is an oddity; the fact that he's a lovable oddity is a kind of a plus – we all feel very fond of Doddy. Audiences are devoted to him, and I think when he kids about going on and on, and the fact that they've missed their buses home, it's part of something he's inflicting on us.'

But perhaps George Melly is closest to the mark when he offers the fascinating possibility that Dodd needs the audience more than they need him, and that he only permits them to leave when he has got what he needs from them – i.e., love: 'I think for him his relationship with the audience is all in his life. He doesn't seem to have many close friends, though he obviously knows people on the halls. And he's marvellous on the stage – I mean, nobody resents sitting there for three hours when they thought it was only going to be twenty minutes. He gets them. He has a spell that he puts on them.

'I went to see him in Blackpool and he talked nonsense for three hours really. You couldn't come out and say, "I loved his joke about . . ." because it's not about anything. It's just a kind of inner world. You go in there and you don't get out till he's got enough out of you. I came out weak with laughter, deaf as I am. He pulls out of the audience the love he needs, I think. This was three hours – it was meant to be an hour. There was a queue waiting outside in the rain – none of them resented it.'

Dodd himself sticks to his value-for-money argument: 'I think people pay you the greatest compliment in the world when they pay hard-earned cash to see your live show. I feel very, very responsible that I give them a good time. It's more important what people say when they go out of a show than when they come in. My job as a jester is to see that people go out full of happiness and laughter.'

When *Desert Island Discs'* presenter Sue Lawley asked why his shows went on so long, he replied matter-of-factly, 'Because I enjoy it – you shouldn't break up a good party.' She quizzed him further, and mentioned the maxim that you should always leave them wanting more, to which he commented, 'Like a lot of other maxims, sometimes it works and sometimes it doesn't.'

Still, you cannot help but wonder whether it was with a sense of irony that at the end of that first phenomenal Palladium season in 1966, Dodd was presented with an inscribed watch for breaking every known record for the theatre. In any case, it certainly didn't help with his future time-keeping. And time is definitely a problem for Dodd, as it is not just the question of overrunning – there is also the issue of punctuality.

'He's late for everything,' says Mike Craig, 'although he was on time for my leaving do at the BBC . . . and he only did about fifteen minutes!' In fact, Dodd's time-keeping skills (or lack of them) had been a problem from the moment Craig and Dodd first met in the mid-1960s, when the comedian was appearing at the Opera House in Blackpool with Tessie O'Shea, the ebullient Cardiff-born singer of music-hall songs. There was a lavish twelve-minute opening number and every night the show would start before Dodd had even arrived.

'He came in and made no effort at all to hurry up,' Craig recalls with no small admiration. 'He went upstairs, got into his suit, put his make-up on, wrote on his fingers, walked down, kissed Anita, the lift was ready for him, and walked on to the stage straight out of the lift bang on cue.'

Craig also remembers a radio interview they both gave: 'He loved his mother a lot and she taught him to read very early. He said, "My mother taught me to read when I was four." I said, "It's a pity she didn't tell you how to tell the time!" He didn't like that. I always say that Ken Dodd was born two hours early. If he'd been born two hours later he would have been on time all his life.'

Indeed, Craig once told him, 'One day I'm going to book you for the day before, so I know you'll be there on time.'

The question of punctuality was one of the areas later pursued by Dr Antony Clare in the radio programme *In the Psychiatrist's Chair*. As any psychologist will tell you, the issue of power is paramount in this matter. It is about controlling other people and asserting your superiority. Like many of those little ploys of one-upmanship, used to great effect by the character C. J. in David Nobbs's comedy, *The Fall and Rise of Reginald Perrin*. 'One, two, three, four. Let 'em sweat outside the door,' he would say to himself as some underling waited to gain entry to his office. 'Five, six, seven, eight. It always pays to make 'em wait . . . Come!'

Dodd says that his notoriously unreliable timekeeping is a kind of anarchy. He hates the notion of being ruled by the clock. 'Rigidity,' he told *Women's Realm* readers, 'it's death. That's why I'm unpunctual.' Author John Hind, however, wonders if there are other reasons: by tempting fate he is relishing the adrenalin-rush of arriving late; or perhaps it is his way of saying that the show cannot go on without him, but that too would be a kind of power game.

Still, despite such eccentricities, in the mid-1960s it seemed that whatever Dodd touched turned to gold, and it appeared that he couldn't put a foot wrong. However, real long-lasting success in one important sphere of entertainment continued to elude him – television.

Some comics – Dick Emery, Benny Hill, Tony Hancock, Morecambe and Wise, Stanley Baxter, even Frankie Howerd – had been able to make the transition from stage to small screen with comparative ease. In fact, Hill and Hancock certainly thrived on the new medium as neither was particularly happy before a live theatre audience. Hancock, the miniaturist, appreciated television's ability to capture the smallest detail, while Hill relished the opportunity it afforded for special effects and disguises. Neither of these advantages were likely to appeal to Dodd. He had more in common with Eric and Ernie, who, against the odds, turned out to be the biggest TV stars of the lot.

Whereas the others were essentially comic actors who assumed characters and utilized the 'magic' of television, Morecambe and Wise were an old-fashioned, cross-talking, variety double act. They succeeded rather smartly by never attempting to hide their stage roots; they simply evolved into something more telly-friendly. Theirs remained a stage act; they still used the curtain – the front cloth – for example, and never lost contact with their audience. When they joined the BBC they had the stage built four feet up so that they could play over the cameras. Of course, they were lucky that Bill Cotton paired them with ex-Dodd writer Eddie Braben, who gave them both a distinctive personality, which was vital for TV audiences to respond to. Their producer, John Ammonds, also played a crucial role in cleverly tempering their stage-bound patter with highly visual, TV-friendly musical numbers and guest stars. Ultimately, the duo astutely melded the worlds of end-of-the-pier variety and television, but Dodd, lacking the guiding hand of someone like Ammonds to help him tailor his own singular talents to television, was never able to achieve that same success.

Although, like Eric and Ern, Dodd's best television work has been rooted in his stage work – *The Good Old Days* and, in later years, his two *An Audience With . . .* programmes – generally speaking, he learned that television is not kind to stand-up comedians. Robbed of audience reactions, unsure whether to play to the punters out front or the people at home, often even brilliant live comics fail to hit the mark. Rather like filmed stage plays or circuses, televised stand-up

comedy often comes across as stilted and lifeless, totally lacking in any atmosphere, which is why television created its
own comedians and its own comedy – the sitcom and, before
that, the sketch show. That is also why, despite his 1964
Christmas special pulling in nigh on 34 million viewers, Ken
Dodd never had much of a future on television after variety
went into decline, which was signalled by the demise of
Sunday Night at the London Palladium in the late 1960s. He
had neither the discipline nor, one suspects, the inclination to
subjugate his own character. Other actors would only inter-
fere with the pace he was setting – he has always been a
maverick. He could no more become a sitcom star than
Wendy Craig could play the Palladium for forty-two weeks.
Similarly, one could not imagine Dodd presenting *The
Generation Game* or *The Golden Shot*. He was far too anar-
chic for such things.

Dodd is doubtless aware of his own shortcomings regarding a career on the new breed of programmes, which is why
he mourns the passing of variety from the TV schedules.
'Unfortunately,' he told John Stapleton in *My Favourite
Hymns*, 'the people who run television – not in their wisdom
– have decided that there's no place for variety. Variety is a
wonderful form of show business because everything's different, it's all full of surprises and creative ideas.'

That may have been the case when Dodd was at his peak
during his Palladium successes, but the attitude of the viewing public had changed over the years. Modern audiences no
longer care for smörgåsbord-style snacks; they want a proper
meal. They have ceased to be interested in different elements,
and prefer their entertainment to be specialized. Nowadays
comedians, or rather comic actors, are seen mainly on comedy programmes, magicians are to be found on magic
programmes and musicians on music programmes – jugglers,
ventriloquists and dog acts, unless they can find a novel form

of presentation, have more or less disappeared altogether. As Steve Punt puts it: 'Why would you want to watch snatches of acts when you could watch the whole thing?'

Of course, it is madness to dwell too much in the past. Things change – indeed it is healthy that they do – and in the same way that variety had taken over where music hall left off, the sitcom and the sketch show began to reign supreme on the box.

Dodd's inability to transfer his talents to television successfully has often been a source of frustration, not only to him but also to his producers and directors. On the odd occasion when a director was indisposed, Dodd's then producer Bill Cotton assumed the directorial reins for a number of Dodd's earlier TV efforts in the 1960s. Cotton's most abiding memory is of experiencing a sinking feeling during filming – knowing full well that viewers at home would get only the merest hint of what the studio audience was enjoying. The main problem, he remembers, was getting Dodd to bear in mind that there were viewers at home – instinctively, he would play to those in front of him, and no one seemed to be able to encourage him otherwise. This was not uncommon, though, as television and even radio were still fairly new to these performers; they were learning as they went along. Indeed, Frankie Howerd had the same difficulty adapting to the microphone, and also found it hard not to give a 'stage' performance, pulling faces on the radio. Another significant recollection that Cotton had of those shows was of standing beside the camera, frantically making 'cut' gestures in an attempt to prevent Dodd from overrunning, but it was always to no avail.

Mike Craig thinks that despite the many visual elements to his act, Dodd works much better on radio than television. 'It's not his medium,' he says of TV. 'It's because he's not in charge: the vision mixer's in charge – or ultimately it's the

director who calls the shots. They'll cut away to take in
audience and Ken'll say: "What did you cut away for? N
facial expression there was brilliant!"'

Part of the reason for Dodd's relative lack of success on television is also due to the fact that he never appeared to take it
quite as seriously as his live stage work. Rather like his real
life, TV was something to fill in the moments before he got
back on stage. Even at the beginning of his television career in
the late 1950s, when the BBC offered him his first series and it
was given a Saturday evening prime-time slot, he insisted the
show be recorded in Bolton with only one day's preparation.
His stage work, he told them, meant that he could not spare
them any more time. That the BBC went along with Dodd's
request is indicative of their faith in him. In the event, there
was little to lose. *The Ken Dodd Show* – recorded at 7 p.m. at
the Continental Theatre on a Sunday – was basically a TV
version of a stage show. Even so, critics enjoyed his performance. 'I imagine that most viewers watch mesmerized,' wrote
The People's Kenneth Bailey in 1960, 'unable to decide
whether he is just a jumped-up funny man from the end of
some pier – or a sheer genius.' It is an observation that has
remained unerringly relevant to this day.

No, I feel his heart wasn't quite in television and he didn't
understand the level of commitment required. Of the really
successful TV comedians of the period, such as Morecambe
and Wise and Tony Hancock, it is immediately apparent that
they threw their lot in with the cathode-ray tube; they
revered and courted it as much as Dodd did the theatre.
Dodd, on the other hand, was irritated by the paraphernalia
of television; he is known to have become tetchy with cameras, calling them 'a load of scrap iron'.

That said, for many years there was no shortage of TV
engagements for Dodd. *The Ken Dodd Show* made its BBC
debut at 8.20 p.m. on Saturday 25 July 1959. Written in the

main by Eddie Braben and Dodd himself, the series, which included many specials, ran intermittently for a decade. Supported on occasions by Patricia Hayes, Graham Stark and the Diddymen (either dressed-up stage-school children or Roger Stevenson's puppets), the shows were, on the whole, unashamedly stage-based with the usual panoply of spangly, high-kicking dancing girls and guest stars. The July 1966 vintage episode somewhat bizarrely featured Harry H. Corbett and Wilfred Brambell in a Ray Galton and Alan Simpson-scripted *Steptoe and Son* sketch.

One of the later specials, arranged to mark Prince Charles's investiture in 1969, was recorded at the Golders Green Empire. Dodd asked Mike Craig and his then writing partner Laurie Kinsey to provide some material for it, albeit in a somewhat unconventional manner. 'I had a phone call from Ken Dodd at three in the morning. "Michael, it's Ken!" "Who?" "Ken. Ken Dodd." "It's three o'clock in the morning, Ken." "I've only just got in – I couldn't ring any earlier. What are you like on rush jobs?" He then explained what he wanted and said, "Can you ring me at nine in the morning and tell me what you've got?" "But Ken, it's three o'clock in the morning now." "Well, you've got six hours then!"' As ever, time had no meaning for Dodd.

Incidentally, on the day that this memorable special was recorded, the producer Michael Hurll took the precaution of having Dodd film the finale first, just in case the programme overran and he found himself without a live audience to watch the real thing.

Although he continued to make the specials for the BBC, from 1967–8 Dodd, Braben and new stooge 'Diddy' David Hamilton also made two series' for ABC called *Doddy's Music Box*. Ironically, however, Dodd probably made the greatest impact on television with a children's programme, *Ken Dodd and the Diddymen*, in which he played second

fiddle to some puppets. Roger Stevenson's marionette versions
of Dickie Mint, Mick the Marmaliser, the Hon. Nigel
Ponsonby Smallpiece and the others had proved to be enormously popular on *The Ken Dodd Show,* and so in January
1969 they made their debut in a show of their own. Written
by Bob Block, the man who later gave us *Rentaghost*, it ran
for four series and a number of specials.

Dodd never really understood the importance of writers –
especially in television and radio, where material is eaten up
at a rate of knots. He regarded them as an expense – an area
in which money could be saved. Dodd often clashed with
Mike Craig when the latter was producing his radio show in
Manchester. Writers, it should be explained, are paid by the
minute, and when Craig told Dodd that so-and-so had been
given twenty minutes' worth of payment, Dodd would hit
the roof. 'How much?!' he would scream. Craig would then
point out that as he was the producer it was his responsibility to organize the money, and besides, it was the BBC's
money: '"You can't pay them that sort of money!" "Yes, you
can. They're writers, Ken. You need them. Without writers
you're buggered." That was the big argument always.'

Dodd couldn't understand that they were being given
twenty minutes each when the show was only thirty minutes
long. 'Yes, Ken,' Craig would patiently point out. 'The
finished show is only half an hour, but you want to do an
hour and a half.'

It is interesting to note that Dodd was as careful with
Auntie's purse strings as he was with his own. Perhaps it was
just a principle. Nonetheless, over the years he (or various tel-
evision companies) provided work for, among others, Barry
Cryer, Michael Palin, Terry Jones, Griff Rhys Jones and
Reggie Perrin author, David Nobbs. A Cambridge graduate,
Nobbs's sketches were first performed on *That Was The Week
That Was* in the early 1960s, and as a BBC comedy writer he

soon found himself writing TV and radio material for Frankie Howerd, Dick Emery, Tommy Cooper, Les Dawson and the Two Ronnies as well as Dodd. He feels that he did not do his best work for the latter. 'I don't think I can put my hand on my heart and say that I was a wonderful provider for Ken . . . I don't know how much contribution I made, really. I can't remember. But I enjoyed working on his show.'

And Dodd seemed fairly happy with the gags with which he had been provided. Unlike Frankie Howerd, for example, who was forever having strops about the quality of material, Dodd changed very little of what Nobbs had produced: 'I think we were quite professional and would give him things he could say. It was little sketches and quickies rather than stand-up that he needed writers for. Ken could do his own stand-up for hours on end obviously. But for the construction of a sketch, he needed writers.

'I first saw Ken when I interviewed him along with Peter Tinniswood when we were both reporters on the *Sheffield Star* and we went to see him doing his act, which in those days was the dying embers of the music hall. I don't remember whether he was top of the bill or not, but it was still a bill and he did his thirty minutes or whatever. He came on singing "On the Road to Mandalay" . . . It was very pleasant afterwards – he was very nice to us. I never dreamed that one day I'd be writing for him.'

Without a doubt it was the stage where Dodd was in his element, and no one knows this better than Roy Hudd: 'Every comic worth his salt is ten times more effective seeing him on his own patch with a live audience rather than having been distilled through this box. Ken was marvellous on that *Audience With* programme, but it was his best stuff. It wasn't written for television.

'Whenever you do a show in the theatre,' says Hudd, 'people always come round or meet you in the bar afterwards and say, "Oh, why don't you do that on television, that was marvellous?" And you sort of hesitate to say to them it's taken me twenty-five years to get that right. Which is what Ken has done with all his routines. Every line is a laugh and worked out, but he's worked on them for twenty-five years. The way things happen at the moment we will never, ever produce the brilliant clowns that we produced in the past because they had time to work on their routine – they would cut out the dead wood, they'd find an ad lib there . . . well, Ken does that all the time because he tours. It's great to tour – I love it. It's like an opening night every night.'

Hot from his Palladium triumph, in June 1966 Dodd returned to the Opera House, Blackpool – this time as a bona fide star – for a reputed £2,500 a week. Triumph followed triumph. Dodd could not put a foot wrong. Still, as he told Barry Norman, 'Success doesn't close doors, you know; it opens them.' And there was further success in the offing as he was also informed that the Variety Club of Great Britain had named him as Show Business Personality of 1965. But then with hit TV and radio series', the accolade of having a waxwork figure of himself at Madame Tussaud's, a record-breaking stint at the Palladium, a Royal Variety Performance appearance and his records going gold, there couldn't have been much competition for the prize.

In June 1967 Dodd made a triumphant return to the Palladium. This time the bill included the Bluebell Girls from Paris, the Diddymen (care of Peggy O'Farrell's stage school) and singer Rosemary Squires. Again, Dave Forrester was on hand to steer the proceedings in the right direction. He was particularly keen to surround his client with the very best support acts – it heightened the sense of expectation, he said. And despite the expense involved in bringing the Bluebell Girls over from Paris for shows at the Palladium and the Blackpool Opera House, Forrester felt it was all worth it, because it was so important 'to surround an artist like Ken with something exotic'. He was right, as always. Although based in Paris, the Bluebell Girls had been launched by Liverpudlian Margaret Kelly in 1946, and in early 1967 the sixteen-strong group had made their British debut on *Doddy's Music Box.*

This second Palladium extravaganza – *Doddy's Here Again!* – turned out to be practically a re-run of the first: the illustrious dressing-room visitors (including 'Appy 'Arold Wilson again), the plaudits, the overrunning . . . Yes, 1967 turned out to be another high-water mark in Dodd's career – at Christmas he was invited to Windsor Castle to appear before the Queen and Prince Philip at the royal household staff party. The Queen Mother, Grade recalls, was a great Doddyphile. He once apologized to her for the late running of a show she was attending (guess who was responsible?), but she cared not a jot; she loved Ken Dodd, she told him.

However, it was his own mother who was beginning to occupy more of Dodd's thoughts. As he told Sue Lawley: 'I was very proud when I was able to invite her to the Palladium. And she saw a couple of royal shows at the Palladium. I remember just before I said goodbye to her she was very thrilled because we went to the royal Christmas household party at Windsor Castle. She was only a little lady, but she had a heart as big as Knotty Ash.'

In May 1968, when his mother died of stomach cancer at the age of seventy-one, the news hit Dodd hard. 'I thought I'd never be able to tell another joke again,' he said, 'but I had to go out and face the audience. It stems from a colossal desire to be loved . . .'

6

Cross-gartered Dodd

Back in his home town, the enterprising Dodd next turned his attentions to rescuing the Royal Court Theatre from ruin. In 1970 the place was, in Dodd's words, 'desolate'. It was failing and its future, or rather lack of it, seemed sealed. In an effort to do something about saving the venue, before it was too late, Dodd decided to put on a show. In June he contacted Bernard Delfont and Dave Forrester, and the three of them signed a twelve-week lease for the theatre. Dodd himself organized the publicity and engaged Dickie Hurran to direct. It paid off handsomely, to the tune of £50,000 in advance bookings. It wasn't the last the theatre was to see of Dodd.

In the meantime, however, it was back to Blackpool's Opera House to collect more plaudits, including the following from the *Guardian*'s Robin Thornber. '*Doddy's Laughter Spectacular* is just that,' he wrote. 'The most expensive, the most hilarious, the one with a real live waterfall on the stage at the end of the first half. Dodd himself is Blackpool at its best – it's his ninth season here since 1955. An aristocrat of true vulgarity, he knows exactly what people want and gives them a little bit more. He does it by taking the same corny gags that the rest of them use, but teasing out the logic to its zany limit and out the other side; it's the only act in Blackpool that stretches the imagination or strikes true chords. The tickling stick's still there, but now it's yards long; a Scarfean phallus nodding over the stalls. "Are there any honeymoon couples in?" he asks. "Good morning!"'

Dodd loved Blackpool audiences. They were, after all, on holiday, carefree, and therefore hungry for fun. When Alexandra Connor asked what he thought made a good audience, he replied, 'A good artiste, a good entertainer. There's no such thing as a bad audience – all audiences are wonderful. They've paid you the greatest compliment in the world because they've actually chosen to see you, and so you have to work very, very hard for them. You can only be as good as the audience. You can only be as good as the audience will let you be.'

Luckily, his audiences let him be very good indeed – and his enjoyment of their enjoyment is palpable. As Griff Rhys Jones noted in *Heroes of Comedy*, 'He has a great joy of performing. When he comes on stage he looks like somebody who absolutely adores being there, and somehow that makes the audience come in to him. We feel his pleasure of being on stage. It energizes him. He himself has got this fantastic bubble of fun coming out of him. That's a marvellous thing to have.'

Television work continued to fill his diary, and, despite the visual quality of Dodd's natural performance, he was also in demand to appear on various radio shows, including the panel game *Pull the Other One*. But both mediums played second fiddle to his first love: the theatre. Never one to rest on his laurels, however, by the 1970s Dodd was keen to extend his range. After spending yet another summer at Blackpool's

Opera House, in November 1971 he appeared as Malvolio in *Twelfth Night* (a role, incidentally, Barry Humphries has always been keen to play) at the Liverpool Playhouse.

There are honourable exceptions, but front-cloth comics rarely make good ensemble actors, in spite of their stage presence, confidence and ability to control an audience. They may be good at 'star' performances, but they can often be too weird, too singular or too used to working alone to meld with the company. In Benny Hill's movies, for example, all his scenes could have been from an entirely different film, and even in a *Carry On* production, Frankie Howerd appeared a solitary performer, curiously divorced from the rest of the team. The comedian is also perhaps too keen to subjugate his comic persona; he is anxious to prove his worth and 'be someone else'. Consequently there's a great danger that this earnestness can topple over into melodrama . . . as anyone who has seen Peter Sellers's straight acting film debut in *Never Let Go* can attest.

Ken Dodd's Malvolio, however, perhaps because like Roman or Restoration comedy it affords the actor the opportunity to address the audience directly, proved to be one of those honourable exceptions. Of course it is not unknown for stand-up comics to take on the Bard – witness George Robey's Falstaff or performances of Bottom by Frankie Howerd, Ronnie Barker and Russ Abbott – and, as ever, Dodd had done his homework. He studied critical works on Shakespeare and carefully took on board notes from his director, Anthony Tuckey.

Tuckey had told him that he did not want him to get any laughs for the first half of his performance. 'Let the play do the work,' he said, advising Dodd simply to embrace the role. 'In the second part, I'll let you have your head a bit.' Indeed, such was Dodd's composure and appearance – with his trademark teeth less obviously displayed and his unruly hair tamed by a parting – that he was on stage a full seven minutes before many of those in the audience even recognized him.

Years later, Dodd felt that the month he spent as Malvolio taught him a lot about teamwork: 'When you're a solo comic, it's just you and the audience – you have no other responsibility. But when you're doing a play, you become part of a team.'

He had always had trouble working with 'real' actors in his radio series' – primarily because his unpunctual tendencies often meant his co-stars were kept waiting, which consequently created tensions – but he was on home ground in that situation: in comedy programmes, the serious actors were the guests. Possibly because he was appearing on stage in a Shakespeare play, it made him more determined to be part of the team because, if anything, *he* was the guest. That is not to say that it was an easy experience for him, as he freely admitted to finding it occasionally tricky: 'You have to wait for other people's cues – not too long – and they have to wait for your cues – not too long. Sometimes you have to wait for the pistol to go off and it doesn't go off. Then you have to make it up as you go along.

'When I was Malvolio they said to me: "Doddy, you'll never stick to the script." I said: "What are you talking about. Of course I will. What do you think I am, a moron?" I did ad lib one night. Malvolio is a steward with his chain and I got so enthusiastic I pulled it and the whole thing fell to pieces all over the stage. And the audience gasped. I waited, and then I said to the Countess, "My lady, when I am with thee I have the strength of twenty men!" And the audience went, "Hurray!" And I looked up and I said, "Sorry, Willie!"'

Although he was commendably restrained, Tuckey recalls that he had to dissuade Dodd from making a first-night speech. The director was absolutely right, of course, when he pointed out that the audience and critics would immediately declare, 'See – he couldn't resist it.' In fact, Tuckey revealed, theatregoers were surprised when Dodd kept quiet, and simply took his bow alongside his co-actors. By the third night, however, the comedian couldn't help but succumb to his natural instincts, and made a curtain speech. Old habits die hard.

Dodd was particularly concerned about losing that much-cherished rapport with the audience: 'With acting . . . you never refer to the audience, except in *Twelfth Night* Malvolio does speak directly to the audience. And there are quite a number of plays where the comedian or the kingpin talks to the audience as a sort of interlocutor, as a sort of interpreter, as a sort of guide to the play.'

For the most part, the critics approved of his Malvolio. Many claimed that his appearance was the highlight of an otherwise lacklustre production, while Michael Billington believed that Dodd kept to the Shakespearean ideal much more closely than any of his co-actors. Meanwhile, the *Daily Telegraph*'s John Barber made a particular point of noting what was, for him, Dodd's highpoint in the play, the moment when for the first time 'he turned on . . . the requested smile for his lady – a toothless grin that melted slowly into the ecstatic radiance of the Professor of Tickleology himself.' Barber was also impressed by the comedian's 'attack and enunciation', and praised Dodd for giving Malvolio 'a super-proper voice of clarity that is a lesson to the rest of the soft-spoken, tentative cast'.

Clearly all those years acting out jokes in a bid to sell them had paid off. Such was the success of the production that he was invited to take it first to Oxford and then the West End. Wary of being caught up in a long run, however, he declined and they went without him, but he had enjoyed the experience enough to toy with the idea of playing more 'serious' roles, possibly *Hobson's Choice*, *Billy Liar* or *The*

Card. While Anthony Tuckey was particularly anxious for the comedian to play *The Miser*, Dodd also told Billington that he would like to try his hand at Molière and Sheridan, if he could iron out his accent, but since that time, none of these projects ever materialized.

More than three decades later, memories of Dodd's Shakespearean exploits still linger in the minds of certain theatre reviewers: in Quentin Letts' appraisal of the 2005 production of *Twelfth Night* at Regent's Park Open Air Theatre for the *Daily Mail*, the critic lamented that the role of Feste was not played by someone like Ken Dodd.

When Tuckey was later asked by writer Gus Smith to judge Dodd's performance objectively, the director said that much of the success was down to the novelty value of having Dodd in the role, playing it under control and word-perfect: 'Ken has charisma on stage, but whether it was a better or even different performance than any other good actor would have given, I cannot say.'

Nonetheless, given his success as Malvolio, Michael Grade finds it odd that Dodd has not been tempted to add more dramatic entries to his CV: 'The thing that's surprised me about Ken is that he hasn't done more acting, because he's got a comic intelligence. I'd like to have seen him doing more acting. Many comedians have made a marvellous transition to straight acting: Jimmy Jewel, Arthur English . . . very good actors.'

Perhaps there was a financial reason for Dodd's reluctance to pursue more acting roles, because although he was paid 'a substantial salary by Playhouse standards', it was, according to Tuckey, chicken feed compared to the money he normally earned as a solo comic. Still, he proved that monetary rewards were not always at the forefront of his mind when, to satisfy his growing restlessness, Dodd found a new outlet for his talents. In April 1973, staying on at the Liverpool

Playhouse with its relatively modest salaries, he fulfilled his ambition to do a one-man show. Entitled *Ha-Ha*, the show – his first time without supporting acts – was in many ways Dodd's pet project: a three-hour exploration and celebration of humour – the fruits of his many years of comic analysis. Again, it was heralded as a triumph, but it started off very differently.

Initially, Dodd the comedy student wanted the show to be a fairly serious, scholarly, theory-heavy production – almost a comedy lecture. He changed his mind, however, after he tried it out at a couple of dates while he was playing in *Robinson Crusoe* at the Nottingham Empire a few months previously. After the third attempt he understood with absolute certainty that the audience didn't want to know about comedy theory – they wanted comedy practice. They wanted to see Ken Dodd being Ken Dodd, not Ken Dodd telling them that Stephen Leacock's theory of comedy is that all humour is based on aggression and superiority. Dodd confessed to Michael Billington that even though the audience were perfectly nice about it, rather crucially they didn't laugh: 'I realized that if I was going to have a show that was entertaining, it would also have to be funny.'

And so it was. Billington wrote in the *Guardian* that it was the 'funniest evening he'd spent in the theatre since he first saw *Beyond the Fringe* in Edinburgh in 1960'. Unaware of the show's first faltering steps, he praised Dodd's decision to concentrate on comic practice rather than theory, though he didn't miss the fact that there were also a few lessons wrapped up in the laughs. 'For a start,' he wrote, 'Dodd confirms something that all the great theorists assert: that comedy appeals to the head and never the heart. Bergson refers to the absence of feeling which usually accompanies laughter and says that in a society composed of pure intelligences there would be no tears, whereas one made up of highly emotional souls would neither know or understand laughter.'

For this bravura performance Dodd threw everything into the brew – as well as the analysis, he impersonated well-known comics including, of course, Billy Bennett, and there was even a soupçon of Malvolio. While taking his audience on a canter through the history of humour, he mentioned how at one time we used to go to Bedlam to laugh at the lunatics, whereupon he immediately pulled on a hat, gurned and burst into one of the youthful Eric Morecambe's favourite ditties, 'I'm Not All There'. Indeed, elements of *Ha-Ha* have become part of his stage act to this day, and as with *Twelfth Night*, critics and audiences alike lapped it up. Author Eric Midwinter remembers that the show started at 7.30, but he had to leave at 11.40 'aching and fatigued' to ensure that he didn't miss his last bus home: 'I have watched him live many times and the result is normally the same – a gasping, panting audience.'

Dodd's former producer James Casey, too, was blown away by his performance: 'At the time I could not think of any other comic who could attempt it without bringing on someone else to fill out the three hours or have something to break it up. It was a phenomenal achievement on his part to do it solo.'

With *Ha-Ha* – subtitled 'A Celebration of Humour' – Dodd clocked up another triumph and again there was talk of taking it to London, but the lack of a suitable venue and the physical demands made on Dodd stymied that idea. However, he clearly loved the experience, and at one time was keen to follow it up with a sequel. In that, he explained, he particularly wanted to demonstrate what he called the fascination that people have for physical skills, for example the extraordinary feats achieved by gymnasts. As ever, he had a theory: 'It's something in the back of your primitive mind. I think you have lots of minds – layers of minds – and I think in one of your primitive minds there's a great admiration for men who can leap over bars and swing from ropes, and I think it's far more than just a modern thing. I think there's something in the darker recesses of your mind that recognizes this animal skill that some people have. I think it comes from your primeval past. There's a little Stone-Age man in everybody.'

Spurred on by his lengthy one-man show, Dodd decided that he would like to earn a place in the *Guinness Book of Records* for the longest non-stop joke-telling period. To that end, at 1.19 p.m. on 5 June 1974, he took to the stage of the Royal Court, Liverpool, to perform a Marathon Mirthquake, while all the time hooked up to a heart machine that recorded his stress levels. To add to the pressure there was also a live link-up with BBC Radio Two's Jimmy Young programme. Undeterred, for three hours, six minutes and thirty seconds he told 1,500 jokes. What the record book didn't explain, however, was that just prior to the performance he had also undertaken a two-hour press conference. The audience was admitted free of charge, but they were encouraged to make charity donations. Dodd started the ball rolling by coughing up 100 guineas himself. In the event, £1,000 was raised.

In the same year Dodd made yet another return to the Palladium. As ever, he was adored by both audiences and the critics. Indeed, many said that this latest appearance was his best so far – he was by now more relaxed and confident. 'Without the tragic undertone of Edward Lear,' wrote one London reviewer, 'or the minute characterization of Dan Leno, Dodd is, in fact, a superb exponent of that line of nonsense that stretches back to the Middle Ages. His jam-butty mines and broken-biscuit repair works belong to the fourteenth-century Land of Cockaigne, where the churches have black puddings for bell ropes. Spreading plumptiousness with his multi-coloured tickling stick, he is a reincarnation of the Doctor in the old mummers' play, come from Itty Titty to restore the hero with Alicumpane. And he is himself a tonic.'

He followed up the Palladium engagement with a further BBC television series in November 1974 – *Ken Dodd's World of Laughter*, featuring Windsor Davies, Bill Tidy and Miriam Margolyes – before returning to Liverpool's Royal Court at Christmas with *The Ken Dodd Laughter Spectacular*, which he also produced. Again, it was a success – the show ran until March 1975. It was significant in that it marked his debut as an impresario, the greatest surprise being that it was the first time in twenty years that he'd ever produced his own show. After all, Dodd is a man who knows his own mind, and is very much used to getting his own way. He is not a man short of either confidence or entrepreneurial skill. He is, he has often claimed, a businessman. 'The satisfaction,' he later said, 'was being able to say for once in my life, "I want that scenery because it's that colour. I want those dresses on those girls. I want this act in the show."' He went on to explain that he was keen to control his own destiny and was willing to give producing another whirl. The experience of being his own boss once again was, in a sense, not a million miles from his old Kaydee days.

It was at this time that Dodd turned his attention to the world of politics. Over the years, his staunch Conservative views had changed not one iota; in fact, if anything, by 1979 he had become an even more vociferous political animal. So much so that, armed with a blue tickling stick, he hit the campaign trail on behalf of the Tories, which was not exactly a popular choice in the Labour stronghold of Liverpool. Predictably, it was not all smooth running. While Dodd was canvassing on behalf of a Tory candidate in the city, he was once taken to task by a woman for betraying his working-class roots. When he asked her what she did for a living, she said she was a cleaner. For once Dodd misjudged the

(*Right*) With his unruly hair and trademark 'sticky-out' teeth, Ken Dodd poses with a diddy likeness of the Hon. Nigel Ponsonby Smallpiece, one of his famous Diddymen.

(*Below*) Dodd and his fiancée Anita Boutin, pictured on Dodd's twenty-eighth birthday in 1955. Though the couple were engaged for many years, they never married.

(*Left*) 17 April 1965: Dodd in his dressing room on the opening night of *Here's Doddy!* The show at the London Palladium would run for a record-breaking forty-two weeks.

(*Below*) In September 1965, Liverpool MP and Dodd fan Mrs Bessie Braddock (*right*) invited Prime Minister Harold Wilson and his wife Mary (*left*) to see Dodd in action at the Palladium.

(*Right*) By appointment: Dodd on stage at his first Royal Variety Performance in November 1965. He became a regular at this annual charity event, and performed before the Queen and other members of the royal family on numerous occasions.

Music-hall heroes: Among Dodd's earliest influences were Billy Bennett (*below*), whose penchant for spoof Victorian monologues resulted in utter nonsense; and 'The Cheeky Chappie' himself, Max Miller (*below right*).

(*Left*) In addition to enjoying success as a comedian, Dodd was also a formidable recording artist. After selling more than 100,000 copies of his 1965 number-one single 'Tears', he was presented with a gold disc.

A favourite of the then Prime Minister Margaret Thatcher (*below left*), Dodd was made an OBE in the 1982 New Year's Honours list in recognition of his unstinting charity work. He received his award from the Queen in February 1982 (*below*).

In 1954, Dodd made his debut on the BBC's music-hall-inspired, TV variety show *The Good Old Days* (*pictured above in the mid-1960s*).

In November 1971, Dodd made his Shakespearean debut as Malvolio (*above right*) in *Twelfth Night* at the Liverpool Playhouse, for which he received critical acclaim.

(*Right*) Among his many television appearances, in 1987 he played the part of 'Tollmaster' in an episode of the cult BBC sci-fi show *Doctor Who* (*seen here in costume with co-star Bonnie Langford*).

In June 1988, Dodd's world was turned upside down when he was charged with several counts of tax fraud. He engaged renowned defence barrister George Carman QC (*above left*), and a year later his case was heard at Liverpool Crown Court. Though it was a difficult time for the comedian, the tension all too evident in his face (*above right*), throughout the ordeal his long-term partner Anne Jones (*left*) was unstinting in her support. After a five-week trial, Dodd was found not guilty of all charges.

Despite the tribulations of the previous two years, it didn't take long for Dodd to bounce back. In April 1990, he returned to the Palladium for six weeks with his new show *How Tickled I Am!*

Back on stage (*below*) he was eager to make maximum comic mileage out of his recent clash with the Inland Revenue; in fact, as he himself admitted, 'I got a whole new act out of it!'

In May 2001, Dodd received the ultimate honour from his place of birth when he was granted the Freedom of the City of Liverpool.

'Do you give in?' Still plying his comic trade well into his ninetieth year, Dodd continued to delight and entertain audiences across the UK.

moment, and jokingly remarked, 'Oh, so you're a scrubber.' Reaching into her shopping bag the woman pulled out a frozen leg of lamb and cracked him over the head with it. 'And that's my tickling stick,' she replied.

It was all a far cry from the cosier days of his first Palladium appearance in 1965, when Mrs Bessie Braddock, the MP for Liverpool Exchange, invited him for tea at the House of Commons, and later suggested that she and the then Labour Prime Minister Harold Wilson should take in Dodd's show. From his seat in Row G of the stalls, Wilson, accompanied by Mrs Braddock, his wife Mary and son Giles, became yet another Dodd convert. Dodd, in turn, laid aside his political leanings and thought him 'a nice friendly man'. It is worth noting that at this time Dodd's reputed annual earnings were something in the region of £50,000, while the PM's were £15,250. Eric Midwinter notes that when theatrical impresario William D'Oyly Carte remarked to librettist W. S. Gilbert that Gilbert earned more than the prime minister, Gilbert simply replied, 'I give more pleasure.' He had a point, and perhaps Dodd would agree.

Whatever he thought of 'Appy 'Arold personally, by the time of the 1979 general election Dodd was terrified at the thought of another Labour government. He was very keen to see the back of the existing administration and what he saw as its crippling tax regime. Ordinary people, he argued, needed applause as much as an artiste, but under the Socialists they had little encouragement as they were taxed and bullied: 'How can you expect people to work hard for a goal when the Chancellor said he would squeeze until the pips squeaked?'

Addressing the class issue, he made a point of stressing the difference between Tories and Conservatives. He explained that he didn't hunt foxes and pheasants and was not a member of the landed gentry, but he was a Conservative and he believed that individuals should be able to decide how to live their own lives and receive just rewards for their achievements and hard work. He also thought that the Conservative Party, headed by Margaret Thatcher, whom he regarded as a fellow Conservative as opposed to a Tory, would be able to deal with the increasingly powerful trade unions. In words worthy of a politician, he explained, 'At the present time I feel that many honest trade unionists are being led by the vociferous minority. In my own actors' union it's the left-wing element that is causing all the trouble.'

He closely allied himself to Thatcher and was often seen pictured with her. 'That was probably a mistake in Liverpool,' recalls the *Echo*'s Joe Riley. 'He never got over-ribbed about it, I think, because they so loved Doddy – he was voted in the *Liverpool Echo* survey as the greatest Scouser ever, so they've obviously forgotten that side of him – but in one sense it was a very silly thing to do in Liverpool because Mrs Thatcher was hated here. An entertainer shouldn't really get involved in politics either way.'

There were, however, a few contretemps on the political campaign trail, and it soon became apparent to Dodd that politics could be a messy, unpleasant business, as the leg of lamb incident was not the only time he ran into trouble. At Speke market he witnessed an ugly crowd kicking and punching the Conservative entourage, ripping up their banners and shouting them down. A Conservative spokesman later commented that, 'Mr Dodd was subjected to the most vicious abuse I have seen in fifteen years of political campaigning.'

Despite being pelted with eggs on another occasion, he carried on canvassing, albeit perplexed that these same people opposing him were also those who comprised his audience. It was decidedly odd for Dodd to put his head above the parapet in this fashion, risking possible alienation from those who paid to see him, but it clearly indicates the depth of feeling he had regarding this issue. Consequently, few were more pleased than Ken Dodd when Margaret Thatcher swept to victory at the 1979 general election. This new Prime Minister, he thought, would give Britain back its pride . . . and, who knows, might even cut taxes.

Dodd always appealed to the Tories. Obviously his name had pulling power, but they genuinely seemed to like him. The most recent Tory MP to declare herself a fan has been Ann Widdecombe. Not only could she and her mother be seen chortling away at Dodd in his second *Audience With . . .* appearance, but in January 2004 she saluted him in a *Times* article, in which she began by explaining that she fell in love with *The Ken Dodd Show* at the age of eleven. The other girls at school in Bath, she said, talked endlessly about what they'd seen on ITV, but she was more than content to watch Dodd. 'To a child,' she remembered, 'the buck teeth, wild hair and crazily improbable words were hilarious enough in their own right, while Gran liked his singing and my elder brother made what I now recognize as mildly rude jokes about tickling sticks. It was family entertainment then, and it is now, which is probably why it no longer features as a regular Saturday night primetime show.'

Dodd was doubtless chuffed by this observation, particularly as the 'family' had always been the target for his talents, appealing, as he does, to everyone in the family unit, albeit on different levels: the parents he keeps entertained through his wordplay and innuendos, while among the children he provokes laughter through his physical clowning.

Widdecombe went on to make the point that Dodd is as at home making sharp, sophisticated gags about Labour politicians as he is telling jokes about Diddymen: 'Slapstick without custard pies, cleverness without cynicism, rudeness without vulgarity, innocence without childishness – he will probably last a long while yet.'

In later life he has become a little more circumspect about his political leanings, and has been at pains to point out that although Thatcher went to see him three times, he also entertained Edward Heath and former Labour leaders Harold Wilson and James Callaghan. 'Politics is a very personal thing. I don't think I agree with any one party,' he now says, adding that he would never want to get closely involved with politics again. He has stressed, however, that he still holds strong ideas about individualism and hard work.

So, by the mid-1970s, it seems that apart from the odd, piffling little blip, Dodd's life had been one long round of success. At alarming speed he commuted from triumph to triumph, from applause and plaudits to even greater achievements and awards. He had hardly known failure, and excepting the sadness he had experienced on the death of his mother in 1968, he had not known much unhappiness either. All that changed in July 1975, however, when doctors at Clatterbridge Hospital on the Wirral gave him the shocking news that his fiancée Anita Boutin had been diagnosed with a brain tumour. The prognosis was not good.

Never one to share his problems, Dodd carried on working while Anita was undergoing radiotherapy. He drew great strength from her courage, but admitted that it was tough to go on stage and make people laugh when inside all he wanted to do was to weep. But still Dodd refused to go public. Each evening, after a show, he would rush to her hospital bedside, hold her hand and tell her how it went. Sometimes she would fall asleep, only to wake up to find him still there.

By the end of June 1976 Dodd was told that nothing more could be done. Early one morning, with Dodd, and both their families round her bed, his forty-three-year-old fiancée died. After a relationship lasting twenty-two years Anita Boutin had still got no closer to becoming Mrs Ken Dodd. When asked some time later why they never married, the comedian refused to discuss the matter, saying, 'That's a private thing, too personal to talk about.'

The *Liverpool Echo*'s Joe Riley has known Dodd for thirty years – they have met professionally and socially many times, and have been in contact on a regular basis. Riley has his own theory as to why Dodd never married. He is anxious to stress, however, that it is just that – his own personal theory. 'I'm not casting aspersions on anything to do with his sexuality, I'm not doing anything nasty, I'm not implying anything,' he says. 'But there are certain people that you meet – not just well-known people – who were so influenced by their parents they can't break from them in a funny sort of way. And nobody will ever quite match up to the parents. I don't think it affects their sexuality, as in what they're attracted to or even what they do sexually or romantically, but I do think there's a psychological step they cannot take – which is to leave behind or break with, or even fracture, the sacredness of what they had with their family – to forming another family.

'There are half a dozen people I've encountered in my life who have fallen into that category. They're not gay and they're not odd, they're not anything – they're just not able to step over the threshold into a full-time relationship. They're so entrenched in the idea that nothing was like their childhood, nothing was like their family, nothing was like their parents, nothing was like their home . . . which would explain why Ken Dodd still lives in the house he was born in and the table is permanently set in the way his mother used to set it – the HP sauce is out as it always was.'

But it wasn't just his mother who influenced Dodd, says Riley – he held both parents in equal regard: 'It's a very sort of urban working-class thing, really. It's to do with the matriarchal and patriarchal society where for one reason or another – whether it was through the church or through just very strict morals or through very hard work or thrift –

certain values were imposed on people from which they couldn't break free. Even when he was younger it would have been against his whole morality to go off with dancing girls and spend a few thousand pounds in a gambling casino.

'Every time he talks about his parents he's always reverential. He never badmouths them. He obviously holds them still – even in his old age – in great esteem.'

Anita's funeral was held at St John's Church, Knotty Ash, where eight years previously Dodd had witnessed his own mother's funeral service. After listening to the Reverend Siviter's thoughtful words of comfort and encouragement, in which he advised the grieving comedian to continue to bring happiness to others to honour the memory of both his mother and his fiancée, the funeral party moved on to Anfield cemetery for Anita's burial.

Afterwards, Dodd returned to his home in Thomas Lane, where he continued to live with his father. Understandably, at this difficult time, he withdrew from the world. His sister June described him as 'grief-stricken'. 'He has taken Nita's death very badly,' she explained. 'It must have been a terrible strain for him to go on stage and be his usual self, knowing he was going to lose the only woman he has ever loved. But it was Anita who helped him to keep going. That was the kind of wonderful, courageous girl she was. The whole family loved her.'

The telling advice given to him by the vicar must surely have stayed with Dodd, because over time he was gradually able to come to terms with his grief and, to borrow Roy Hudd's colourful phrase, 'he pulled up his knickers' and threw himself back into his work, which included an agreement to be the subject of an episode of the *South Bank Show*, broadcast in March 1978.

Also on the agenda was the saving of a few theatres. Liverpool's Royal Court had lain waste for a year and the

Grand Theatre, Blackpool, was also in severe difficulty. Dodd later became closely involved with a £350,000 fundraising scheme for the latter in 1978, and pledged that if they were successful in buying the Grand from EMI, and running it as a full-time theatre, he would hire it for a summer season.

By the late 1970s there was, alas, no shortage of theatres in trouble. Unable to pay their way without grants and subsidies, managements found it difficult to resist the tempting wads waved under their noses by developers. Ever the northerner, Dodd was particularly suspicious of those in the capital. 'Today's managements in London think they can run halls in the provinces,' he said, adding bluntly, 'but they can't.'

And it got worse. While appearing at the Palace Theatre in Manchester, Dodd learned that its future was also in the balance – he immediately offered to finance his own Christmas *Laughter Show* to the tune of £100,000 to help it out of a hole. Of course he wasn't taking too much of a gamble, as from mid-December the 2,200-seat auditorium was host to sell-out shows, and thus another theatre was saved from ruin. During this time Dodd became an ever more vociferous advocate of live theatre. 'How dare people say live entertainment is dead,' he told the *Liverpool Post*'s Joe Steeples. 'When you watch a theatre show, you don't just watch it, you're in it. As far as I'm concerned, a live audience is the most important part of entertainment. You can't clown away in a vacuum. You can't tell jokes to yourself!'

After a further two-week sell-out season at the London Palladium, Dodd found himself spending the Christmas of 1980 at the Alexandra Theatre, Birmingham. Playing the Good Fairy in *Dick Whittington* was forty-five-year-old ex-Bluebell Girl, Sybil (also called Sybie) Jones. Known to her friends as Anne, she had been acquainted with Dodd for a number of years, but it soon became apparent to those around them that the two had fallen in love. As ever, despite the blossoming romance, there was to be no talk of marriage. This time, Dodd's excuse was that he thought that marriage could lead to complacency in a relationship, and caused some couples to stop putting in any effort. As far as he was concerned, when two people lived together the fact that either could walk out at any time meant that each would have an incentive to treat their partner with respect and not take the other for granted.

Possibly he was not aware of the tax advantages of being married.

After making an appearance on the John Fisher-produced *Parkinson* chat show in 1981, in which the veteran interrogator unearthed precisely nothing about the comic, Dodd made another radio series. Produced in Manchester, this time James Casey had the enviable (or unenviable, depending on how you look at it) job of trying to cut and edit the hours of material, while coping with the star's unpunctuality. Like Bobby Jaye and Mike Craig before him, Casey found producing *The Ken Dodd Show* a frustrating business. As Dodd would be needed at rehearsals by noon, Casey took the precaution of changing his contract to state that his start time was 10.30 a.m. Needless to say, Dodd arrived at midday.

On one occasion, when Jaye attempted to upbraid his star for overrunning, Dodd, staring into his dressing-room mirror initially acquiesced. Then, just as his producer was about to leave, without taking his eyes off the mirror, he added, 'There's just one thing, Bob . . .' 'What's that, Ken?' 'Remember . . . you need me more than I need you.' Both men understood the reality of that statement – it was clear that they both knew where they stood.

The 1982 New Year's Honours List brought – not altogether unsurprisingly, given his unstinting work for charity and the fact that he was Margaret Thatcher's favourite comedian – an OBE ('One boiled egg'). Dodd was, he said 'full of plumptiousness' to receive the award. After the ceremony in February he told reporters: 'Oh yes, I was on time for Her Majesty. I mean, no one is allowed to be late for the Queen.' On that occasion, it was Dodd who knew where he stood.

The 1980s for Dodd started out much like the previous two decades: the more or less constant touring interspersed with a few longer dates for pantos and summer shows. The *Financial Times*'s Michael Coveney remained one of Dodd's staunchest supporters. 'As usual,' he wrote in December 1983, 'he moved me instantly to tears, to laughter, to tears of laughter. There is no one in whose company I would rather spend my last moments on earth – if I had to be in a theatre, that is.'

During a summer season at Scarborough in 1985, Coveney noted, 'Dodd is the very spirit of tireless vaudeville and, as ever, he impresses as an animal who only exists in the glare of a spotlight, in the palms of our hands. This is what people unfortunate enough to have only seen Dodd on television do not understand.'

As the decade progressed Dodd's working patterns started to alter – there were more one-night stands ('One night is all they can stand'), and fewer pantos and summer shows. The pantomime was increasingly being given over to Aussie soap 'stars' and one-hit wonders, and the summer season was suffering due to the ever-growing popularity of the package holiday and the lure of cheap tequila. Indeed, in 1985, journalist Alan Frank charted the demise of the end-of-the-pier show for *The Times*. Twenty years earlier, he noted, it was common for performers to play twenty-three-week seasons, by the mid-1980s the seasons had fallen to five or six weeks. Then there was the recession. A popular Blackpool show in 1965 would have cost about £50,000 to stage; two decades later the cost had doubled. Financially, the summer show had become increasingly less profitable.

It was, of course, impossible to discuss the summer show without speaking to Dodd in the year that he was at Scarborough. 'Oh, they've been writing off the summer show for years,' he told Frank. 'You see, the trouble is that every year the town's newspaper, in whatever resort it might be, gives the show a right old roasting, complaining about the old gags and stale routines. But I'll tell you, even the old chestnuts like the landlady jokes, when they're properly delivered, are the best in the world.' He went on to explain that he thought TV was a mixed blessing for the summer show. Television provided names big enough to fill a large theatre, but it produced artists who found it difficult to adapt from one medium to another. He had a point. Whereas the old school entertainers could turn their hands to practically anything, the younger fry were in many ways severely hampered by the lack of a suitable training ground. In any case, Dodd had not appreciated was that his summer shows were an exception – most of the others were dying on their feet. The tide had changed.

Dodd reckoned that in order to survive, a performer had to make radical alterations to his or her act every seven years or so. 'I used to be a salesman,' he told Frank, 'and I had a round, the same as I do now. Only these days, it's what I would call a laughter round, a giggle round, where you have built up a range of customers who know what you offer. But you can't stand still. Every seven years you have to pass a new test; you could call it the public responsibility exam. The audience gets fed up. They know you like an old friend, and like any other old friend they can get tired of you if you are always saying the same things.'

Meanwhile, in the world of television, an opportunity arose for Dodd to demonstrate his acting skills once again. Given the fact that he is fond of seeking out strange new worlds and boldly going where no other comedian has been before, it is no surprise to learn that Dodd is a fan of science fiction. For someone interested in weaving and creating their own warped universe, sci-fi obviously holds great appeal. Therefore, in 1987 he was delighted to be asked to appear in an episode of the cult BBC TV series, *Doctor Who*.

Featuring Sylvester McCoy as the eponymous Time Lord, 'Delta and the Bannermen' is generally considered by *Doctor Who* aficionados to be one of the weakest entries in the long-running and recently revived series. Then in its twenty-fourth season, the programme's producers seemed unsure where to go next – hence the cast for this jokey three-parter also included comedy stalwarts Stubby Kaye, Hugh Lloyd and Richard Davies. Originally entitled 'Flight of the Chimeron', the plot involved the Doctor and his assistant, Mel, landing at a tollport, being hailed as the one billionth customer, and consequently winning a holiday to Disneyland. While travelling in the Tardis, the Doctor is knocked off course, and ends up at the Shangri-La holiday camp in Wales. (This being budget BBC, it was filmed at Butlins in Barry Island, south Wales). Complete with an infuriating 1950s soundtrack, there was more than a whiff of the then popular *Hi-De-Hi!* about the whole sad enterprise. Dodd, cast as the Tollmaster, adorned in shimmery turquoise livery, more or less played it as himself. It was all a far cry from *Twelfth Night*.

The following year Dodd found himself back in Wales, where he was appearing in a seaside summer season at the Arcadia Theatre in Llandudno. It was not a wholly happy return, however, as it was during this engagement, after a performance on Tuesday 7 June 1988, that Dodd was compelled to make an extraordinary announcement.

'I haven't done anything wrong,' he assured a packed audience. 'All I have done is made a very, very stupid mistake and then admitted to it.' As he left the theatre, he addressed the circling press decamped outside the theatre, simply saying, 'The matter is in the hands of my solicitors. I can't say any more.'

The statements were made in response to various stories that had been recently plastered all over the papers. *The Times*'s headline – 'Ken Dodd faces eighteen tax charges' – said it all.

The Llandudno faithful had given Dodd a standing ovation, but the same could not be said for the Inland Revenue. It had spent the previous three years sifting through Dodd's accounts in England, the Isle of Man and the Channel Islands, looking into his various companies, Ken Dodd Enterprises, Diddy Scripts and Happiness Music. It was the start of what was to be the lowest point of Dodd's life.

7

Opening Pandora's Box

'KEN DODD'S SO STARSTRUCK he won't come off . . . if he gets two years, he'll do four!' So went a joke – attributed to both Bernard Manning and Les Dawson – that was in circulation during the time of the Ken Dodd tax trial. With its blurring of accepted Dodd lore with the cold, harsh truth of his uncertain future, the joke somehow seemed an appropriate metaphor for the events that took centre stage at Liverpool Crown Court over a five-week period in the summer of 1989.

There is a certain ghoulish fascination about seeing a familiar face in the dock – even more so in one as loved and revered as Dodd's. His was the kind of face that would normally be featured in a courtroom comedy sketch on TV, but unfortunately for Dodd, this was the real thing. The papers, of course, rustled with anticipation.

It was an extraordinary spectacle – almost on a par with the high-profile court case of Oscar Wilde more than ninety years previously: both were successful, flamboyant men at the peak of their profession; both had exceptional wit; and both, it could be argued, lived in a kind of fantasy world, each with their own unique take on society and the world at large.

In the public's mind, however, there was one crucial difference between the likes of Wilde and Dodd: whereas Wilde's love that dared not speak its name made him a pariah, a clear-cut, bona fide hate figure in late Victorian England, Dodd's 'enemy' was, in a sense, *our* 'enemy' – the Inland Revenue. There was, undeniably, an undercurrent of 'good on you, mate' running through the whole trial – more perhaps in the north than in the south. After all, here was a man who had entertained thousands, a man who had illuminated the dark corners of many lives, a man who had given himself unstintingly to countless good causes, and what was his perceived vice? He liked a few bob.

'He's a money fetishist really, I'd have thought,' says George Melly. 'Doddy is obviously fascinated by money and less by possessions. He hates paying out money. He doesn't spend it.'

This singular attitude to money – it is not without irony that 'Ken Dodd' has become rhyming slang for a 'wad' – is what many of his acquaintances first note about him. After writing a spoof protest song for Dodd that the comedian had liked, in the mid-1960s Mike Craig had been invited to meet with him in Blackpool. Craig lived seventy miles away, and though he managed to arrive at the rendezvous point on time, he had to wait and wait for Dodd to turn up. When the comedian eventually appeared at 10.20, he uttered the improbable line: 'I've had to go for a fitting for a new suit!' It was a thin excuse, as John Fisher's *Heroes of Comedy* programme laid bare so graphically, since Dodd has been wearing the same silver-grey, generously-lapelled suit for decades. 'He's had that suit so long it's come back into fashion,' recalls Craig.

After the meeting Dodd took Craig and his writing partner Laurie Kinsey over the road for a drink with himself and Anne: 'The bar was open and he said, "What would you like to drink?" Laurie said, "I'll have half a lager, Ken." And I didn't drink much in those days so I said, "I'll have a fruit juice." And Anne said, "I'll have a gin and tonic." He put his hand in his pocket and he worked it out what it would cost and he gave Anne exactly the right money – if he'd given her a ten-bob note she might have got a double gin!

'But this is a man who had Anne do everything on an Amstrad word processor. I tried to get him to buy a computer. I told him you can buy one for five hundred quid. "Crikey! Five hundred quid!" I said, "Ken, it's allowable against tax."'

Few would argue with Roy Hudd when he observed that Dodd has a bad case of 'the comic's disease' – it is not exactly unknown in showbiz circles, and there is no shortage of stories to demonstrate his . . . shall we say, 'carefulness'.

For example, writer David Nobbs recalls a rare post-show drink at the Captain's Cabin pub in Piccadilly. Dodd had promised the cast that he'd buy them all a drink after the recording, so they all went off to the pub and bought a couple of rounds of drinks between them. Then, Nobbs explains, 'At one minute to eleven, Ken came in and said, "Sorry about that – I had to talk to some people. What are you all having?" He got out a piece of paper and took down all the drinks, went up to the bar and came back with a light ale and said, "I'm sorry. It's after eleven and they're closed, but they gave me one because I hadn't had one all evening." But we didn't resent it – it was part of the experience of working with Ken Dodd and I think to a certain extent that he was probably living his own legend. Obviously a comedian is fairly self-centred – I mean, how can you go on night after night?'

But then in the same way that cabbies would ask Jack Benny not to tip them so they could tell family and friends how mean he was, Nobbs feels almost cheated by the fact that on one occasion, Dodd actually paid for his stay in a hotel. The comedian had wanted Nobbs to write for him, and had requested that the writer came to see his act. As the performance wasn't local to Nobbs, he had to stay in a hotel, but because Dodd had been so eager for Nobbs to see him, uncharacteristically he was prepared to settle his account. 'Ken Dodd paid my hotel bill!' expostulates a still-shocked Nobbs.

Roy Hudd, too, has had first-hand experience of Dodd's remarkably long pockets . . . when he was asking for an important favour. It was the time Dodd turned up at a theatre in Clwyd – where Hudd was appearing in a play called *The Birth of Merlin* – specifically to ask Hudd whether he'd agree to be a character witness at his forthcoming trial. Hudd recalls: 'A message comes round – "Ken Dodd's in the bar – he wants to know what you'd like to drink." What? It was like getting a drink out of Max Miller – a miracle! Anyway, Ken was there in the bar and he said, "Ah, young man, what would you like to drink?' and I said, "I'll have a bitter please, Ken." "Certainly – a half of bitter for this young man!" *Half* a bitter! I thought: he hasn't let me down!'

Dodd is not just careful with money, he can be an extremely astute businessman. David Nobbs remembers a time when he was writing a TV series for Dodd, and it was decided that it would be a great idea to end each of the shows by showering foam over the audience: 'So every week we did this episode where we'd cover the audience with foam. And he always said it didn't quite work, it wasn't quite right. Eventually by episode six I think he was happy, but an awful lot of foam was wasted. When the BBC got the invoice it was from Diddy Foam Products of Knotty Ash.'

Michael Grade has described Dodd's relationship with money as 'peculiar', and has jokingly suggested that 'he's still got the first penny he ever earned': 'For reasons I wouldn't begin to guess at – and I don't mean this in a judgemental way – he is a miser. You'd go backstage. "Would you like a drink, guvnor?" "That's very kind of you, Ken." And he'd go into his cupboard and pull out a bottle of Double Diamond, which he used to get free because he would plug it in the show.'

None of these stories concerning his perceived meanness would come as a surprise to Dodd. So aware is he of this particular foible that he once revealed a telling insight into his unusual point of view: 'I am not mean, but I am nervous about money. Nervous of having it, nervous of not having it. I'm not a tycoon – not a rich man who shows it. In fact, I'm not rich at all. I'm only as rich as my last show.'

On the business side of things, however, Grade remembers Dodd as a bit of a tough cookie when it came to financial negotiations: 'Money was always important to him. I wouldn't say he was greedy, but he was always very tough on deals. He took the money side of it very seriously.'

And it certainly paid off. At his peak in 1970, Dodd was said to be earning £10,000 a week, yet he still preferred to eat Irish stew at home rather than dine at expensive restaurants. When he bought a set of encyclopaedias, it was on hire purchase. With Dodd, there was never any outward sign of wealth, but whether that was because he was keen to remain 'one of the people', or because he was mean is anybody's guess. One thing was certain: he loathed the way that people behaved differently when the issue of his fortune arose. 'Once I had achieved a degree of success and met again people I had known for years, I could see in their faces the change in their feelings towards me,' Dodd declared in the 1970s. 'But with a very steady northern brain, trained to caution, I have managed to sidestep the temptation to think that money can buy you anything.'

The subject of money arose again in a late-1970s interview in the *Liverpool Post*: 'What is money except a lot of noughts on a bank book?' asked Dodd. 'It's only there for the taxman – and how do you think it feels to write a cheque for £39,000 for the Inland Revenue and know that's only an initial investment?' As a lifelong supporter of private enterprise, he has never made an excuse for having money – 'I am a one-man industry,' he once declared – and having watched other celebrities fritter away thousands through inept financial management, he has been extremely careful about how he has invested his own hard-earned cash, and merely limited himself to a country house – 'my little piece of England'.

The *Liverpool Echo*'s Joe Riley is acutely aware of Dodd's paradoxical attitude to money. 'People say he's very tight with his money, but he's very generous with his time. I think it's more telling if you're generous with your time.' He also points out that Dodd has raised hundreds of thousands of pounds for charity over the years, so when it comes to responding to good causes, Dodd is certainly no slouch, and has led by example on many different occasions.

Riley also points out that although people might expect him to throw money around all over the place, as a rich man, the reality is that he is cautious: 'What I'm talking about is if you went out for a meal with him, as I did once after the London Palladium, we looked at the menu to which he said, "The liver and onions is very good here" – brackets: don't be thinking of anything else. So he can occasionally give the idea of being scrupulously tight, but he's not mean-spirited.'

In analysing the root cause of his views about financial matters, Riley can understand why Dodd has developed his odd attitude to money: 'He comes from a background of thrift, an old-fashioned background where his father was a coal merchant, counted the pennies and put them away for a rainy day. And he's been in that mould all his life and he can't get out of it. It's a sort of Protestant work-ethic mode of old Liverpool.'

The general public's attitude to the wealth of others is often contrary: if, for example, someone scoops the pools or wins the lottery, people tend to say, 'Good luck to you, mate.' If, however, someone toils honestly and diligently for decades to accumulate a few bob, the public somehow resents it, and in this case, 'the comics' disease' – meanness – hardly helps matters. Where that particular trait comes from is a bit of a mystery. It has often been thought that it was pre- and post-war childhood poverty that fuelled it but, according to Arthur Smith, the disease shows no sign of dying out. He says that it is not just the old-guard comedians who suffer from that particular malady; many younger comics are equally 'careful'. However, it could be argued that it is often what is seen as a character 'flaw' that makes a comic human; what makes him of the people. Dodd's apparent tightness really reinforces the fact that he is just an ordinary working bloke. Those comedians who really connect with their audiences are those who are willing to put human frailties on display. As Bob Monkhouse said of Tommy Cooper: 'I could see why he was a goof . . . and it made me love him all the more. I knew he had these flaws in his character [a fondness for alcohol that occasionally spilled over into violence] – who hasn't? You love a man for his flaws. Every comedian, as soon as you identify what's wrong with them, you love them even more, because they represent you.'

★

When Dodd's brush with the Revenue first made headlines in June 1988, the case of Lester Piggott was also in the news.

Convicted of a £3 million tax fraud, the jockey was then serving a three-year jail sentence – it was reported that he broke down in tears in his prison cell when news reached him that the Queen had stripped him of his precious OBE. Piggott's plight must have focused Dodd's thoughts very closely, and doubtless drove home the gravity of the situation. It was no bad lesson to learn; this was not something that could be flippantly brushed aside. Dodd was in deep, deep trouble.

Then, to compound matters, things got worse for Dodd. He did not attend the preliminary hearing in Liverpool in June 1988, because he was in Sussex at the Jewish cemetery in Hove, attending the funeral of Dave Forrester, the man who helped him earn all those pounds in the first place. In Dodd's absence in the courtroom, it was revealed that he would now be facing tax charges dating back to 1972 relating to his three companies and various bank accounts, as it was alleged that he had given false returns under-estimating income and profit.

Furthermore, on 10 August, at Liverpool Magistrates' Court, Dodd was ordered by Norman Wootton, the stipendiary magistrate, to surrender his passport, to safeguard against his fleeing the country to avoid facing the charges. Peter Cockin, prosecuting counsel for the Inland Revenue, told the court that the tax authority had requested that Dodd give up his passport because the 'new offences are non-extraditable, should he want to leave these shores'. To Dodd, the patriot par excellence, this was a particularly cruel blow, especially as this was a man who had never even left the country for fifty-odd years. Nor would it ever have occurred to him to leave Britain. 'There is no place he could go,' stated his barrister, Miss Susan Klonin, 'because he would be instantly recognized.' She explained that Dodd had never owned property abroad and had no intention of being 'a fugitive on the run'.

The list of charges had also grown since June, as the Inland Revenue had added a further nine to the original eighteen relating to tax fraud made at the first hearing. Three of these new charges alleged false accounts at Ken Dodd Enterprises in 1986; the other six were of criminal theft, involving alleged falsifying of the cash book of Ken Dodd Enterprises, which related to services at three hotels. David Hartnett, senior principal inspector of taxes in charge of the investigation, told the twenty-five-minute hearing: 'The Inland Revenue view makes this case much more serious than we originally thought.'

Cross-examined by Klonin, Hartnett agreed that Dodd had been aware of an Inland Revenue investigation and that it had been going through his affairs 'with a fine-tooth comb for some years'. Klonin told the court that within the last two days Dodd had made efforts to pay all the money the Revenue claimed was owing, by placing £350,000 in tax reserve certificates (a bond issued by the Inland Revenue), and £475,000 on deposit with the Revenue. She went on to explain that Dodd had decided to apply for reporting restrictions to be lifted because he was anxious for wide media coverage of his protestations of innocence. 'He proposes to stand his trial,' she said. 'He has been fully co-operative with the Inland Revenue.' She then added that he was in desperate need of a break: 'He suffers from bronchitis and emphysema. His doctor advises that he should go abroad for his health.' Dodd was duly permitted to apply to the court to have his passport restored for specific periods.

He was committed for trial at Liverpool Crown Court, and was due to be tried the following June. Bail was granted: Dodd's brother Bill and his partner Anne Jones each put up £25,000.

Outside the magistrates' court, Dodd waved and managed a thin smile as he signed autographs. Back home in Thomas

Lane, goodwill messages flooded in. 'Nothing will stop the laughter,' he maintained. And, true to his word, despite the Inland Revenue's Sword of Damacles hanging over him, he continued to honour his professional commitments. At the Floral Hall in Southport, he bounded on stage, his energy and dedication undimmed. Even Dodd's booking agent, Keith McAndrew, was amazed by his resilience, and his ability to block out his worries and soldier on for the sake of his fans. 'Ken knows they are behind him,' he remarked, 'and it helps him to carry on. That's why he keeps working so hard – he'd hate to think that anyone had missed out on the fun.'

One audience did miss out, however. As *The Times*'s City Diary pointed out on 14 October, Dodd was due to perform that day at Camber Sands in Sussex, but the hosts, the Civil Service Motoring Association, decided to replace him with Little and Large. The reason? A large number of the association's members were tax inspectors.

Throughout this difficult time in his life, it appears that Dodd kept hold of his sense of humour. In December 1988, while appearing as Idle Jack in *Puss in Boots* at the Civic Theatre, Halifax, someone in a gambling scene had the line, 'Money is no object,' to which Dodd replied, 'I must remember that line!' Then, in a scene in which Dodd and the Dame were making lumpy dumplings in the kitchen, she asked the audience, 'Is he kneading the dough?' 'About a million quid!' was Dodd's cheeky riposte.

Dodd was now compelled to play the waiting game. In many ways, the ten months leading up to the trial were the most painful of all, but he found that work was a constant balm. Being on stage seemed to take his mind off his mounting worries in a way that no other pursuit could. 'You manage for a few minutes to forget it all and it's as if you're getting messages from the audience of goodwill. It's wonderful.'

Throughout this period, Dodd kept a high public profile, particularly in and around Liverpool – there he was still opening galas and attending civic functions, as well as reciting John Betjeman's poem 'Christmas' in Liverpool Cathedral. The strain must have been enormous, but he clearly felt it was the best course of action. He did the right thing, too, by not being drawn into public brawls by the press. Unlike the local newspapers, who generally remained loyal to Dodd, some of the Fleet Street nationals were not quite so generous. Stories of his parsimony vied with each other for attention. One newspaper was particularly uncharitable, alleging that Dodd had broken his promise to pay for Anita's gravestone. It was an accusation that infuriated Anita's brother, Bill. 'I didn't like what the papers wrote,' he later revealed. He went on to say that he had always admired the way that Dodd had treated his sister, and that he and the comic were still good friends. It is little wonder that Dodd holds scant regard for certain members of the press, who seemed to delight in kicking the man when he was down.

However, even his fellow Liverpudlians were not beyond having the odd pop at him – although they tended to do so not only with affection, but also with wit. For example, there were the convicts in HMP Liverpool who hung a placard from their cell windows, which read: 'Appearing here soon – Ken Dodd.' Despite the seriousness of his circumstances, I imagine that even he couldn't resist a laugh at that.

But for Dodd, it was not only his liberty that was at stake; even if he was found innocent, he was concerned that perhaps his career would suffer. Radio producer James Casey once said that he thought Dodd only wanted to be a comic and not a star: 'His simple lifestyle has demonstrated this. I think it is important to him to have the respect of his showbiz colleagues and he has always had that. I've yet to meet a performer who didn't think Ken was a great comic.' Though he might have been right about Dodd wanting respect, I have my doubts about Casey's belief that the comedian did not want to be a star. It is arguable that status is very important to Dodd – he was always very concerned about maintaining his position. 'I still want to be starring, to be up front,' he said. 'Anything else would be humiliation.' Perhaps he was recalling one of Frankie Howerd's more public slides down the showbiz ladder, when, during a run in Great Yarmouth with Tommy Steele, Howerd suffered the ignominy of being billed as a supporting player, his name reduced commensurately on the poster. It was a fall from grace that no well-established comic would wish to experience.

For Dodd, the interminable wait came to an end at 10.30 a.m. on Tuesday 6 June 1989, in Court 5-1 at Liverpool Crown Court, almost exactly a year after the allegations had first hit the headlines. To defend himself he had engaged one of the most respected, most successful, most famous, most feared (and most expensive) lawyers, George Carman QC. Northern, working-class, and almost as steeped in showbiz as his client, Carman was the ideal choice to defend Dodd, but this legal heavyweight did not come cheap. That Dodd was willing to dig deep to secure Carman's services indicates the gravity he placed on the matter. But the price would be higher than he could have ever imagined. In order to save Dodd's skin, Carman would be compelled to open the Pandora's Box of his client's private life by making public many of the more intimate details about Dodd's past, which the comedian had spent the previous thirty years attempting to conceal. The great irony is, of course, that to save his successful career and protect his cherished liberty, a man who prized money and privacy above all else should have had to spend so much of the former in order to expose the latter.

Born in Blackpool, the son of a furniture salesman, Oxford-educated Carman was called to the Bar in 1953, and first came to prominence in 1979 when he defended the Liberal Party leader, Jeremy Thorpe, at the Old Bailey. It was to be the first of many big-name, high-profile cases. In fact, having successfully represented such luminaries as Elton John, Norman Tebbit, Imran Khan, Richard Branson and Tom Cruise, Carman's client list reads like a veritable *Who's Who*.

Like Dodd, Carman was a showman. He could be positively dramatic and was always eminently quotable. Particularly cherishable was his description of David Mellor, who, he said 'behaved like an ostrich and put his head in the sand, thereby exposing his thinking parts'. But despite such theatricality, he rejected the view that barristers were purely actors. 'In the theatre,' he once said, 'the actor holds the audience, but when the curtain comes down, everyone goes home and knows it's a play. In the courtroom, there's no rehearsal and it determines, possibly conclusively, the happiness or misery of the people involved in the case.' How right he was.

Within minutes of the opening of Dodd's case, Carman delivered his first surprise when he informed the judge, Mr Justice Waterhouse, that he was applying for an adjournment so that his client could undergo further medical tests. Carman explained that Dodd had had a medical examination the previous month and had been told that his heart condition was potentially so life-threatening it would be unsafe for him to face the strain and stress of a criminal trial. It transpired that Dodd had seen Dr Rhys Williams, a GP at North Manchester General Hospital, on 19 May. The doctor detected an abnormality and further tests were carried out involving Dr Geoffrey Howitt, senior consultant cardiologist at Manchester Royal Infirmary, who was one of the country's leading heart specialists. The tests showed that Dodd was suffering from ventricular tachycardia excessive heartbeats.

'It became immediately apparent that he had a grossly irregular pulse,' Dr Williams told the court. 'So abnormal was the rhythm that it became impossible to record satisfactory blood pressure.' Doubt was also thrown on the possibility of Dodd ever undertaking live work ever again.

This all came as something of a shock to everyone, not least the judge, who said that it was 'inexcusable and inexplicable' that the development should take place at the start of the trial. Carman stressed that his client had no wish to avoid facing trial and was anxious to disprove the Inland Revenue allegations. Actually, avid Doddwatchers had first caught wind of possible problems some time earlier, when Dodd pulled out of a gala benefit in aid of the ninety-five victims who died in the Hillsborough disaster in April. Anyone who knew him would have recognized that he would have had very good reasons for withdrawing from such an important event. Although the judge was far from happy – 'I suspect it [the medical report] could be written about an awful lot of people in this country in their sixties' – he nonetheless agreed to halt the trial until Monday 19 June.

The intervening two weeks worked wonders for Dodd. A fortnight later, accompanied by his brother and girlfriend, a far more confident and upbeat Dodd returned to the court. He even took time out to joke with the waiting crowd. 'I can't get in,' he told them, 'there's not enough seats.'

In court, Carman explained that medical tests now indicated that his client had no cardiac or arterial disease and was therefore fit for trial. Standing in the dock Dodd replied, 'Not guilty, my Lord' as he denied seven charges of cheating the public revenue, dating from 1973 to 1986, and four counts of false accounting between 1982 and 1988. The jury of seven men and five women were then sworn in, and with Anne Jones sitting at the back of the courtroom taking copious notes throughout, the scene was set.

For the prosecution, Brian Leveson QC kicked off the proceedings by admitting that Dodd was one of this generation's greatest entertainers and a national institution, but alleged that there was another side to him. He claimed that although Dodd earned more in a month than most people earned in a year, he had been dishonest with the Inland Revenue and even his own accountants.

The court heard that the Revenue had begun its investigation into Dodd's affairs in June 1984, when a couple of tax inspectors spoke to him about his financial affairs. They asked him if the details of his finances were correct, adding that if they were not, criminal prosecution was unlikely if he owned up. Dodd replied that if there were any inaccuracies then it was either a genuine mistake or an accountancy error. Using the information provided by Dodd, his accountants Thornton Baker (now called Grant Thornton) spent the next nineteen months compiling their report, which they submitted to the tax authorities in January 1986.

Leveson revealed that Dodd had signed certified statements of his assets and bank accounts in October 1986, but he alleged that Dodd had made no mention of any Isle of Man or Jersey accounts in these documents. He described how Dodd had had a further meeting with tax inspectors in December 1986, during the course of which they asked for permission to speak to a bank on the Isle of Man. Although he still denied the existence of any Manx accounts, Leveson said that Dodd signed the authority, but then revoked it the next day after abandoning Thornton Baker and engaging the services of another firm of international accountants, Arthur Young.

He then instructed his new accountants to produce another, very different, report, to which were attached letters from Margaret Thatcher and two former prime ministers, Edward Heath and Harold Wilson, which, Mr Leveson suggested, sought to persuade the Inland Revenue that the man they were investigating deserved special treatment. 'During inquiries for this [the report],' Leveson told the court, 'the accountants and the Revenue learned of more than £700,000 in Jersey and the Isle of Man, and Mr Dodd was interviewed by tax officers in October 1987. Further material then came to light, and it learned how he was paid for some shows partly by cheque, which went through the books, and partly in cash, which did not.'

Leveson suggested that all Dodd's accountants wanted was honesty, but instead, he alleged, they had been engulfed by a blanket of lies: 'The accountants acted rather like a computer. If the material they were given was as accurate as it could be but, more importantly, honest, the answer which they reached would itself be reasonable and valid. If they were not told the truth, their results, however well presented, would be worthless. Like a computer, if you put garbage in you will get garbage out. In at least one vital respect Mr Dodd fed his own accountants with absolute garbage. Not once did he lie, but many, many times.' He went on to say that when Dodd was given a chance to come clean and tell the truth, he became devious and deceitful: 'For years and years, he has been reporting to the Revenue that his profits were far less than in truth they have been. He has been receiving cash and putting the cash in his pocket.'

Leveson pointed out that in the 1960s Dodd created a company by the name of Ken Dodd Enterprises in order to make the most of reducing his high tax bill through legitimate means, but added that Dodd's personal affairs and those of the company should have been kept separate. Instead, he suggested that Dodd had treated the money in Ken Dodd Enterprises as if it was his own: 'If somebody does a "foreigner" and receives cash which he puts in his pocket, he knows well that he should declare that money to the Inland Revenue, and if he doesn't, he is defrauding them.'

That, on a grand scale, he alleged, was what Dodd had been doing for years.

The prosecutor also revealed that Dodd had engaged the services of several accountants over the years. In the early 1970s he was associated with Widnes-based Reginald Hunter, who also looked after his personal affairs, in addition to auditing the company accounts. Although there was no evidence to suggest he had dealt fraudulently with Dodd's accounts, it later came to light that Hunter had been prosecuted for false accounting in 1983.

It had been a traumatic morning for Dodd, but the afternoon was not much better as private details of his personal finances were broadcast to all and sundry. Leveson told the court that within a sixteen-week period Dodd had made many trips to the Isle of Man and Jersey, depositing a total of £298,720. After wondering aloud about how much of this money had been declared, he then revealed that by April 1967 Dodd had £777,453 deposited in overseas bank accounts – £371,079 worth of interest had accrued. It was also disclosed that fifteen years earlier, he had bought a six-bedroom country house in Whitchurch, Shropshire – his 'little piece of England' – for £26,500. At the time of the trial its value was estimated at £250,000. He and Anita had originally chosen it as a retreat, but she had died some eighteen months after the purchase.

The next day the revelations continued apace. 'Since Mr Dodd started in show business back in 1949,' the prosecutor informed the court, 'his gross income, up to 1982, was £1,154,566 – the "net income over his entire life available to spend". But in all that time he spent just £23,100 in cash.'

Leveson then took the jury through the Arthur Young report, the contents of which had suggested that Reginald Hunter must have put any amount of money as being spent on business – through Ken Dodd Enterprises – when it appeared that it was Dodd who was really taking possession of the large sums of cash. 'Why should Mr Hunter make this kind of mistake?' Leveson asked the jury. 'And how could Mr Dodd so frequently not make it clear to his accountant that there was money over, which he was accumulating?' He pointed out that if Dodd did know, he was deliberately deceiving the Revenue. The prosecutor dismissed as an excuse the fact that Dodd had blamed the accountant for failing to keep a proper catalogue of his earnings and expenses, claiming it was inconceivable that Dodd did not know what was going on and was not deliberately withholding cash or exaggerating expenses to evade tax.

The comedian had originally denied seven charges of common law cheating and four of false accounting, but after legal discussions three of the charges referring to the former were dropped, though they remained on file.

Leveson then told the court that Dodd had opened new bank accounts not only under his own name, but also under those of Artson and Jones – references to his father's first name and his current partner's surname. Though Dodd explained that his actions had been motivated by a need to protect the account after papers relating to it had been stolen, Leveson refused to accept the validity of this argument, maintaining that the reason it had been done was to confuse the Revenue, not burglars. He went on to say that when the investigation began, Dodd confirmed to his accountants that he did not have any deposits abroad. Seventeen days later, however, the comedian went to the Isle of Man, withdrew £181,000 in cash and hid it in wardrobes, cupboards and under the stairs at his three Liverpool homes (two of which were on Thomas Lane). 'At one time,' said Leveson, 'he had kept £336,000 because he liked having a lot of cash, and he used to carry £1,000 in cash with him in Liverpool, but up to £5,000 if he travelled away from the city.'

It was then revealed to the court that on 21 April 1980, Dodd had flown to the Isle of Man to deposit a total of £110,300 cash into three separate banks. A day later he paid a visit to Jersey, bringing with him a further £44,000 which was duly deposited into two more banks. Between 28 March and 21 April 1980, the total sum that he had paid in to various banks had reached £196,800. He made a return visit to the Isle of Man just over two months later where he deposited £27,000 in the Royal Trust Bank.

As far as Leveson was concerned, here was someone who had not only allegedly 'fiddled' for years, but who had also lied when his affairs were under investigation. He added, tellingly, that the trial was not about how much Dodd owed, but about his honesty.

By Wednesday it was time to call the witnesses for the Revenue. First to the stand was Joseph Atkinson, who had worked at the Revenue's inquiry branch at Liverpool for seven years. It was while he was investigating Reginald Hunter's affairs that he came across copies of letters to Dodd and became suspicious. According to Atkinson, the content of one jokey letter, which referred to the 'Aladdin's Cave of Knotty Ash', implied that some of the assets from Ken Dodd Enterprises could have been overlooked. It read: 'Once again, Ken Dodd Enterprises' balance sheet omits its greatest asset, i.e., the Great Drum, better known in Stock Exchange circles as the Aladdin's Cave of Knotty Ash. Long may that priceless possession remain submerged in the Merseyside mangrove swamps to be seen rarely and by very few.' A second letter, sent in December 1977, began: 'My respects to the Great Drum.'

George Carman QC explained that Atkinson had been told that the 'Aladdin's Cave of Knotty Ash' was a reference to Dodd's home, in which was stored an Aladdin's Cave of stage equipment. He added that the Great Drum was not a hiding place for money undeclared to the Inland Revenue, but merely a stage prop. Though the letters may have been dismissed as meaningless, their existence and subsequent discovery had led to the initiation of the whole investigation.

Details of Dodd's 'frugal existence' were also referred to during the proceedings, specifically concerning his low-key, luxury-free lifestyle, which did not befit his successful wealthy status, as he managed without bodyguards, chose not to travel in chauffeur-driven Rolls-Royces, and nor did he own a mansion with swimming pool. In fact, when Dodd was first subjected to an Inland Revenue investigation he drove a Ford Granada, and though he later bought a Jaguar, he never picked it up and it stayed in the car showroom for months. Eventually it was driven to his home by sales staff, only to remain in the garage untaxed and never to be driven.

Backing up his client's thrifty attitude towards company money, and revealing the size of earlier tax contributions, Carman said: 'In respect of the one million pounds he earned between 1949 and 1982, Mr Dodd paid more in tax in a month than the average man does in a year. Yet he never put in expenses claims for helicopters, a chauffeur or bodyguard, or entertaining people.'

Things turned a little nastier on the fourth day of the trial as it emerged that Dodd had grown angry during an interview with two tax inspectors, Joseph Atkinson and Peter Williams, who had tried very hard to persuade him to allow them access to his home as soon as the meeting had ended. Dodd had told Atkinson that it was not possible to return to his home on that particular occasion because he had to see the widow of a recently deceased cousin to help make arrangements for the funeral the next day. Atkinson refused to delay his visit until later that afternoon, however, and kept pressing Dodd for permission to go straight to his house. It was then that Dodd accused him of using

'Gestapo' tactics. An agreement was finally reached whereby Grant Thompson, an accountant who had attended the interview with Dodd, would accompany the comedian to his home in Thomas Lane in order to be shown how much cash was being stored there. Dodd later produced £4,010, an amount, he maintained, that was all the money he had in the house.

When asked by Carman whether he thought that Dodd was a fool, Atkinson said that in fact he considered Dodd to be a man of above-average intelligence, but felt that he had obvious difficulty understanding the basics of finance. On a similar note, Yvonne Rice, who was employed on a private basis to keep Dodd's books, described the comic as being a 'little scatter-brained' when it came to keeping records. He would often bring her carrier bags filled with receipts that he had collected while on tour across the country, but he rarely had any time to provide her with any details.

By the afternoon of Friday 23 June the first week's proceedings had drawn to a close – it had been quite a week. The press, meanwhile, had been having a field day. 'Doddy's Knotty Stash,' screamed the *Daily Star*, while the *Sun* set a phone-in tongue-twister starting 'Ken Dodd's Dad's Dog's Dead'. It offered a £10 prize for the caller who tripped up the least. The newspaper intended that the 'dotty diddy ditty' should be made a daily event, but George Carman QC had other ideas, declaring how he regretted that a newspaper 'so distinguished for its intellectual integrity' should stoop so low. The judge took note of Carman's complaint, and agreed to refer the matter to the attorney-general as a prima-facie question of contempt. The *Sun* retorted by saying, 'We believe Ken Dodd's brief's beef to be beyond belief!' and then set a new tongue-twister about pheasant pluckers, while 'apologizing in advance to any qualified pheasant plucker' appearing in court in the next twenty-four hours.

In his summing up of the first week for the *Sunday Times*, Brian Moynahan noted Dodd's general demeanour throughout the proceedings: 'Lost in the great open space of an eighteen-seat dock, in a neat lightweight suit, an open briefcase beside him, unmoving except to sip a glass of water or pass forward a note, Dodd looks more like a minor adviser in the case than its allegedly criminal focus. The rabbit teeth show only when he wets his upper lip, the electricity is cut off from the shock of hair, the eyes lack the familiar fires of anarchy. He has been described by Brian Leveson QC, the prosecuting counsel, as a liar, a man who fed his accountants "garbage", a cheat. He does not look angry, or indeed hurt.'

Unfortunately for Dodd, the worst was yet to come.

8

Diddy . . . Or Didn't He?

T HE SECOND WEEK of the trial kicked off with defence barrister George Carman alleging improprieties surrounding unorthodox increases in Dodd's expenses. He described how, without Dodd's knowledge, his first accountancy firm, Reginald Hunter, had vastly inflated his annual expenses to £37,000: general expenses had increased from £1,000 to more than £4,000; his dry-cleaning bill had shot up from a modest £300 to £2,000; monies spent on hotels and travel had risen from £5,401 to £25,400; and various other categories of expenses had also risen substantially.

Carman made the allegation while cross-examining John Collier, who was a partner in the Liverpool office of Grant Thornton, the accountancy firm responsible for preparing the original report on Dodd's financial affairs for the Inland Revenue. Although Collier agreed that Hunter had been careless, he would not concur that it was clear Hunter had been irresponsible or dishonest. Earlier, Collier told the court how his firm had discovered that in one year Dodd had spent £19,000 in cash before it had even appeared in his bank records. Questioned by the prosecuting counsel, Brian Leveson, Collier said: 'Our figures appeared to be showing that cash had been spent while there wasn't any available.'

Collier went on to reveal that he had visited Dodd's house three times, and seen hundreds of stage props, scripts and bric-a-brac which were stored in a rusty old lorry container, stables and in the cottage next door. Taking careful note of these facts, Carman asked Collier for his view on whether his domestic scene in Thomas Lane suggested that Dodd was a man who was 'very busy in his profession as a comedian, artistically inclined, but not very organized'. Collier agreed that that was a fair assessment, and when further questioned about whether there was any kind of extravagance, high living or lavish expenditure evident in the house, the accountant confirmed that there was not.

Describing how the property's exterior contained 'waist-high weeds' and had 'an air of desolation', Carman went on to suggest that the back of the house was 'rather reminiscent of Steptoe's backyard', in an effort to show the jury that if Dodd's home was indeed the 'Aladdin's Cave' referred to in Hunter's letter to him, then it was certainly lacking in the treasure department.

Dodd's expenses claims were further investigated in court later in the week. Roderick Mackinnon, the tax inspector in charge of the Revenue inquiry into the comedian's finances, said he was surprised by the information that Dodd had submitted. In the earlier report prepared by Grant Thornton between 1984 and 1986, it was stated that his expenses had amounted to £12,000 a year, but in a subsequent summary of his spending given to Arthur Young, Dodd claimed annual expenses of £3,500, telling his accountants that he had never been on holiday until he was fifty-one, had not bought a new suit for two or three years, spent only £10 a week entertaining his show-business contacts and paid out £7 a week on lager and £50 a year on wine. To justify the drastic scaling down of his estimated living expenses, Dodd was adamant that he had merely overestimated the original figure, and he also pointed out that 'a lot' of items, including milk and meat, were paid through his company, Ken Dodd Enterprises. Not surprisingly, Mackinnon expressed astonishment at the difference between the content of the two reports.

The last day of the week unearthed even further eccentricity on Dodd's part. The court heard how he had hoarded more than £330,000 in cash at three of his homes because he feared that Britain was on the brink of civil war. He refuted the notion that he had kept the money at home in order to conceal it from the Revenue. In a six-hour interview with two tax officials in October 1987, he explained how the events of 1979 and the winter of discontent in the days before the Conservatives came to power had caused him great concern: 'I would have been taxed at ninety-eight pence in the pound. Banks were collapsing and the pound was collapsing. I thought we were nearly up to civil war in this country.'

It was revealed that between 1979 and 1981 Dodd had moved this money from his homes and deposited a total of £336,370 at banks and financial institutions on the Isle of Man and Jersey. Throughout the interview he said he thought his offshore deposits were not subject to tax, telling the officials: 'At the time I did not think I had committed an offence. I did not think it had to be on the [tax] return. I saw many advertisements in newspapers saying that interest in the Isle of Man was not liable to tax.' To support his claims he then presented to the tax men examples of such advertisements, which had since been outlawed in the United Kingdom because they were 'potentially misleading'.

When asked why he had revoked a mandate that would have given the Revenue licence to examine his Manx deposits, Dodd replied: 'I thought I had nothing to fear in the first place. Then I discovered I had committed an offence after speaking to some friends and various people.'

At the same meeting, Dodd's solicitor David Freeman had informed the tax men that his client wanted to avoid legal action: 'All our efforts have been towards a successful conclusion on this matter without prosecution. I would ask that you recommend that there is no prosecution. Mr Dodd has apologized not only once, but two or three times today for his misunderstanding and lack of appreciation of the Revenue laws affecting the Isle of Man. I would ask that any report carries a request that this matter be settled in monetary form.'

Despite the efforts made by both Dodd and his solicitor to clear his name of any wrongdoing, the tax officials were in no position to grant such a wish at that stage, or as it turned out, at any time subsequently. As far as the tax authorities were concerned, prosecution was the only way in which the situation could be resolved.

In the first two weeks of his trial, apart from pleading 'not guilty', Dodd had said very little. However, the third week saw Carman open the case for the defence, which meant that Dodd's presence in the witness box would be guaranteed.

'To the allegations that Mr Dodd has lived in a world of fantasy, a world on occasion of folly and a world of insecurity, we say "yes",' Carman began Thursday's proceedings. 'To the allegation that this man is devious, this man is deceitful, this man is dishonest, we say "no", and we shall continue to say "no". His conduct, so obviously eccentric, was to be explained not by dishonesty but by the close-knit family upbringing of which he was so much a part for most of his adult life. It was an upbringing which stamped on him for the rest of his life the values almost of another age: thrift, relentless hard work, close family loyalty and great charity for others. Money is not the beginning and end of Ken Dodd, far from it.'

On the afternoon of Thursday 6 July Dodd took the stand, and in a hoarse voice he spoke of his early life. He told the court that his grandmother was the first lady magistrate in Liverpool and chairman of the Old Swan Labour party. 'And she had sixteen children?' Carman enquired. 'She knew all about labour, yes,' Dodd replied, which prompted much laughter.

He explained that his father had founded a coal business in Knotty Ash, which his elder brother Bill still ran, and that two years after war broke out, at the age of fourteen, he began working alongside his father and brother in the family business, and stayed there until the age of twenty. He went on to describe his daily routine of what was generally manual work: 'We would go down to the railway yard, load the coal in hundredweight sacks, stack it in the lorry and take it to places around Knotty Ash and West Derby. I think I started off on about £2 10s a week when I was fourteen. I think I probably got to about £5 a week, something like that. But I enjoyed it. I worked with Billy and we had a great time.'

He also described how both his parents worked from morning to late at night, and how his mother was the family support. She was, Dodd said, the person who kept the foundering ship afloat and it was lessons from her that guided his future. He explained how the family had always kept their cash in the house where it was readily available: 'We saved money because we didn't want to go back to the bad old days. It sounds old-fashioned, but my mother and father didn't trust banks and it rubbed off on us.'

Encouraged by his parents, and patriotic calls to save for Britain during the war, he had simply continued in the family tradition.

As his alternative career as a part-time entertainer developed, he received cash payments for each appearance. The money was stored in labelled envelopes at home, mostly under the care of his mother, and even when he became a star he kept his cash at home because he had nothing else to spend it on: 'I had no children, I'm sorry to say. I had no Rolls-Royce, I had no villa in Spain. I didn't want anything else. I wanted to live as I had always lived and be a successful comedian. But you have to have something to show that you are successful. I had a nest egg. It was my security and reassurance that I had made it. It made me proud that I had generated that kind of cash.' Dodd described how money was unimportant to him, and that it acted merely as a measure of success to prove that he was 'a star'.

He also explained how, in his early teenage years, he discovered he had a special talent: 'I found that I had been given – blessed with – a magical gift, the gift of making people laugh. Over the years I have tried to develop it and look after it and share that gift with everyone.'

By the age of twenty-six he had earned about £4,000, of which every penny was stored in cash in the attic. Seven years later it had grown to £30,000, and by 1963 his career had progressed to such an extent that his guaranteed weekly earnings had reached about £1,500. A measure of his success came that year when the Beatles appeared as guests on his radio show. Two years later, Dodd was starring at the London Palladium earning £3,000 a week. He also revealed that eighteen months before her death, in 1966, his mother had entrusted him with her life savings of £15,000 instead of giving it to her husband, who liked to gamble. By 1980 Dodd's cash savings had increased to more than £330,000.

The insights into Dodd's background and the openness he was displaying when questioned by Carman made the situation seem more like a TV chat show than a court of law. By any standards, it was developing into an extraordinary case.

Carman said that Dodd was devoted to bringing happiness to other people, but behind the scenes he was possessed 'by haunting insecurity in his personal life'. The barrister also maintained that his client had made no secret of depositing money in banks on the Isle of Man and the Channel Isles, and therefore Dodd was far from dishonest or deceitful: 'At the end of the day we shall establish that deviousness is not part of his make-up. Insecurity is the theme. Caution is the theme. Reserve about private affairs and, on occasion, a little bit obstinate, a little bit of blinkered vision. Outside his own special world, where he is a master, he is a really very ordinary man from Knotty Ash.'

The last day of the third week revealed even more about Dodd's unusual lifestyle, with events in the courtroom taking an increasingly surreal turn. Two TV sets showed the jury a six-minute video recording of a tour of his home in Knotty Ash, while Dodd treated them to a kind of director's commentary. They saw the exterior of the Georgian house and the dilapidated outbuildings surrounded by the overgrown garden, which Dodd declared were 'unsafe' and had to be propped up. He indicated the burglar alarm and the lean-to kitchen his father had constructed in 1935. Video images of the inside of the house revealed it to be in a state of some neglect, with sparsely furnished rooms filled with untidy piles of scripts, pages of jokes and books. The study contained just a desk and telephone, while the living room appeared to have very few home comforts.

'Here you see the Aladdin's Cave of Knotty Ash,' Dodd remarked, as the scene changed to another indoor view of the property. 'It is a double garage containing all sorts of props and instruments. There's a Diddyman's body and costumes from various shows. And there is one of the Great Drums of Knotty Ash together with instruments.'

As had previously been claimed, it was hardly the type of home and lifestyle enjoyed by the majority of multi-millionaire celebrities. It was obvious that Dodd cared not a jot for possessions – his home was indeed merely a base. He lived for his work. Carman was clearly making an excellent job of establishing his client's frugal and eccentric way of life . . . but at what cost to Dodd's privacy? That the comedian would have shown a video of his less than salubrious home to a host of strangers or discussed the details of bank accounts would have been unthinkable under any other circumstances, and proves just how the threat of losing one's liberty helps to loosen one's tongue.

Led by Carman, Dodd then spoke of how he thought fame and fortune affected people. 'It is a strange thing that happens to you when you get paid a lot of money,' he said. 'Some people go crazy and go in for all sorts of things and some people don't. Most entertainers suffer from fear of not getting any more work – the basis of stage fright, when you wonder what the audience will be like and whether they will like you – but the big fear is that maybe next week or next year you might not get a summer season or a panto season. Show business is littered with people who have gone bankrupt.' He went on to give relevant examples of the time, including the singers P. J. Proby and Kathy Kirby, and the comedy actor Terry-Thomas, who had been struck down by Parkinson's disease, and who was reportedly living in a one-room flat at the time of the trial.

After being cautioned by the judge to speed up his evidence, there was a short adjournment after which Dodd admitted that he had opened his first account with the Isle of Man Bank Ltd with £600 on 20 December 1979; by the end of the year the account held £3,000. He also confirmed that he opened his first Jersey bank account on 22 February 1980. In that year he split £256,000 between five Manx banks and £57,000 between three Jersey banks. Denying that there was anything secretive about his actions, Dodd maintained that he had simply opened a number of accounts because he did not want to put all his eggs in one basket. 'I enjoyed going to the banks,' he said. 'The bank manager would say, "Oh, it's you, Ken Dodd." They would bring all the staff out. I would sign autographs and they would take photographs. We would have morning coffee. Each bank has a different character and it was nice to go shopping in different banks.'

Prompted again by Carman, Dodd confessed that being a celebrity was a double-edged sword. While the downside of being well-known was that the press were often intrusive, especially during difficult times, he explained that on the positive side it was nice to walk down a street and have people come up to you and say hello. He added that there was quite a carnival spirit when he visited the offshore banks. When Carman asked if he had been invited into private offices to distance him from customers or staff, Dodd replied that it was 'quite the reverse'.

In response to Carman's question about why he had not deposited money in UK banks, Dodd replied that after his father died in 1979, he realized that the family home (where he had been storing vast sums of money) had a serious case of dry rot, and therefore needed urgent attention. Thus, he realized that he would have to move all his cash savings before he could admit workmen to the house. It was at this time that he saw the advertisements which he thought contained claims that interest earned in Jersey and the Isle of Man was tax free: 'I was paying 83 per cent, the top rate of tax plus 15 per cent on top of that. I would get £2 out of every £100 I earned in interest.'

Dodd added that he wasn't aware that, according to the law, if you lived in England but invested money abroad – whatever the law of that country – you still had to pay tax on the interest earned in that country. He said again that the advertisements did not make that clear and that he had been misled, but on discovering his error he immediately informed the Inland Revenue about each of the Manx and Jersey bank accounts.

After the third week of the trial Dodd could have been forgiven for thinking that it was all going reasonably well. However, the price had been high, and unfortunately for the comedian it was to get even higher.

Monday 10 July marked the start of the fourth week of the trial. After asking Dodd about his extensive charity work, Carmen went on to mention the M-reg Jaguar that Dodd had bought, but which he had left in the garage for years. Dodd denied that this behaviour was abnormal, but did concede that it was a little eccentric. Again he pressed home the point that possessions meant little to him – 'The most precious thing in the world is time. You cannot do four hundred shows a year and go floating around in Jags.' It transpired that he was far happier to use his old estate car for work as it was more practical for lugging round theatrical props.

Things took a more intimate turn when it came to light that Dodd and Anne Jones, then forty-five, had been trying to start a family. On one occasion in October 1986, the day before Dodd was due to meet his accountants, he and Anne had attended a charity dinner in Liverpool, before driving to Lincolnshire to another engagement and then on to the Princess Theatre in Hunstanton in Norfolk for an evening performance. At the time, Anne had been undergoing a course of injections to increase her chances of becoming pregnant, and for the treatment to work properly it was essential that intercourse took place between twenty-four and thirty-six hours after the last injection, which clearly put them under intense pressure while fulfilling work commitments across the country. After the show in Norfolk, Dodd embarked on an eight-hour drive back to Liverpool, to be back in time for his appointment with Grant Thornton accountants the next day.

Among the papers he signed at the five-hour meeting were statements of assets and certificates of disclosure on bank accounts that were to be forwarded to the Inland Revenue. Not surprisingly, Dodd was 'shattered' after the previous day's exertions, and in court he revealed that he had put his signature to a vital record of an interview with the Revenue without properly reading it first. Dodd said that the pressure he was under was compounded by domestic stress, which was clearly a reference to the difficulties surrounding the couple's attempts to conceive a child.

The extent of the stress that Dodd had been coping with for some time soon became apparent, as Carman's probing questions continued. As the barrister asked him whether he had ever taken the Revenue's investigation into his affairs lightly, Dodd clutched his forehead. In a voice filled with emotion, he replied, 'I have had five years during which I have not had one happy day,' adding that since 1988 he had suffered eighteen months of torture.

Later, perhaps in an effort to lighten the mood, Dodd's humorous reference to one of the accountants at Grant Thornton provoked laughter when he described Anthony Brown as 'a cross between Bertie Wooster and Brian Rix'. Recounting how Brown wanted receipts for everything, including bus tickets, Dodd recalled: 'He said it was like a Chinese laundry – no tickee, no laundry. I thought that strange for an accountant.'

At this the judge interrupted to tell him to 'get on with it' because they didn't want a character sketch of everything, but Dodd was at pains to point out that it was relevant because he had lost confidence in the accountant. He claimed the firm did not explain things and seemed to be strangers to the workings of show business. He had also been subjected to a series of embarrassing and offensive questions about his financial affairs: 'They asked me who I lived with and who did my washing, who cleaned the house. They even asked me how many pairs of underpants I bought a year, how many pairs of socks.'

He added that he was also asked personal questions about his mother, as well as Anita's illness, whose death from a brain tumour had even been recorded in a report. In a voice shaking with emotion, Dodd described how he had made it clear to the accountants that her death had nothing to do with the investigation, but that they had said 'they would put it in to get a bit of sympathy'.

In the afternoon Dodd faced Brian Leveson QC. He explained to the prosecuting counsel that he had not declared his overseas savings as part of his assets because he didn't think it had anything to do with the Inland Revenue: 'I thought they were just being nosey. You know how they want to know everything about your lifestyle? At the time I thought this is no business of theirs. I had already paid tax on it. Was I expected to pay tax on it again?'

Leveson suggested that Dodd could have told them, 'What has it got to do with you?' to which the comedian replied, 'Well, you don't really talk to tax inspectors like that . . . you just answer what they ask you. You don't enter into a jolly conversation with them.'

When asked why he had told the Inland Revenue about other savings – including £45 in the Co-op Bank and the contents of some other private accounts in the UK – but not about his money in offshore banks, Dodd was adamant that he hadn't declared them because he was under the impression that the tax had already been paid: 'I believed I had found a tax-efficient investment for my savings in the Isle of Man and Jersey outside the scope of the British tax system.'

When it was revealed to the court that Dodd had brought back £181,000 in a briefcase from the Isle of Man to Liverpool, the judge asked, 'What does it look like – all this money in a briefcase?' 'The notes are very light, my lord,' came Dodd's infamous response.

Questioned about any other assets including jewellery, Dodd replied that apart from his watch he didn't wear jewellery and nor did he own any diamonds. He explained again that his mother had given him her life's savings in order to keep it from his father, and that he had added it to his own savings without informing his accountants because 'it was a very private, personal thing'. He also explained that over twelve years Anita Boutin had received about £50,000 from Ken Dodd Enterprises. 'She didn't actually physically get a weekly pay packet,' explained Dodd. 'We were living together. Ladies always know where the man's inside pocket is.'

Leveson then pointed out that the tax inspector had also asked Dodd whether anyone was holding his assets in safe-keeping, to which Dodd had replied in the negative. Casting doubt on the validity of Dodd's reported response, Leveson asked, 'But who was living at 66 Bankfield Road?' The comedian then revealed that the occupant had been his late fiancée's brother, though he confirmed that Billy Boutin had not been looking after any of his assets. When Leveson asked how much money was kept in the house, Dodd's surprising reply was, 'Just over £100,000.'

The prosecutor's later description of the money in Dodd's three Liverpool homes as 'cash hoards' provoked indignant protest from the comedian: 'I would not use the word "hoard". It sounds like something out of Long John Silver.'

When asked about his failure to share information with Grant Thornton regarding his overseas accounts, Dodd insisted he had not purposely withheld details from the firm: 'It was not a concern of theirs and had nothing to do with UK tax. I believed I did not have to tell them.'

Earlier, Leveson asked Dodd whether he had been made aware of the Hansard system, an arrangement whereby a person could avoid prosecution by the Revenue as long as they fully disclosed all the facts concerning their investigation. He replied that it had been explained to him, but he insisted there was nothing wrong with his accounts: 'They said it was a chance to come clean, but before coming clean you have to do something wrong, and I didn't know I had done anything wrong.'

At the start of the next day's proceedings in court, the unusual contents of Dodd's home came under the spotlight after he admitted keeping 'tremendous amounts of money' in his attic, which he had saved out of his taxed earnings, and which by 1979 had risen to more than £300,000.

He explained that there was nothing secretive about the fact that when builders were at work in his home he had taken the cash personally to a bank on the Isle of Man, not realizing that he could have transferred it via a local bank. When Leveson asked if he thought it was risky to have kept so much money in his attic, Dodd replied that since being burgled on one occasion he had had alarms installed and steel window grilles fitted to his home, and when quizzed about the possibility of losing all his savings in a fire, Dodd replied, 'There are worse things in life.'

Describing his modest leisure interests, he explained that he rarely backed horses, never did the pools, and did not drink much. He said that when he left school at the age of fourteen he had £100. When he started his own business in 1949, he 'probably had several hundred pounds'. By January 1966, he agreed that the maximum capital available to him was the £61,753 given in his tax return forms, but as Dodd had accrued cash savings of £336,000 by 1979, Leveson was interested to know where the money had come from. 'I had saved tremendous amounts of money out of my own legal earnings, my taxed earnings,' Dodd replied.

At this point the judge asked the question, 'If it was in the attic, how could it be declared for tax?' to which Dodd replied that it had been declared by his agents: 'I know it is old-fashioned probably and eccentric, but I liked having those savings. It proved to me I was someone.' He added that his former accountant, Reginald Hunter, would send him blank tax return forms with two pencil marks and a note saying: 'Sign here. I will fill it in for you.'

Leveson continued to probe him further about the money, and put it to Dodd that from 1966 until 1979 it would not have been possible for him to have built up cash savings of £336,000 out of taxed income. Dodd replied simply, 'Well, I did.'

The comedian grew angry at Leveson's accusation that Dodd had only disclosed his Manx and Jersey accounts after he knew the Revenue had been made aware of them, and dismissed the suggestion as 'rubbish': 'I earned every penny in those accounts perfectly legitimately in my own name . . . I am an honest man and I realized I had made a mistake. I have done nothing dishonest. Mistaken, maybe, not dishonest.'

The following day a pale and emotional Dodd returned to the dock to listen to various show-business colleagues present themselves as character witnesses. Shedding a few tears as each came forward to praise him, he was clearly overwhelmed.

Ken Dodd

Eric Sykes told the jury that he had known Dodd for almost thirty years, and proclaimed him as 'one of the kings' of his trade: 'He has my wholehearted admiration because I know happiness is the best medicine and this nation owes a great debt to what Ken Dodd has given.' Describing how Dodd was regarded with genuine affection by the profession and held in awe over his many accomplishments, Sykes went on to tell the court of a time he went to see Dodd in Blackpool: 'I had never seen such a wonderful performance in my life. I thought: "This is the way an entertainer should be." There were people who had to leave for the last bus home, but they were not walking up the aisle. They were backing up the aisle so they would not miss anything. To me, he is the greatest contributor to comedy in this country. I volunteered to come up here. I thought it was the least I could do to pay my homage.'

John Fisher, then head of variety at Thames Television and a former producer of several Ken Dodd shows, said that he considered Dodd to be the greatest stand-up comedian of his lifetime, and possibly the greatest that Britain had ever produced. Fisher remarked that he knew that although Dodd showed dedication, generosity of time and effort, the comic was also totally disorganized in his working habits and frequently unpunctual: 'The telephone is a beast unknown to him and he is a frustration to producer and production staff. But you soon learn, because of the spirit of the man, to fit in with his way of doing things.' Speaking of a ten-page letter Dodd wrote to comfort him when his wife was in hospital with cancer, Fisher went on to describe him as 'the most life-enhancing personality I have ever met in show business'.

Roy Hudd, in his capacity as chairman of the Entertainment Artists Benevolent Fund, revealed that he thought Dodd was one of the most admired comics in the land, as well as being wholly dedicated to his job. 'The obsession of his life is the perfection of his art as a comedian,' said Hudd. He also pointed out that Dodd's work for charity was unlike that of any other star. Many celebrities, he said, worked for high-profile charities that obtained the greatest publicity, but Dodd was not like that, preferring to get involved with the smaller, less well-known organizations: 'He has always been a great supporter of Cinderella charities.'

It turned out to be an extremely emotional day for Dodd, as he found himself fighting back more tears while Anne Jones told the jury of their attempts to have a child over a five-year period. 'It was,' she said, 'the most important thing in my life at that time.' After she had described the fertility treatment she underwent between 1982 and 1987, George Carman QC questioned her about the effect it had had on them both. 'Great stress,' she answered. 'I felt probably it put more stress on him.'

On the subject of Dodd's professional life, she described how he had always been insecure: 'He was too severe on himself, too critical. He never put any store on what he had achieved and was always striving for something better.' When asked by Carman if the comedian was also insecure in his personal life, after a lengthy silence she replied, 'I felt very protective towards him.'

She told the defence barrister that she was responsible for organizing all of Dodd's engagements on his hectic schedule, and for paying the various artists who worked with him. Although she had failed O-level book-keeping, she took over the management of some of Dodd's accountancy records as he had no enthusiasm or any time available for taking care of such things.

In response to questions about the couple's lifestyle, Anne said Dodd was not interested in expensive clothes or luxury vacations: he bought his suits from Marks & Spencer and Debenhams and they had package holidays. Carman then asked how their lifestyle compared with that of other famous people. 'To be quite honest I'm uncomfortable with people who live a very flamboyant, exquisitely dressed life,' she said. 'We like a simple straightforward life.'

With regard to the allegation that Dodd had dishonestly changed the cash elements of engagements to put the money in his pocket and make a secret profit that was not declared to the Inland Revenue, Carman asked Dodd's partner whether there was any truth in that allegation. 'None whatsoever,' Anne replied.

The last day of the fourth week of the trial brought further tributes. Michael Billington, theatre critic of the *Guardian,* was unstinting in his praise: 'Ken Dodd is a comic genius. He has superabundant energy on stage, phenomenal inventiveness, and an exuberant love of performing. He comes to life as a person at his fullest on stage.' But with regard to Dodd's life off-stage, Billington thought it appeared crowded. Stressing the comedian's unpunctuality, he described how Dodd 'always ran into jams of appointments and his life was often very hectic and frenetic', which gave him the impression that 'he had too many things to do'.

Sheila Murray, secretary of the Clatterbridge Hospital cancer research trust, told the court that Dodd had agreed to be the nationally known figure whom the trust needed to lead a £1 million appeal fund for the hospital. He was, in fact, the trust's sole patron, and had become actively involved with the charity after Anita Boutin's death at the hospital in 1976. Describing Dodd as 'absolutely wonderful', she revealed that he had done as much as he could for the research trust and had put them on the map: 'He is a giving person who really got us off the ground and under his patronage we have raised £10 million. For a small regional charity that is an amazing sum of money and without his help I do not think it would have been possible.'

Next on the stand was William Tankard, the organizer for the northern branch of the actors' union Equity, who said that as far as young artists were concerned, Dodd was always very supportive and encouraging, 'And he has regularly performed at concerts to help older artists who have perhaps fallen on hard times.'

With so much heartfelt praise ringing in his ears, Dodd must surely have returned to Knotty Ash for the weekend in far better spirits than expected, despite the fact that the trial was far from over.

The resumption of the trial on the following Monday brought the inevitable reply from Leveson. The jury, he said, should only be interested in Dodd's attitude to the Inland Revenue. The praise heaped on him in the last couple of days was irrelevant. 'If this trial was about Mr Dodd's rating as a comedian and entertainer it would not have lasted very long; my words about four weeks ago were that Mr Dodd is one of the great entertainers of our generation,' he said. 'If this trial had been about the extent of his charitable activities it would not have lasted very long; I described them as undoubted. If it had been about his love of the theatre, the assistance he has given to younger artists or his relation with his fellow man, it would have been over very quickly. What you are concerned with are not these issues, but whether Mr Dodd had a very different attitude towards a very different institution which affects every one of us – the Inland Revenue.'

The next day, in his summary for the defence, Carman pulled off a masterstroke by accusing the Inland Revenue of failing to produce Reginald Hunter – the one man who might have helped to throw light on the case – as a key witness at the trial. The barrister raised the question that the fact Hunter was never called was because he might jeopardize a prosecution where the stakes were high. 'It is a disgraceful avoidance of the truth,' said Carman.

According to press reports, in 1983 Hunter had pleaded guilty to eleven charges of false accounting at Mold Crown Court, in north Wales, and was fined £6,000. It was due, Carman suggested, to the 'disgraceful way' that Hunter kept his client's accounts from 1972 until 1982 that Dodd was now in a mess. 'One thing we have learned from this trial,' Carman famously said, 'is that comedians are not chartered accountants, but sometimes chartered accountants are comedians.'

Carman also accused the Inland Revenue of 'moving the goalposts' during the trial, by suggesting that they had moved the focus from the issue of cash received to that of inflated expenses. The former, he said, would have necessitated Dodd being paid for his work in cash by reputable promoters, but despite searches, the Revenue had not produced any evidence that this was the case, hence the switch towards the matter of inflated expenses. He pointed out, too, that Dodd had opened the offshore accounts in person – hardly the actions of a criminal.

On the subject of the testimonies given by Dodd's colleagues and associates, Carman reasoned that they were not intended to provoke sympathy, but simply 'to reveal the true nature of the man'. He freely admitted that his client's behaviour could be strange and eccentric, and that Dodd had a natural mistrust of strangers, but that in stark contrast, when he was on stage he was the most outgoing, fun-loving creator of happiness in the country.

Later that day, the judge, Mr Justice Waterhouse, began his summing up, explaining that it was for the prosecution to prove that Dodd has deliberately acted dishonestly. Continuing his crucial summary the following day, he maintained that Dodd's good character *was* relevant to the case and advised the jury: 'All the witnesses agreed that the defendant is a very hard-working man and a dedicated performer.' He added that it was obviously necessary for the jury to discuss the part played by Reginald Hunter in the whole affair, and mentioned Carman's attack on the prosecution for failing to call Hunter to give evidence. 'You will give appropriate weight, according to your assessment, to that comment,' said the judge.

The fifth-floor courtroom was packed to the rafters with members of the public. At the start of the hearing many people had been left to queue outside the courtroom in the lobby area, unable to witness the unfolding drama inside as the case drew nearer to a close. Dodd kept looking straight at the judge, making occasional notes, while Anne appeared to be writing down the judge's speech word for word.

Ending his nine-hour summary of the evidence given by forty-four witnesses the next day, on Thursday 20 July, the judge told the jury that the crux of the case for the prosecution was whether the defendant dishonestly required a payment in cash because the balance of the fee for a performance was not to be recorded. He asked the jury to 'remember that the essence of all the charges was the allegation of deliberate dishonesty on the part of the defendant. If you are left in any little doubt about an essential ingredient of the count you are considering, then it is your duty to acquit the defendant on that count.'

He pointed out that Dodd had denied that he openly defied the Revenue by continuing to receive fees in cash for his performances while the investigation was under way. Adding that he wanted the jury to return unanimous verdicts in respect of all the counts, he brought his summary to a close: 'That is the whole of the evidence. I am afraid it has taken a considerable time.'

At 11.45 a.m. on Friday 22 July, after deliberating for almost ten hours, the jury eventually arrived at its first decision. With regard to the four charges of false accounting and one of intent to defraud, Dodd was cleared unanimously, which then left the three substantial fraud charges on which the judge said he would accept a majority verdict.

At 1.30 p.m., shortly after the lunch break, the jury returned to announce its second verdict. Sitting in the dock, his head bowed, Dodd played nervously with a pen, and took from his pocket two small jewellery boxes, which, at the time, were believed to contain Anita's engagement ring and his OBE. As each verdict was announced, he looked up at the foreman. After the third not-guilty announcement, the spectators in the public gallery cheered. Dodd was in tears, while Anne had collapsed, overcome with emotion. Even the prison officer standing behind Dodd gave him a pat on the shoulder. Dodd embraced Carman and then thanked the jury. He was free – shaking and struggling to fight back further tears, his relief was palpable. The twenty-three-day trial was finally over.

Outside the court, champagne corks popped and such was the mass of people outside, from jubilant members of the public to press photographers anxious to get a good shot, that Dodd was unable to exit the courthouse. Fortunately, police reinforcements soon arrived and a line of officers linked arms to hold back the crowd. Emerging from the court a free man, Dodd addressed his supporters: 'Thank you, thank you all. Thank God it is all over. Thanks for the thousands of people in Liverpool and Merseyside who have said their prayers for me. God bless you all.'

After thanking Anne Jones and his defence barrister George Carman QC, he continued: 'All I want to do is put it all behind me and get back to work. Anyone know where I can get a drink?' At that, a plastic cup full of champagne was thrust into his hand and the celebrations began, and later continued at a party held at St George's Hotel in Liverpool.

A Revenue statement issued on the day of the verdict said that the decision to prosecute was made only after Mr Dodd had failed to disclose his bank account in the Isle of Man and

Jersey. 'It was agreed by the defence that the Revenue acted responsibly in bringing a prosecution. There was never any issue about the certificates being incomplete or inaccurate. The issue for the jury concerned Mr Dodd's honesty and it is on that issue they have returned their verdict.'

Though the court case was over, and Dodd had been exonerated, he now had to face up to paying the price for establishing his innocence. Not only was there a financial penalty – the fees for the defence alone were estimated to be £300,000 – but there was also a personal price. In an interview with the *News of the World* he revealed that he feared his health would fail during the trial: 'I have to take tablets just to keep breathing. There were moments when I found it very hard to catch my breath. It came in waves and was a very scary feeling on top of everything else that was happening to me.' His emotional health had also taken a bashing, and he had rightly pointed out during the trial that he had been 'stripped naked' by the court. Each day, with lip-smacking relish, the papers had gleefully exposed what they interpreted as his eccentricities.

Psychiatrists and psychologists also attempted to find out what made Dodd tick – Dr David Lewis interpreted his hoarding as 'some sort of ritual magic where . . . it is dangerous and threatening to throw anything away. He is cocooned in his past and his money, and it makes him feel better.' But I think that in reality it was just a family trait, the only difference being that his family had kept a few bob around the house whereas he had stashed away thousands – it was just a matter of scale.

During the trial, totally unprompted, Dodd had suddenly blurted out: 'Early in show business I fell in love with comedy. The only thing left open to me was to discover the secret of humour and find out how it is created. For forty years I have read every possible book on humour and the psychology of humour. I have formulated formulas for the creation of jokes and comedy and believe that I have cracked it.' He went on to reveal that his joke books were kept in a bank safety deposit box along with his OBE and some love letters, which suggests to me that that is where Dodd's true fortune lay – not in his attic.

The columnists and analysts had a field day in the weekend following the conclusion of the trial. Noting that Dodd's hold on the affections of the nation remained intact, an article in the *Sunday Times* summed up his unique appeal: 'Here is a strange man who tickled his way into the drawing rooms of prime ministers, sang his way to discs of gold, rendered millions helpless and giggling over three decades, and lived like an over-cautious and eccentric squirrel, keeping bundles of money in a cluttered attic and dieting on fish and chips and scouse stew. His has been a life of thrift and laughter, unusual in an age of conspicuous affluence and stern endeavour.'

In the aftermath of the trial, two positives were certain: the experience had brought Anne and Dodd even closer together, and he also learned who his true friends were. Roy Hudd was one of those friends whom Dodd was able to rely on in his hour of need. When Dodd paid him a visit to ask whether he would mind appearing at his trial, Hudd replied honestly: 'I'm happy to do it, Ken. Whether you're an honest man or not I haven't got a bloody clue, but all I can do is go in and give you a character reference.'

Conscious of the work that Dodd does for various charities ('He puts as much effort into it as when he does it for money'), Hudd was keen to help his fellow comedian, but the same could not be said of other high-profile people in the entertainment world. 'Apparently a lot of pros promised they would go,' according to Hudd, 'and when they found it was looking a bit 'umpty [troublesome], they found excuses not to come and talk, which I thought was totally unforgivable

. . . there were some very big names who backed out.' Most noticeable, perhaps, was the absence of fellow Liverpudlians offering some much-needed support.

Financially, on the down side, it was reported that Dodd faced a hefty £2 million bill (though the final amount was later disclosed as being nearer £1 million). In addition to the £825,000 he had promised to pay the Revenue whatever the outcome of the trial (£450,000 of which had already been paid and a further £375,000 lodged with the Revenue in tax certificates and bonds before the case began), there was £51,000 for two previous solicitors, as well as £54,000 for Grant Thornton and £25,000 for Arthur Young, and of course George Carman's sizeable fee.

During the pre-trial discussions he had with George Carman, Hudd became fascinated by the way the barrister's mind worked when preparing for a case such as this. When Carman asked Hudd to give him some insight into Dodd's character, Hudd described the time when he was appearing in a concert party in Babbacombe at the same time that Dodd was at Torquay: 'He was a big star, but he did a marvellous thing for me. I'd never met Ken in my life and his producer was a man called James Casey – the head of light entertainment in Manchester. Jimmy was doing this radio series and he booked me for a *Workers' Playtime* – the first time I'd ever done radio.' When Hudd asked Casey how he had got his name, the producer replied: 'I went round to see Ken about the new series. Because I've seen his act a thousand times, I asked him, "What can I see while I'm here?" And he said, "Well, there's a young comic in the concert party up in Babbacombe and people tell me he's very good – why don't you go up and see him?"' So it was due mainly to Dodd's recommendation that led to Roy Hudd making his radio debut. 'I owe a lot to Ken,' Hudd revealed. 'Twenty-six years on *The News Huddlines* came from that.'

Another memory that Hudd shared with Carman concerned an occasion in the early 1960s when he had tried to get a show inside Dartmoor Prison to entertain the prisoners. 'The probation officer from that period was a great fan of our little concert party, "Out of the Blue". So he came to see us and he said, "I've tried all the big stars in Torquay and nobody wants to know, but I'd love to take a show into Dartmoor Prison." He said they might be hardened criminals . . . Of course we'd go anywhere to do a show as we'd only just started – but the only one of the big stars who would go was Ken Dodd. So we got there and he was just terrific – he opened up with "There is a key that will open up all doors", which was one of his songs, and then he said "You've been a lovely audience – I'm taking you all on a cross-country run this afternoon . . ." But it was fantastic of Ken to do that because he was a huge star and it was a little concert party, but he went.'

Having had time to digest the two stories, Carman later phoned Hudd and said, 'Great, you must tell that story – I'll prompt you into that.' 'So I said, "Oh great". Then about a quarter of an hour later he rang back: "Don't tell that story!" I said, "No, but it's there but for the grace of God . . ." He said, "I know, but for Christ's sake don't tell the story." All right. Twenty minutes later he's back: "Tell the story." It kept changing all the time. He was obviously working it all out in his nut – the way it could play with the jury and the judge. So eventually we got to the court in the morning and he changed his mind four times there when I'm waiting to go into the dock! Do tell the story . . . don't tell the story . . . I don't think I did tell the story. I can't remember whether I told it or not. I didn't know whether I was on my arse or my elbow!'

Michael Grade also thought the trial was quite extraordinary: 'I think the jury was so gobsmacked that here was a man who had earned all this money, but what had he done with it? Absolutely nothing! There were no flash cars, holidays in the Bahamas, cigars, birds, booze, gambling, race horses, a flash lifestyle . . . He'd never been abroad for a holiday, never been out of the UK – whereas Lester Piggott had a pretty good lifestyle – Rolls-Royces and all that. You never see Doddy with all that,' adding with a broad grin, 'he's too mean.' Hudd also notes that Dodd never flaunted his money. 'No! In any way, shape or form! People in Liverpool appreciate someone who grafts and he's always grafted for a living. They appreciate people who work for a living.'

Dodd, in many ways, is the product of a bygone era. A Sunday newspaper columnist noted that when he was appearing at the Palladium in 1965 his dressing room was like a booking office with Dodd 'selling tickets for cash to a queue of working-class friends, thumbing through a ready-reckoner because each friend wants tickets for coachloads of friends.' Not quite the sort of behaviour one would expect of a star earning £10,000 a week.

Comedian Steve Punt remembers that the court case had just started when he, Hugh Dennis, David Baddiel and Rob Newman started performing *The Mary Whitehouse Experience* on the radio. It therefore became a running gag. 'It really interested me because I'd been reading stuff about Morecambe and Wise and that whole variety hall era, and Ken Dodd seemed to live as if he was still in the 1950s,' says Punt. 'You know, always being paid in cash and going round the country slipping tips to stage managers and putting his money under the bed. It just seemed extraordinary – like time had caught up with him rather than anything else.'

As the *Sunday Times* had pointed out, Dodd's appeal remained undimmed, and it wasn't long before he was back in action. In early August, he went to Southport to announce details of his first post-trial stage appearance, which was to be held at Southport Theatre on 3 September in aid of the NSPCC and several other local and national organizations.

'I want to celebrate all sorts of happy events over the past few weeks,' said Dodd, 'to celebrate the fact that so many people supported me.'

He had been inundated with offers of work, including a host of live shows, a BBC radio series, two books, and some straight theatre, and acknowledged that Doddmania was about to sweep the nation: 'I am what they call "hot" at the moment!'

9

Fallout

'I T TOOK THREE MONTHS of my life. Two years, if I'm truthful, worrying about it. It's so f**king boring. I don't give a bugger who else talks about it, because I won. But I don't like discussing it. It interferes with my career.'

It was in these earthy words that Ken Dodd later spoke of his trial in 2001. But however much he would wish it, the courtroom drama that unfolded is not likely to be forgotten in his lifetime. It is unfortunate that his name is now as synonymous with 'tax trial' as it is with 'jam-butty mines', and though he might want to draw a veil over the whole ghastly business, quite clearly that can never be done.

As a true pro, however, he has turned a lemon into lemonade and it has furnished him with a whole new raft of material – 'My name is Kenneth Arthur Dodd, artist's model and failed accountant'; 'Self-assessment – that's an idea they got from me'; 'One tip: never trust an accountant who wears mittens'. But off-stage it has obviously changed him, particularly in the way that it has made an already private man almost pathologically insular. It was unjust that many newspapers paid scant regard to his forty-year body of work or his charitable activities, preferring instead to concentrate on salacious tittle-tattle about a host of various personal matters. The trial had made public much of his private life; things he had spent a lifetime attempting to keep hidden from view.

Nowadays, in the age of kiss and tell, almost nothing is private. Numerous so-called celebrities have quite often only attained their dubious status by selling their stories about affairs with *real* celebrities to the highest bidder. How different it was for Dodd's generation, who were far more reluctant to wash their dirty linen in public. The sad fact remains that bad news sells. People love to see the rich and famous on the ropes. Doubtless it will continue for as long as all those people who moan about scandalous stories in the press continue to buy the very same newspapers carrying these tabloid tales.

Roy Hudd is particularly sympathetic to Dodd and is still angry about the way the press treated him. 'All the business that came out at the trial was so sad – stripping everything away from his private life which he's always protected. And why shouldn't he protect his private life? Nobody does now, that's the tragedy of it. Not when you sell your wedding and your bloody divorce to *OK!* magazine. It's all wrong. People are not used to that thing of being a private person. We've lost the mystique.'

The years since the trial had certainly changed Dodd. Although in August 1989 at a press conference, he had spoken in mock bravado of his being 'hot', by 2001 he was saying that the trial had affected his career. This may well have been the case, but he is wrong if he thinks it has had an adverse effect. Being an enemy of the taxman does not carry the same stigma as being a murderer – in fact, the former can even make you a bit of a hero. In truth, it did his reputation no harm at all, and if anything it revived interest in him.

Fallout

One of Dodd's first appearances after the trial was at the annual ball of the Grand Order of Water Rats, the showbiz charity. It had been due to the influence and encouragement of Roy Hudd, an active member of the organization and 'King Rat' in 1989, that Dodd had agreed to attend the function. After Hudd had provided a crucial testimony as a character witness at the trial, he quite rightly presumed that Dodd owed him one. According to Hudd, the event was most significant for featuring one of the greatest gags the Water Rats had ever pulled off: 'I knew nothing about it, as God is my judge!' It was just as Dodd rose to his feet to address the audience that from the balcony behind him two casefuls of fivers came fluttering down. Hudd went on to assure me: 'I can tell you that he picked up every one before he spoke!'

Hudd was delighted that Dodd came along; not just because he paralysed the audience with his gags and repartee, but also because it was rare that he made many speeches at occasions of this kind. 'I don't think he likes it very much – it's a different ball game,' says Hudd. 'I know great comics, marvellous stage comics, who can't do an after-dinner speech to save their lives, but he did it. And of course it was just after the trial and the whole audience just adored him. When he stood up to speak it was like Jesus Christ walked in – they were so thrilled to see him and that he wasn't inside. I mean, it would have killed him.'

Despite his reluctance to speak to national newspapers, Dodd was willing to talk to those he trusted – the local press. The *Liverpool Echo*'s Joe Riley was the first person to interview the comedian after his acquittal. Riley's first post-trial impression of him was that he was a mightily relieved man: 'He did say it had been the worst time of his life. He opened up a bit in the sense that nobody could play it down and pretend that it was anything but terrible. I don't know if he did those things, but there was a certain amount of self-effacement and self-humiliation involved about his health and about his general capacity to understand pounds, shillings and pence. Once the thing was thrown out he sort of bounced off it, and his standard joke for many months afterwards was, "Oh, penny in the pound – I thought it still was!" So he told open jokes about the Inland Revenue and himself in a way that Lester Piggott couldn't. But it was a very close and scary brush with what could have been a far darker story.' I suspect that it was not just the loss of privacy, the financial cost and the enormous stress of the trial that smarted with Dodd. Riley's point about humiliation is undoubtedly valid, particularly when one recalls the remark that Dodd made to Michael Billington many years ago that business brings out the 'manliness and masculinity' in you, and that running a competitive business was a 'matter of pride'. This very public revelation that he was perhaps not the great businessman he had always claimed to be must have been a difficult pill to swallow.

Almost as if nothing had happened, on 27 August 1989 Dodd returned to the Arcadia Theatre, Llandudno, the scene of the earlier pre-trial press announcement, where the 1,100-odd seats had sold out in a matter of days. Armed with his fresh battery of Revenue-inspired material, it won him another standing ovation. He celebrated by donating £500 from the sale of the £1 souvenir programmes to a local hospice appeal, of which he was president. Notably the show contained a delicious Revenue-related ad lib. During one routine he asked, 'I don't get overpaid, do I?' When someone in the audience shouted, 'Yes,' Dodd replied, 'Not you as well!' It brought the house down.

Dodd was back in the saddle and seemingly none the worse for his travails. Some held the view that the experience might even have done him some good. 'The fact that he's flavour of the month is undoubtedly partly due to the publicity of the court case,' noted then comedy producer Paul Jackson, 'but if he hadn't been so hugely talented in the first place, the sensation would have died quickly. This man can dominate a theatre as few others can.'

In September, Dodd joined presenters Richard Madeley and Judy Finnigan on *This Morning* for his first national television interview since his acquittal. And in April 1990 he finally agreed to appear on *This Is Your Life*, after he'd twice foiled earlier attempts to be ensnared. This time, however, presenter Michael Aspel pounced on him at the London Palladium when he arrived there for talks about his new autumn show. 'They brought me down to look at a poster and then, from behind the pillar, came the man with the red book. It frightened the life out of me, I thought he was the VAT man,' said Dodd. 'I'd heard whispers of it twice before, but I had never had much of a life up to then.' For the occasion, the show's researchers managed to unearth one of his schoolteachers, then ninety years old, who still remembered her naughty pupil.

The TV tribute must have been somewhat of a double-edged sword to this most intensely private of men, but Dodd realized the programme was always a fairly innocuous one, and it also generated some brilliant publicity for his forthcoming Palladium appearance. In fact he had already apprised *Desert Island Discs* listeners of his planned return earlier in the year. 'I want to put a really big show back on at the Palladium,' he said. 'They've had musicals now for the past seven or eight years, so I want to show what a really big, spectacular Palladium show is like: sixteen beautiful girls, a theatre orchestra, speciality acts from all over the world, men diving off a two-hundred-foot pole on to a wet flannel, that sort of thing . . .'

And that is exactly what he did. The new £1 million show *How Tickled I Am!* saw Dodd supported (or rather interrupted) by the Williams Brothers tap dancers, magician Omar Pasha, the Stutz Bear Cats singing group, the Brian Rogers TV Dancers and the Diddymen (ten girls from a Manchester theatre school). The modest six-week season was his first there in a decade and he was the first to admit that the taxman would be sure to figure in the show: 'Nineteen-eighty-nine was an exciting year for me, but I got a whole new act out of it.' And in one particular reference to the Inland Revenue, he was to say, 'They wrote to me from their head office – it's in Andover.'

Among those in the first night audience were Eric Sykes, who reiterated that Dodd was his favourite comic, and magician Paul Daniels. 'He's the only person you will ever see who can make people physically fall off their seats with laughter – and I mean that literally,' said Daniels.

The three-hour show won Dodd his by-now customary standing ovation. Afterwards he remarked, 'I never realized until last year how rich I was. Not in money, but in friends.'

This time, however, the press reviews were mixed. Both *The Times* and the *Financial Times*, for example, were luke-warm. 'Dodd is a master comedian,' wrote Tony Patrick in the latter, 'but his command of rapid one-liners, building ever more fantastic pictures of comic disaster, was undercut by a too-ready recourse to the great British humorous staples: flatulence and frustration. More than a few jokes were at the expense of homosexuals, foreigners and "our colonial friends".'

The *Independent*'s Tristan Davies concluded: 'Doddy can make 'em laugh . . . he can make 'em dance . . . and he can make 'em cry. As Dodd changed his expression from that of Jack Nicholson in *The Shining* to Ingrid Bergman in *St Joan*, the lights transformed Knotty Ash into a chapel. At which point, he gave thanks for it all – "for laughter, for children, for beautiful theatres" – by singing the hymn "How Great

Thou Art" with as straight a face as one blessed with his can muster. He is closer to heaven than he thinks.'

Michael Billington still continued to fight Dodd's corner, admitting to *Guardian* readers that Dodd never ceased to astonish him: 'What is it that makes this man a comic genius? It has, I think, to do with that mysterious quality of ecstasy. He doesn't dispense gags warily with parsimonious thrift, but uses them to build great aching pyramids of laughter. He also doesn't just pelt us with corn, but gives a slightly surreal spin to the everyday so that next time I pass motorway cones piled on top of each other I shall think of his suggestion that they are mysteriously breeding overnight. I doubt that we shall look upon Dodd's like again. There is a wild new comedy abroad today full of talent. What it doesn't have is roots in a pre-permissive society, where sex was still a bit naughty, nor does it have that music-hall ability to run the whole gamut from verbal patter to ventriloquism, cod Kipling and medleys of ballads old and new.'

Thames Television broadcast a John Fisher-produced version of the West End show, imaginatively titled *Ken Dodd at the London Palladium*, in 1990. That it was aired at prime time on Christmas Day indicates the regard in which he was suddenly held. Dodd was still at the top, and he remained genuinely grateful that his public had stood by him: 'Your life is full of triumphs and excitement, and then there are other times when there are sad times; when there's bereavements and difficulties. But we're very, very lucky – show-business people – to have so many kind and thoughtful and really nice people who pray for you and send you letters. It gets right to you and you're very grateful.'

For his earlier appearance on *Desert Island Discs,* Dodd had selected a number of classic songs: Perry Como, 'For The Good Times'; Al Jolson, 'Mammy'; Frank Sinatra, 'You Make Me Feel So Young'; Frank Chacksfield and his orchestra, 'Love Is Like A Violin'; Nat 'King' Cole, 'I Wish You Love'; Stevie Wonder, 'I Just Called To Say I Love You'; and Elizabeth Schwarzkopf (whom he re-christened Betty Blackhead), 'En Chambre Separate'. 'On With The Motley' from the Leoncavallo opera *Pagliacci*, also featured in his music choices, though I don't think he would like to be seen as a Pagliacci-like clown figure whose heart is breaking inside, as he has scant regard for the 'tears of a clown' notion. Though he has had downs as well as ups, and confessed to having regrets, by anyone's standards Dodd's life must be counted as hugely successful, and, for the most part, happy. His act has always embodied positivity and jollity, rather than focusing on the bleaker, less whimsical side of life, and he certainly doesn't share the view held by many comics that comedy is the channelling of a private misery. As Bob Monkhouse has remarked, 'No one wants a self-pitying comedian. We all know about the tears of a clown – that's OK, it's part of the performance. But when we go back stage to see that the guy we were laughing at is actually cutting his wrists, we're not that amused.'

Essentially Dodd is a silly, jovial clown; a simple (though clever) jester, who brings warmth, fun and happiness to his audiences. He is a stranger to the introspective ramblings of Tony Hancock or Les Dawson, and the dark, angst-ridden mutterings of Frankie Howerd are alien to him. Morose self-analysis was their stock-in-trade; failure was grist to their particular comic mill. But as Howerd once wisely said, the sad clown would be even sadder if he wasn't a clown.

In Roy Hudd's professional opinion, Dodd puts his all into doing the best job that a comic could possibly do. 'He's never courted controversy or anything like that. Unlike Bernard Manning, Ken doesn't get up to do an after-dinner speech and cause chaos with all the politically correct people walking out; he doesn't eff or blind; he doesn't do anything that's likely to make headlines, all he does is, quite simply, his job – better than anyone else in the country.'

In summing up Ken Dodd's personality, Monkhouse has said, 'He is a man with a very great heart. He's a very complex man, a difficult man to get to know. A man who protects himself very much, a man who likes repetition and safety within his own discipline of his life. But I think really the reason that he will never come off stage and will give the audience so much is that he's a naturally generous man and wants to give, give, give, give, give until it hurts. But I don't think it hurts him.'

Many journalists and interviewers have tried to learn something of the man behind the tombstone teeth and the aerial hair. Perversely, of course, the less someone gives away about themselves the more our curiosity is aroused, but Dodd's no pushover – he's been a professional obfuscator too long to fall into the traps set by cunning journalists. He will give away precisely as much as he wants: no more, no less.

On *Desert Island Discs* he explained to Sue Lawley about his dual personality: 'You're two people, you see. You're Ken Dodd the ordinary fella from Knotty Ash, and there's another one – there's a Ken Dodd who's on the stage. He's quite different from me, honestly – a totally different man.' In an attempt to find out more about the real Ken Dodd, Lawley pressed him further on this subject, but he was wise to her techniques, noting aloud that he could discern the journalist in her revealing itself: 'Arthur Askey gave me some good advice. He said, "Ken, when confronted with a journalist, close the front door and keep it closed." I keep my personal life, my private life, very, very close to my heart, because I think it's only fair to your family and your friends not to embarrass them.' Undeterred, Lawley tried another tack and quoted him as having once described himself as being difficult to live with and a bit of a loner, but Dodd simply pointed out that it had been a throwaway line: 'You've got to say that, haven't you? Always throw a journalist a titbit.'

Dodd's non-committal approach to media questioning was not acceptable practice to everyone, however. In June 1990, the *Sunday Times*'s Paul Donovan wrote a scathing piece which heavily criticized the fact that Dodd hadn't been forced to address the issue of his court case during his *Desert Island Discs* interview. It transpired that although Sue Lawley had asked her castaway about the trial during the recording, he had made it clear that he wouldn't discuss it and so producer Olivia Seligman had to edit out their interchange on the subject. 'Silences are not very good on radio,' explained Caroline Millington, head of current affairs magazine programmes.

Donovan went on to say that *Desert Island Discs* was supposed to reveal a person's life and that the trial was one of the most important events in Dodd's: 'As a result of it he has been "reborn", in the words of his publicist, Robert Holmes.' What had riled Donovan most of all, though, was the perceived role of the BBC in the course of events. 'Obviously Dodd can refuse to discuss the past if he wants to,' said Donovan, 'but it seems bizarre for the BBC actually to suppress Lawley's efforts, taken on behalf of the listeners and licence-payers, to get him to talk about it.'

The reference to Dodd's duality – 'the ordinary fella from Knotty Ash' and 'the Ken Dodd who is on the stage' – is in many ways the key to understanding what makes Dodd Dodd. His very ordinariness has also been a useful barometer of Joe Soap – he's never lost the common touch – but he happens to have a talent that propels him into the limelight and takes him into public arenas where he would not normally be invited. We are therefore presented with a man who one moment is shaking the hand of his monarch and the next is returning home to 'Steptoe's yard' in Knotty Ash. This is the man who held the West End in thrall, but who stacked complimentary bottles of lager in the empty shower in his dressing room. On one hand we have a man who works tirelessly for innumerable Cinderella charities (it has been estimated that he has raised £2 million for charity), yet many people have shared their stories of his almost unbelievable Dickensian meanness.

His singular, peripatetic lifestyle also results in moments of eccentricity. Mike Craig recalls writing a radio show for Dodd many years ago and waiting at home for Dodd and Anne to arrive. The two of them had been working two hundred miles away the previous night and they eventually arrived at Craig's house after midday. To his surprise the producer noticed that Dodd had also brought a complete meal with him: 'Anne had got his lunch ready for him. It was a steak covered in gravy with chips. The gravy was thick and it was there ready for him to eat. It had all gone cold and the gravy was solid.' After they had finished their meeting, Craig remembers, 'He said goodbye to me and then they went out. He got in the car with his plate on his knee, a knife and fork and started eating it as he drove off . . .'

It is unlikely that Dodd would see anything eccentric about his life at all – but, of course, that is the mark of true eccentricity. Even at this advanced age he spends much of his waking hours holed up in his silver people-carrier traversing the country, but apart from the lengthy tenures at the Palladium or Blackpool, it is all he has ever known. His hobbies appear to be few: he watches a lot of satellite television, is a keen reader (science fiction is a favourite) and has only recently discovered the joy of travel. Roy Hudd, incidentally, remembers how he and some friends once persuaded Dodd to go away for a rest. 'We said, "Ken, why don't you go on holiday? You need a break. It doesn't cost much to go abroad." So he eventually went on holiday, and he said, "It's marvellous – I did enjoy it. We went for a week to Majorca – it was a hundred and twenty quid!"'

It was certainly his ordinariness that took the nation by surprise as they devoured the newspapers during the trial. Dodd, however, remains convinced that he is not a freak: 'I don't know that show-business people *do* live this glamorous and exciting jet-setting life. I think most of them are so shattered when they've done their show, all they want to do is go home and close the front door or read a book or put the video on.'

He has also never let the glitter of showbiz obscure his vision; he has remained acutely aware that it gives those involved with it a warped view of the world. 'Show business is the happiness business,' he has said. 'Probably you may get a false sense of life, always wanting to make people laugh, always wanting to be surrounded by laughing people, but it's a great life and I enjoy every second of it.'

He has also been keen to stress that his life is not one of frugality. 'No, I have the time of my life. I love food. I first discovered nice food when I came into show business. I discovered the joys of eating and I've got the paunch to prove it,' he told Sue Lawley. And as well as enjoying his home and other properties, he spends money on books, and is fond of buying gadgets. Indeed, Dodd had one of the first home video cameras. According to Roy Hudd, he used it once to film the postman coming up to the house in order to play a joke on the man: 'He said to him, "Come in here – I've just seen a wonderful programme on the television. Good Lord! It's you! I didn't realize you were a star!" You can't help loving the guy whatever he does.'

In George Melly's view, although he was a great admirer of his work, he says that he did not particularly like Dodd: 'He struck me as odd. You couldn't get on a wavelength with him. He didn't give out any warmth, you see. I think he's like a ventriloquist's doll: you've got him out of the box, pushed him on stage and he's brilliant, really brilliant. He gives the impression of being of the people – I don't know if it's a front or not, or just one of his devices – but he doesn't strike me as such. He doesn't go out and you don't see him in pubs.'

Dodd himself has acknowledged his temperament: 'I think I'm normal. I think I'm probably liverish in the morning and full of the joys of spring by three o'clock in the morning . . . when I should be going to bed.'

Although nothing like in the Tony ('I don't expect happiness') Hancock league, there is a certain sadness there. As a close friend of his told me: 'I think he's a very lonely man. Very lonely. My wife will tell you about how he used to talk about children. He'd say, "What are you doing at Christmas?" She'd tell him about the rituals with the children waiting round the tree to open their presents. He listened, enraptured.' Then, when asked what he would be doing for Christmas, he would reply, 'You don't want to know,' and it transpired that part of his Christmas Day ritual involved laying flowers on the graves of Anita and his mother.

Many have tried to catch Dodd off guard and get him to talk about a world less sunny, and on such occasions he had revealed a very human side to his character. 'Lots of things bring me down,' he admitted to John Stapleton. 'When you feel that life is turning against you, when you can't get your own way . . . We're told God is love and God does love you. He can't always help you in the way you want to be helped because that's something we don't understand. But there are things we don't understand, I think, that we're not supposed to understand.'

He went on to add: 'We all have regrets. There are lots of things I wish I'd had the courage to do. There are lots of things I wish I hadn't said. And there's one or two things I wish I hadn't done . . . but that's life. Your life is like a garden: there's bound to be a lot of sweet peas, but there's also going to be a lot of weeds as well.'

Alexandra Connor also did her best to coax him into talking about the lows as well as the highs. 'I've had my moments – it's not all been up; I've had one or two downs as well,' was about as far as he would go. 'Why talk about downs? Everybody has highs and lows and troughs, you have times of gladness and times of sadness. And you have to try to sustain yourself through those moments and sustain yourself with optimism, with laughter, with prayer.

'Of course I have some regrets; I have lots of regrets. I regret that earlier on I didn't . . . If I was to advise anyone these days, being an entertainer, I would say get some formal training as well. It would have helped me a great deal – because you have to learn how to move, to stand, to speak . . . Along the way I still have drama lessons and I still have speech lessons. I was helped enormously by the Northern College of Music.'

There we have it: a masterclass in evasion, side-stepping and ducking the issue. Any self-respecting politician would have been proud. Just as he was on the verge of revealing something that might have come back to haunt him, he deftly changed the subject to work – back on safe ground. By studying the replies given to various journalists and interviewers, it soon becomes apparent that Dodd's performances on chat shows and the quotes he gives to reporters are as well rehearsed as his stage act.

One can't help thinking that it has taken enormous self-control for a man like Dodd, a man who has confessed an interest in psychology, not to have given in to temptation and opened up a little more. Perhaps the nearest he came to revealing more about his inner workings was when he appeared on Dr Anthony Clare's Radio Four series *In The Psychiatrist's Chair* in July 1987.

After five years behind the microphone, Dr Clare had earned himself a reputation as a fairly tough inquisitor. It was therefore somewhat surprising that the notoriously private Dodd leaped at the invitation to submit himself to the psychiatrist's probing questions. Flattery, no doubt, was a potent force. To be asked on the programme was indeed an honour, and Dodd has always been a bit of a sucker for intellectual recognition. In fact many comics of a certain age like to be thought of as intellectual in some way: Les Dawson wrote novels, as did Eric Morecambe – both regarded them as their finest achievements – while Tony Hancock and Frankie Howerd would sit long into the night pondering philosophy.

As usual, Dodd attempted to use the programme as a platform for his comic theories. On this occasion, however, Dr Clare was wise to it. As he explained to Gus Smith, author of *Ken Dodd: Laughter and Tears*: 'I found that when people talked theoretically about acting or politics, it was a way of keeping me at bay. I sensed that Doddy wanted to theorize.'

That said, the seasoned broadcaster continued to chip away at Dodd's tattifilarious façade. Dr Clare was not interested in the Palladium or the Diddymen: he wanted to know why Dodd had not married Anita Boutin. Dodd trotted out the standard reply: 'To be honest with you, I was, as you know, engaged for a long time; I know it sounds amazing, but we were too busy to wed. Every television series that came along, every stage show, posed for us a fresh set of emotional challenges.'

Although Dodd admitted that Anita had wanted to get married, he continued to stress that there was never time. Later in the conversation he casually let slip that he had been too busy to get his hair cut before the recording. 'You know,'

Dr Clare pointed out to Dodd, 'that is the second time you've used "too busy" as an explanation for why you didn't do something. What it really means to me is that if you're too busy to do something, it really is relatively low on your list of priorities.'

'Oh no, I don't think that's correct,' Dodd hastily replied. 'No, it wasn't necessary to have my hair cut and it wasn't necessary for me to marry.' Dr Clare, and indeed his audience, was to conclude that the reason Dodd had never married was simply because – regardless of his fiancée's wishes on the matter – it did not figure highly in his priorities.

'Every one of us has something to hide,' Dr Clare told Gus Smith, 'and this is true of Ken Dodd. He is thrifty and this is because money loomed large in his early life; you find that people rarely admit that they are thrifty, but in Dodd's case it is a recurring theme.' He went on to explain that having an overly frugal attitude was often the result of experiencing financial insecurity in childhood: 'Lack of money in early life can frighten you later on, with the result that you never take a spending view of life.'

Tellingly, Dr Clare also observed that despite Dodd's emphasis on building a rapport with his audience, his style of quick-fire, gag-telling was actually opposed to this, and that the tirade of laughs he was provoking in the viewing public was much more likely to keep them at bay. He used Tony Hancock as an example: whereas Hancock used his failings and suffering to forge a bond with his audience, Dodd's audience is never permitted to enter into a relationship with him: 'It is distanced from him and it's his way of ensuring that it is under his control.'

This point is echoed by Steve Punt: 'Just because he may himself be interested in analysis, his sort of act is the least interesting to try to analyse. It doesn't really tell you anything about the person, and that always feel odd to me. You can analyse Billy Connolly because his jokes are clearly coming from somewhere and there's clearly a very personal psychology behind what he finds funny and what he's prepared to confront; the fact that he enjoys saying, "I used to be very poor and now I'm loaded." But I always think with the sort of club comic, gags-driven style, you're not really learning anything about the person. What you're learning about is the general sociology of jokes rather than the psychology of jokes.'

It is an opinion with which Arthur Smith concurs. 'He never gives anything away in his act,' Smith remarks. 'You never learn anything about Ken Dodd.' This point of view is one of the schisms between comics of the old and newer schools. The younger breed clearly think that comedy has to be about something and to say something about the comedian; the old pros of Dodd's generation think the opposite is true. Funny is funny: no more, no less.

Although Dodd was undoubtedly flattered to be following in the wake of such luminaries as opera singer Dame Janet Baker and composer Sir Michael Tippett on *In the Psychiatrist's Chair*, as the probing progressed he must have wondered whether he'd done the right thing in accepting Dr Clare's invitation. At any rate he would never again volunteer himself for such clever analysis under the media spotlight.

*

Following up the success of his 1990 Christmas Day Palladium show, four years later Dodd was back on the small screen again in London Weekend Television's *An Audience With Ken Dodd*. Here he was doing what he did best, but this time it was in front of an audience of his celebrity peers.

It was a triumph; in fact for many it was considered the high-light of his television career.

In this celebrity-fuelled age it is no longer acceptable to have just a couple of big names and a few chorus girls in spangly tights on stage – nowadays, viewers want to see names, and the more names the better. A brilliant idea incorporating a clever spin on the variety format, these *An Audience With . . .* specials are extremely popular, and provide a great showcase for the chosen performer. The formula is deceptively simple: you take a prominent, proficient celeb and get him or her to field a few questions from a specially invited audience of old pals and admirers, thereby providing the perfect vehicle for his or her comedic talents. Crucial to the success of the show is, of course, the subject. Former boxing champion Muhammad Ali was the first to test the water, but very soon it became the province of the comedian or raconteur; subsequent performers included Dudley Moore, Peter Ustinov, Kenneth Williams, Mel Brooks, Jackie Mason, Victoria Wood, Joan Rivers, Billy Connolly, Bob Monkhouse, Jimmy Tarbuck, Bruce Forsyth, Warren Mitchell (as Alf Garnett) and Ronnie Corbett.

Not all the subjects of the programme have enjoyed appearing on the show, however, as some have found them fraught with tension and emotionally draining. Perhaps because she was six months pregnant at the time, Victoria Wood found her experience a 'hellish' one. 'It was nerve-wracking because I could see all their faces lit up, with the cameras on them,' she later recalled. 'They were a friendly audience, but not a normal one, so I was trying to play to the normal audience behind them and ignore the celebrities.' Despite these apparent difficulties, however, she still won a BAFTA award for her popular performance.

Like all the other subjects, Dodd was permitted a say in which celebrities should be invited to make up the audience.

For his first outing, in December 1994, actors James Fox, Hannah Gordon and Warren Mitchell found themselves rubbing shoulders with the likes of Su Pollard, Josie Lawrence and Paul Daniels. Certain people asked pre-arranged questions, which gave Dodd his cue to move on to a new subject, and the act was peppered with various songs, a Dickie Mint interlude, and ended with a rendition of 'Happiness'.

The show was an enormous success, and although it resembled a mere shadow of his stage routine, it was still a comic tour de force. In a sense there was no excuse, as the show drew heavily on much of his perfectly polished stage material. Because the programme was pure undiluted Dodd, and not subject to being broken up by sketches or guest variety performances, it was perhaps the very first time that modern television audiences got a taste of the real Ken Dodd, as it was the first occasion that he had been granted the time and space to flex his comedy muscles. As Denis Norden points out, 'There was a whole tranche of the population who'd never seem him at full-length before, at full throttle.'

For his second *An Audience With* show, old muckers such as Claire Sweeney, Ricky Tomlinson, Denis Norden, Miriam Margolyes and Sylvester McCoy were joined by Nicholas Parsons, Martin Clunes, Carol Vorderman, Henry Cooper, Frank Bruno and a sprinkling of familiar soap-stars. It was very much a repeat performance – another sizable chunk of his stage act captured for posterity. This time, Sybil (Anne) Jones was credited as production associate, and there was even room for a guest appearance by his old trumpet-playing 'stooge', Joan Hinde. Known as the 'first lady of the trumpet', Hinde had previously appeared in Dodd's *Happiness Show* on tour, and in fact had supported many other comedians throughout her career. In the second *An Audience With Ken Dodd*, she was required to emerge from the front row to interrupt Dodd's singing with some very loud trumpeting. So effective was her contribution that apparently, the audience laughed so much that the recording had to be stopped until everyone had recovered!

Oddly, according to Norden, the show didn't run too far over its expected recording time: 'All the *Audience Withs* overrun because it allows them to choose the best bits, as it were. But it didn't overrun to the extent that all the technical staff were put on triple time.'

Ann Widdecombe was also in the audience on this occasion. 'He was as vibrant as ever,' she recalled, 'falling over his words in his haste to be funny, running vastly over-time without the audience becoming restless, singing in a voice of apparently undiminished strength.

'That was more than four decades after he first crackled on to our ancient television set,' continued Widdecombe. 'During those forty years family entertainment has been given over to soap operas about sad, dysfunctional lives, stand-up comedians have become foul-mouthed and coarse, singing has yielded to cacophony in popular culture, but Dodd's act is essentially unchanged. I detected in that audience a certain protectiveness towards him, a feeling that he and his act were worth preserving for another forty years.'

On Tuesday 19 March 1995, Dodd reported to Shepperton studios in Middlesex to make his somewhat belated film debut. With typical conceit, following on from his successes with his movie versions of *Henry V* and *Much Ado About Nothing*, Kenneth Branagh expanded the part of Yorick (the skull complete with the appropriate triangular dental arrangements) to accommodate Dodd in his film version of *Hamlet*. Shot in 70mm, Branagh's star-studded epic marked Dodd's first – and, to date, last – big-screen appearance. His co-stars included Kate Winslet as Ophelia, Rufus Sewell as Fortinbras, Robin Williams as Osric (a role surely more suited to Dodd), Richard Briers as Polonius,

Billy Crystal as the First Gravedigger, Jack Lemmon as Marcellus and Gérard Depardieu as Reynaldo.

As he told Alexandra Connor: 'He [Branagh] phoned me up one day and said, "How would you like to be in my film of *Hamlet*?" I thought, oh yes, I've got the legs for it. Have you ever seen me in white tights? I look wonderful. He said, "I was thinking of Yorick." I said, "Yorick's a skull!" He said, "That was when he was going to Weight Watchers – now we shall show Yorick in flashback, fully fleshed."

'So there I am one day, in this baronial hall with the Hamlet family at dinner; on my left is Sir Derek Jacobi, on my right is Brian Blessed as the king, resplendent in his red uniform and medals, across here is the young Hamlet – a smashing little lad – and right opposite me is the beautiful and gorgeous and voluptuous Julie Christie. So how could I miss?'

During the making of the film, Branagh's text adviser Russell Jackson kept a diary. In it he described Dodd's appearance on set as 'resplendent in a costume that is a cross between a classic nineteenth-century clown (Joey Grimaldi) and the Mad Hatter'. Dodd's performance centres on his entertaining the royal family at dinner. In the finished film, he appears to be performing a mime routine, to the amusement of the characters on screen, but during filming, while the cameras kept moving in semi-circles to record this particular scene, Dodd was telling real jokes from his routine, including one about cat food, which made all the actors laugh hysterically. Unfortunately for the crew, they were standing too far away from the action and couldn't hear the joke, only the guffaws emanating from the cast.

Jackson went on to describe how they did a close-up of 'Doddy' displaying his teeth in order to match their shots of Yorick's skull in later scenes. He then recalls how, during a break in filming, Dodd talked about the variety comics whom he admired, 'particularly those who seemed like beings from another planet (Tommy Cooper, Frankie Howerd)', and also observed how when Dodd's face in make-up is seen close up, 'his features seem strangely delicate'. He concluded by saying how Dodd was tickled pink to have his photograph taken with his name printed on a chair back, and to have been given the Yorick skull as a memento.

Though Dodd did not have any scripted lines to deliver in the film, being limited to keeping the royal family amused while they dined, it was still an extremely clever use of his singular talents.

In 1998, alongside the likes of Imelda Staunton and Sean Bean, Dodd lent his voice to an animated version of the *Canterbury Tales*, playing the part of the Canon. A year later he took on the role of Mr Mouse in Nick Willing's production of Lewis Carroll's *Alice in Wonderland*. Although the Mad Hatter character was surely made for Dodd (he is the living embodiment of Tenniel's Mad Hatter drawings), it was doubtless because it was an American production that US actor Martin Short landed the part.

'I played Mr Mouse in *Alice in Wonderland*,' Dodd told Alexandra Connor. 'Not the dormouse – he's the one that falls asleep in the teapot – this was Mr Mouse who rescues Alice from the Pool of Tears. In the new film I'm with Whoopi Goldberg, Gene Wilder and the gorgeous Miranda Richardson, Ben Kingsley . . . all these wonderful people. I didn't go to Hollywood – it was done over here. They'll all come to Britain for *Alice in Wonderland*.'

Though it has been suggested that Lewis Carroll, with his unique, surreal and rather warped view of the world had been one of Dodd's influences, in truth the delicate young Ken had found him 'menacing'.

★

Fallout

Back on home ground, in May 2001, Dodd received the ultimate accolade as a staunch Liverpudlian when he was made a Freeman of the City of Liverpool. At the ceremony held at the town hall, tribute was paid to his outstanding career in comedy, as well as his tireless work for good causes and charity fundraising. Described by the Lord Mayor of Liverpool as 'a legendary figure in the entertainment world who has constantly promoted the city', Dodd was tremendously proud to have received such an honour. In accordance with his rights as a Freeman, he joked that he would be taking advantage of the ancient laws that enable him to drive sheep through the city centre and on to a Mersey ferry, as well as grazing some goats in local parks. This award was the second to have originated in his home town in four years, after he was made an honorary fellow of Liverpool's John Moores University.

Regrettably for Dodd, the year would not continue in quite such a positive vein, for as well as attracting the attention of various Liverpool dignitaries, in the autumn it soon became apparent that he had become the focus for the unwanted attentions of an obsessed female fan.

After a period of relative calm since his brush with the Inland Revenue, Dodd was to learn the hard way that the innocent device of flirting with his audience ('I'm a sex symbol for women who don't care'), i.e., the 'By Jove, Missus!' element of his act that was part of his bridge-building exercise, could sometimes have frightening consequences. The whole unfortunate experience proved to be yet another unwelcome intrusion into Dodd's cosy world. After all, it's never a beautiful day for posting a dead rat doused in perfume through someone's front door or sticking burning rags through a letterbox. But these are examples of exactly what thirty-five-year-old Bristol-born Ruth Tagg did to Dodd over a period of several months.

'I was depressed at the time,' Tagg later explained, 'having just resigned from a job because of bullying, and I was searching for a new interest in life. Comedy was what I felt I needed and, on the suggestion of a penpal, I decided to hire out a Ken Dodd video and laugh away my sorrows.'

Though Tagg couldn't trace any copies of his videos, she did find some of his singles, and discovered that he had 'a superb tenor's singing voice' and soon realized that she enjoyed listening to his romantic songs. Eventually she started attending his shows, and while sitting in the front row on one occasion, Dodd happened to ask her her name. 'I told him and he replied, "That's Hebrew. It means spirit of beauty." From then on, he spoke to me from the stage all evening. He was saucy, and made a lot of remarks about my breasts such as, "You don't get many of them to a pound!" Far from being offended, I felt flattered and thrilled.'

After the show she went backstage to meet him. 'When Dodd eventually appeared,' Tagg recalled, 'he had his hair swept back and was wearing a smart tweed suit. He looked so different to the wild-haired comic on stage. Privately, I thought he looked rather handsome. I expected him to recognize me as the girl he'd spoken to all evening, but he didn't seem to remember. When I told him I'd travelled all the way from Bristol, he seemed touched and asked for a kiss. I was over the moon with excitement as he drew me near and pressed his cheek against mine. He whispered in my ear, asking me to come to another show. I was walking on air, and felt as though I had fallen in love for the first time.'

Tagg then spent the next two months, working twelve hours a day, creating a tapestry portrait of Dodd. She sent it to him as a present and he replied with a note of thanks. While attending another of his performances in Weston-super-Mare, she claimed that towards the end of the show he approached the edge of the stage and asked her, 'Do you fancy me?' Such was the extent of her growing feelings for him that she had to admit to herself that, yes, she really was attracted to him.

The deeply troubled woman could not understand that the Doddy she saw on stage was merely putting on an act, and so at a backstage meeting with fans after the show, she was deeply upset when he appeared not to acknowledge her. Indeed, by this time Dodd had become extremely wary of her and on this occasion had already told staff that she might be a stalker.

It was not the first time Dodd had had trouble with a member of his audience. He once told the *Yorkshire Post* that many years earlier when he was appearing on stage singing 'Love Is Like A Violin' in Bristol, while the theatre was in darkness and the spotlight was on his face, he suddenly felt the presence of someone standing beside him. Slowly turning his head to the side, he was met by the staring glaring gaze of a man swaying right next to him. At the time, Dodd feared the worst, and convinced himself that he was carrying a gun or a knife, intent on doing him harm. 'While I was thinking this, the stagehands had gathered in the wings ready for action and as the last note of the song died away, the spotlight faded and for a moment the entire theatre was in darkness. Out dashed the stagehands. I threw myself one way and the man lunged another. He eluded the stagehands, dashed across the stage, down the steps and out of the first exit. We never saw him again.'

Unfortunately, Ruth Tagg wasn't about to disappear from Dodd's life quite so quickly. She had started to follow Dodd all over the country, always sitting in the front row. After initially sending him anonymous love letters signed 'Your secret love', she then began to use the name Rose Price in her correspondence, in which she would ask, 'What does one have to do to become one of your extended family?' Even more disturbingly, just before Christmas 2001, Anne Jones received a parcel containing three T-shirts with offensive messages emblazoned across them. Dodd himself was sent a pornographic picture of the obsessed stalker wearing a mask in a provocative pose.

The situation was growing out of all proportion in Tagg's mind. At another backstage meeting, she claimed that, out of Anne Jones's hearing, Dodd had told her the tapestry had caused him 'a lot of problems', which she took to mean that it had caused friction between the couple. A fortnight later, the portrait was returned to Tagg. With its glass frame shattered, she believed it to be a deliberate act of vandalism by Anne. It was then, shortly before her arrest, that Tagg sent a parcel to the couple, containing a dead rat sprayed with perfume.

Her obsession grew to such an extent that she had convinced herself that as Dodd wasn't married, she was still in with a chance of catching him for herself. Despite her 'goal', however, she had begun to brood more and more, feeling 'insulted and rejected' by Dodd. It was in this fragile state of mind that she attempted to set fire to the house next door to Dodd's home in Knotty Ash, where he stored his props, by pushing burning rags through the letterbox, causing £11,000 worth of damage. Fortunately Dodd and his partner had been away in Gravesend at the time, so their lives were never in any danger.

Tagg was finally arrested at one of Dodd's shows on Merseyside, and she was detained under the Mental Health Act in November 2003. At Nottingham Crown Court she pleaded guilty to charges of arson and harassment of Anne Jones. In court, Tagg's defence lawyer, Martin Picton, explained that Tagg was now ashamed and apologetic about her actions. The court heard that she suffered from a psychopathic disorder, but she was making good progress and it was hoped she could recover.

On sentencing her, Mr Justice Morland said, 'Clearly viewed from the standpoint of Ken Dodd and his partner, you were a dangerous and all too frequent menace. Your distorted obsession about Ken Dodd was making him and his partner's lives hazardous. There is happily every indication that you are overcoming the problem and that you have made excellent steps towards recovery. At present, you remain a danger to the public at large, and not only to Ken Dodd and his partner.'

The incident left both Dodd and Anne Jones considerably shaken. The day after the trial's conclusion the *Liverpool Echo* reported that the couple's letterbox had been sealed with a piece of timber nailed into place behind the door and that their mail was being kept safely away from the house in a cast-iron Dutch-style letterbox. The paper quoted a friend as saying: 'It affected them both – they were very worried about what she might be capable of. They will both just be glad it's over.'

Tagg's parents later defended their daughter's actions, explaining that she loved Dodd's act and would never want to cause any harm. Although she had admitted that she found Dodd 'incredibly sexy', Tagg herself said that she had made 'a stupid and serious mistake' for which she was sorry.

'Following Dodd's shows felt exciting at the time,' she said. 'There was a magical atmosphere, but the atmosphere is part of the illusion and, off stage, Dodd is quite different – not at all funny, but rather surly and sour. One thing is for sure, the next time I feel lonely and in need of some fun in my life, I won't look to Dodd to provide the laughter.'

Luckily, she was in the minority.

Coming fairly hot on the heels of the tax trial, therefore, this whole unpleasant episode was a further unwelcome invasion into Dodd's private life. He was, after all, only doing his job – audience flirtation has always been one of the most common weapons in a comic's armoury. Dodd had just been unlucky: he had directed his friendly approach at the wrong person, someone who took his joking earnestly. But yet again, Dodd – arguably the world's most unlikely stalker victim – was able to bounce back, seeking solace in his work as ever, and, more importantly, he was still willing to flirt with the punters.

10

The Gospel
According to Doddy

'IF YOU TRY to find out what makes us tick,' Eric Morecambe once said, 'the watch stops.'

Morecambe was one comic wise enough to simply embrace his talent and not analyse it to death. The likes of Tony Hancock and Frankie Howerd, however, were not quite so sanguine: perhaps because they were not 'gag' men and relied more on their personas to prompt laughter, both would spend years in a fruitless search for understanding. At an enormously high price – in Hancock's case, the highest – they tried to find out what it was that made people laugh at them. 'Instead of being content to let the talent lead him,' said Bob Monkhouse, 'Hancock made the mistake of wanting to lead it.'

The general consensus of opinion is that any analysis of comedy is almost certainly doomed to failure. Quantifying what is or is not funny is a sure-fire route to squeezing the last drop of wit out of anything. If you try to coalesce the vapours of humour, you just end up slightly damp. Indeed,

Roy Hudd considers comic analysis both rare and extremely dangerous: 'I remember years ago Norman Wisdom being interviewed. Someone asked him why what he was doing was funny and he said: "Please don't ask me. If I start trying to work out why it's funny, it won't be funny any more. Leave that to the writers, really."'

But what does Doddy care for convention? What has he to do with the general consensus? Why, he's a maverick, a gladiator. He's fearless. Of course, all comics give thought to what they do, but surely only Ken Dodd has made a study of Freud, Bergson and Schopenhauer in order to try to comprehend the psychology of humour. 'He's a scientist as well as a poet,' says George Melly. 'A comedian who cares.'

As Dodd told Sue Lawley: 'I really fell in love with comedy in my teens. My dad used to say: "If you want to know anything go to a library." So I used to look up the word "laughter" and "comedy" . . . and that's where I started this sort of research and I went right back to Aristotle. He said that laughter was a buckled mill wheel.'

However, he also acknowledged that the journey to comic enlightenment was a long and tortuous one: 'The more you go into this wonderful adventure – the more you seek and find reasons in the human mind for what appear on the surface to be fancies, fripperies and little pieces of nonsense – the more you realize that the human mind is such an unbelievably complex instrument; sometimes it completely overwhelms you. It overwhelms you with the sheer immenseness of trying to build a comic map of the mind.'

Although he's compared analysis of humour with 'pulling the wings off a butterfly', he remains convinced that it has benefits: 'Humour ought to be studied in much greater detail, I think. It affects everyday life as much as anything I can think of. It plays a part in communication, in negotiation, in business, in politics, in religion.'

Over the years he has built up his own 10,000-book library. He has also said that one day he would like to write a book about humour and comedy himself because, he reasoned, he had learned a thing or two about it. 'Some people say there are only seven original jokes . . . well, I think there's twenty-seven formulas,' he revealed, somewhat cryptically.

As Dodd intimated, it's all very well studying the theory of comedy: putting it into practice is an entirely different matter. 'The trouble with Freud,' he famously opined, 'is that he never played second house at the Glasgow Empire.' It's a nice glib quote, of course, but then as Roy Hudd points out, if, as Dodd appears to suggest, analysing humour is so important, Freud would have slayed 'em!

Though Dodd may own this vast indexed library of comedy-related volumes, some have cast doubt on his studiousness. 'He has certain pretensions of being a comedy analyst,' says Denis Norden, and Mike Craig agrees. 'He likes to think he's serious. He's got a lot of books, but he doesn't read them.'

Nonetheless, in February 2002, Dodd accepted an intriguing invitation from Dr (later Professor) Richard Wiseman of the University of Hertfordshire to be interviewed as part of the academic's LaughLab experiment for National Science Year. Doubtless flattered by the attentions of the intelligentsia, Dodd would also have been safe in the knowledge that he would not face being quizzed about anything other than his professional abilities at such an intellectual gathering.

LaughLab was a huge event designed to get the public involved in experiments concerning science and humour. It involved people visiting a website, submitting their favourite joke and rating jokes suggested by others. As a kind of spin-off event Wiseman thought it would be interesting to interview a few comedians about the psychology of humour. As one of the country's few remaining gag-tellers, Ken Dodd was the obvious choice. Most comedians nowadays, notes Wiseman, are devoted to observational humour, and that wasn't what LaughLab was about; LaughLab was about jokes. Wiseman also liked the idea of talking to Dodd because of his wealth of experience; not just in the telling of jokes, but in relating the same jokes over and over again. He felt that Dodd would have an ideal insight into the psychology of the best way to phrase jokes.

The idea for the LaughLab live event, which was to take place at a theatre in Wrexham, was simple: after doing his act for some accountancy firms in the afternoon, Dodd would first be introduced to the LaughLab audience, perform ten minutes of stand-up, face an interview conducted by Wiseman for forty-five minutes, and then finish with about an hour of his act. At least that was the plan. In the event Dodd opened with forty minutes of stand-up, was interviewed for about half an hour and then he performed his act for about two-and-a-half hours. But it left Wiseman with a profound memory of the evening. Seeing him work a live audience, he too became a Doddy convert. He was entirely captivated by the comedian's fascinating persona: 'Even backstage – and I had my back to him – you knew he was there, and part of that was that he just attracts people's attention. There's something about him, even off-stage, that is very charismatic – it's not as big or as silly as on-stage, but still there's something there that is very charming and wants to be the centre of attention (and achieves it very easily), and is very funny.'

Wiseman realized that Dodd's sheer force of personality was key to his success. With most comedians it is mainly about material – you have to have good material and you have to deliver it in a convincing way. But Wiseman concluded that Dodd is different. Though many of his jokes are undeniably funny and his delivery is faultless, he felt that a lot of the material is actually not that good, but despite this, it was still able to get a fantastic response from the audience. 'There are not patches when he's dying in any sense,' recalls Wiseman. 'But you think: hold on a second, ninety-nine per cent of comedians standing up there with that material would die on their backsides and never use it again. He's getting huge responses and I think that's because more than any other performer I have seen for a very long time, it's about *him*. This is all about *him*. That you just *love* him. He's a very lovable person.'

That's why, Wiseman observes, it doesn't matter that the audience has heard the routine twenty times before. It doesn't make any difference: 'It's a bit like going to a rock concert and hearing them play the same songs again – you wouldn't want new material.'

He goes further, judging a Ken Dodd evening to be less like a traditional comedy set, and more of a religious event: 'Yes, people were laughing, but the style was more that of a preacher in a sense, whipping up a crowd. The material itself didn't matter after a while. It wasn't about that; it was about being there, having that experience and being converted, in a sense, to what this whole thing was.'

Later during the LaughLab interview, Dodd spoke of his spectrum of humour and Wiseman noted that because his act celebrated all things positive that Dodd's own 'hue' was about as far from the darker end as it was possible to get: 'It's about the joyous laughter of just being alive, and of course laughing at the silly and the absurdities of life. It's not targeted at any one person or any one group for the most part. It's about selling a world view that's kind of joyous.'

He also picked up on the rhythm of Dodd's delivery. According to Wiseman, it is again part of charismatic preaching. 'A television-documentary director told me that if you get a voiceover for your documentary and they get the rhythm right, the audience will believe anything they say. They can say the most absurd thing, but if you get the rhythm right people go into this state of thinking it's all true. And it's the same with Ken Dodd. He gets a rhythm going with the audience and once you get into it – the rhythm is: I say something, you laugh – after a while it doesn't matter what he says. But you enjoy it and you keep going and it takes you over.'

How true that is. Quite often, Dodd's material simply doesn't make sense; it does not bear close examination at all. 'Did you get your free sausage on the way in?' he will enquire of his audience. 'Well, you will on the way out!' If you take the trouble to analyse that second line it makes little or no sense, but it gets a huge laugh nonetheless. And that's mainly down to the rhythm: it's like an aural exclamation mark.

Another similarity between Dodd's show and a religious meeting according to Wiseman is that it's a group experience. We're watching it collectively, which is a further reason why it doesn't work on television, where we are watching it as individuals: 'You have to be there. You have to be in that auditorium. He understands that. That's why I think he's doing live work and has done for pretty much his whole life. His bread and butter is going out and doing those live shows.'

Perhaps the most courageous aspect of Dodd's performance that evening, however, was his willingness to dissect a joke, like a magician showing his audience how he executes a trick. Wiseman agrees that Dodd's studying of comedy is a way of protecting himself: 'Comedians are to some extent insecure and comedy is, of course, a way of trying to assert your security. And so it wouldn't surprise me if there was a sense of trying to prop up those insecurities by saying, "Well, I'm terribly well read. I'm terribly knowledgeable." Of course, what he's doing is what a lot of serious authors aren't doing, which is going out there and putting it all to the test. I think he probably has a lot more insight into humour than pretty much anybody else who's written on the subject.'

Before Dodd made his Palladium debut in 1965, journalist Godfrey Winn was despatched to Liverpool's Royal Court to catch his act and interview him. When the subject of analysis came up, Dodd gave him an insight into his understanding of audience reactions. 'I've read Freud and Jung from cover to cover, but in the end it all comes back to getting the audience with you. When I do my serious singing spot, I can tell how things are by the number of matches being struck to light cigarettes. If there are only a few out there in the darkness, I feel good.' These days he probably gauges how well his show is going down by the sound of sweets being unwrapped.

Oddly, Dodd has never been frightened to voice his opinion that comedians are vulnerable, and are only as good as their last laugh. 'All comedians are conscious of the fact that you're walking a tightrope all the time,' he has said. 'A joke is like a watch mechanism: there can't be one word too many or one word too few. And it's all a rhythm – each word has to be a very special word in a very special place with a very special rhythm.'

And, just like a watchmaker, Dodd used that evening in Wrexham to take apart a gag and put it back together again. He started by telling the joke about the man who is shipwrecked and from the sea comes this beautiful Ursula Andress-like voluptuary in a wetsuit (a gag doubtless familiar to any viewer of *The Two Ronnies*). Unzipping a pocket she offers him a hip flask of whisky, then from another she produces a pack of cigarettes. Finally, unzipping her wetsuit, she says, 'Would you like to play around?' and he says, 'Why? Have you got some golf clubs with you?'

When Dodd first delivered the joke, uttered with little enthusiasm, it wasn't surprising that it didn't get much of a laugh. Then he explained to the audience that the reason the laughs were so few was because he didn't think it was funny at that moment in time: 'I've got to imagine it. I've got to imagine that sexy woman and communicate that to you as an audience. I've got to build that image.' According to Wiseman, he started to do just that, and as he told the joke again and again and again, it became progressively funnier: 'So he had that analysis thing going on there, that he wasn't scared of telling the same joke maybe four or five times to an audience saying, "What I'm going to do now . . ." And by the end of it he got the audience laughing with a gag that had died on its backside ten minutes before.'

A former magician himself, Wiseman thinks there's not a world of difference between what Dodd does and what professional magicians do. 'Ninety per cent of magic is dreadful, but the ten per cent which is any good is about getting people to believe for a moment that the normal rules don't apply; that things can appear and disappear and levitate or whatever. And I think that's what he does in his act. He takes you to another world where you literally forget your problems and your troubles in this mad world where everything's funny and everything's joyful. And that's unlike most comedians. Most comedians are negative.'

During his study of watching Dodd at work, Wiseman was continually impressed by the amount of affection shared by performer and audience: 'He does this thing about going along the front row and saying, "Where are you from?" What was phenomenal about that was that whatever he got it was always a positive thing. He never made the person feel stupid. It was always done in quite a nice sort of jokey way. I've seen so many comedians do it and basically if you're in the front row you're going to have the piss taken out of you and it's going to be a negative experience. With him, it's not like that. He's going to have a go at you – he made a joke about me being bald, for example – but it's done in this incredibly inclusive way. I would imagine that it's a bit like being a guest on *The Morecambe and Wise Show* – you're kind of proud of being the butt of a joke. I don't think he alienates young, old, male or female. I think we're all in it together.'

Wiseman concluded that Dodd's act isn't just a job – it's a vocation. It is simply his life's mission to spread joy and happiness. That's why, he reasons, Dodd is reluctant to leave the stage: 'Most entertainers do what they do for a living and it's a bit like you and I going to work. The idea of the boss saying, "Do you mind working an extra five hours today?" . . . You'd say, "I don't think so. I finish at six-thirty" or whatever. But you talk to preachers and that's their life's mission, so they'd be very happy to do a few more hours. And I think that's what he's engaged in – either consciously or unconsciously – that this is what his life is about, the receiving and giving of a colossal amount of love and adulation for the time he's on stage. Why would you want that to finish?

'It's difficult to think of another example in showbiz of someone who goes on that long. Most of them, you do your job and you get off. That's what you're paid for. So I think it is a unique phenomenon and it will be sad when he's not doing it any more.'

By the end of this extraordinary evening Wiseman found himself entirely won over by Dodd, both as a person and a performer. 'Because I have a background in magic I've seen hundreds of live performances of magicians and comedians over time, but I haven't seen anything that matches what happened in that hall on that day. I was completely unprepared for it. I thought: no, this is not about material, this is entirely about the performer and the relationship with the audience. It's an act of love.'

Wiseman is not the first to have made the religious analogy. When Dodd's on a roll, Denis Norden notes, 'I think he gets possessed, like these revivalist religious groups when the power comes upon them.'

And Liverpool poet Roger McGough recalls the time in

Ken Dodd

1997 the BBC televised a *Songs of Praise* programme from Goodison Park at which Dodd was present: 'It was amazing just watching him going around. He was like a bishop, but he had a tickling stick instead of a crook – in a metaphorical sort of way because he didn't have a tickling stick [with him]. But he would go around from table to table telling jokes, like the laying on of jokes, in a way. People weren't quite kissing his hand, but he was there at the table telling jokes, spreading sunshine, people loving him. I thought there was something very priest-like; this sense of his highness of comedy Ken Dodd walking around and everybody loving him. And they do in Liverpool.'

Given the fact that he had a religious upbringing, courtesy of his mother, it's little wonder Dodd has made no secret of his faith. 'I believe that your life is a quest and you're searching for your communication with your creator,' he explained to John Stapleton. 'I think we're all looking for God and we all hope to find him, and at different times of your life you really feel that you are in the presence of God.'

While discussing the subject of religion with Alexandra Connor, he revealed, 'I think anybody with any sense believes in their creator, and anybody with any sense knows when to ask for help. And if you ask for help you're given help. Have faith and you're given help.'

Dodd is also a great believer in the power of prayer. As he told Stapleton: 'Life is a series of highs and lows. One thing that does help for sure is prayer. Prayer is very, very powerful and very, very unique. I pray all the time. I pray before I go on stage. I pray every day, I pray every evening, I pray every night. They're not very articulate, but I think they are heard. And many, many times when I've been very down I have prayed and I've been lifted up.'

He went on to expand on his theory as to why churches are often empty. 'Sometimes,' he thought, 'the message isn't given in a way that a congregation finds attractive. I believe that when you go into church you should want to go – it shouldn't be a penance, it shouldn't be a duty, it shouldn't be something you don't look forward to. You should look forward to going to church the same as if you would look forward to making a long-distance call to someone you love very much, perhaps on the other side of the world. I've been to several churches where, I have to be honest, I didn't enjoy it, but I go to Liverpool Cathedral on Sunday afternoons sometimes, when I can, and they have evensong and it's wonderful. And they have good preachers who say things that are relevant. Religion has to be relevant.'

That may be so, but there's certainly a time and place for it. The Royal Variety Performance, for example, is far from ideal. Michael Grade recalls a bizarre occurrence on such an occasion a few years ago: 'He wanted to do a song that was rather sentimental and religious – it was not for the Royal Variety Performance – because he'd seen the light; he'd got this idea. We had this terrible row and I said, "We're only going to edit it out, Ken. Don't do it." But he just wouldn't listen and of course it died. People thought: what's he doing? It was strange.'

Similarly, Roy Hudd recalls another Royal Variety Performance and another case of bad judgement on Dodd's part: 'Because he'd just done *Twelfth Night* at the Liverpool Playhouse, he went on the Royal Variety Show and did the opening speech from Malvolio. Well, he died on his arse! I'm sitting there thinking, "What is he doing?" And then suddenly – "But I tell you, Missus!" – he went into the real act and paralysed 'em. Billington said he was brilliant as Malvolio, but you don't do that on the Royal Variety Performance when you're known for the Diddymen and "Tears".

'But he'll try it, Ken. With the ammunition he's got, he's marvellous. He's got the great thing where he'll do so long and then go into a couple of songs – that breaks it all up ter-rifically well. And he's a smashing singer of that style. What a terrific thing to have . . . and he seems to know when to put those songs in. You don't need to do what he does, but he probably needs to do it because he doesn't like things off-stage; he likes things on-stage best. You go to see Ken backstage afterwards and he'll talk for hours . . . but it's usu-ally about comedy. He loves all that – it's his life.'

11

Wither Doddy?

Iᴛ'ꜱ 2004, and I'm in the Watford Colosseum, another featureless authority-run auditorium in Hertfordshire. It's still cold, and it's still grey, but then so am I – fifteen years have passed since the first time I saw the squire of Knotty Ash on stage. The world has moved on beyond recognition, but it would appear that the realm of jam-butty mines and Dickie Mint has not.

Yet again, the place is groaning with punters, with 2,000 eager Doddyphiles in residence, all paying £20 a head. This is just one night in one town, but Dodd still performs three or four nights a week, ten or eleven months of the year. *The Stage*'s Peter Hepple suspects he's cutting down his engagements a little, but still, from July to December 2004 there were approximately sixty dates booked all over the provinces, and for the most part these are fairly large venues. Sixty dates with an estimated average capacity of 1,000 seats means that, potentially, some 60,000 punters will cough up to see Dodd over a period of six months. At £20 a head, box-office receipts are heading towards the £1.2 million mark.

Two and a half million pounds a year is no cottage industry. It's a financial force to be reckoned with, and that's without taking into account the revenue from the sale of programmes, CDs, videos, comic books and tickling sticks that fly off the box-office counter at the interval. 'His money must be fairly astronomical I should think,' opines Hepple. 'He's not greedy, but he'll want several thousand pounds a night.'

This, then, is Dodd's life: one long, exhausting, if lucrative, round of continual touring, mainly appearing in these vast, hangar-like auditoriums. Occasionally, however, he appears at a more pleasant, prestigious venue. In the summer of 2002, for example, as part of his pledge to play every live theatre in the country, he appeared at the Open Air Theatre in Regent's Park, London, where he told his audience: 'After nearly fifty years in the business, at the peak of my profession, admired by all my peers, here I am performing in the middle of a field in a theatre that can't afford a roof!'

In the cold light of day it's an extraordinary way for a man pushing eighty to lead his life, but after more than half a century, Dodd still has no problem packing in the crowds. He has an enormous following, and people will travel miles to see him. 'If he does Scarborough, for instance,' says Hepple, 'he'll get people in from Tyneside, Teeside, Leeds and York.' And it's the same all over the country.

When Steve Punt and his comedy partner Hugh Dennis were touring in the early 1990s, they would find that at virtually every venue there was a stage crew with a Dodd story to tell, invariably involving an overrunning show, and a very late finish. Punt and Dennis became fascinated by the fact that at each theatre they visited they would look at the list of events and realize that Ken Dodd had recently performed there or was due to appear in the near future. 'There's a whole raft of comics who only do that,' says Punt, 'but most of them do it because they're too rude for television, so you get people like Mick Miller and you used to get Roy "Chubby" Brown. You knew why they were doing theatres because they were obviously not suitable for telly and they released videos, but Ken Dodd was entirely different. He was doing what was effectively a family show, but without any kind of broadcast back-up at all. So he seemed to forge this totally unique work ethic of just continually touring and I would imagine that the same people go to see him in the same way that you go to a panto or something.'

Indeed, the Watford audience is a typical one: a pretty mixed bunch, mostly die-hard Doddyphiles split between the sexes, but there's also a contingent of young men dragging reluctant girlfriends to see for themselves what all the fuss is about – there's even a sprinkling of children. There's a palpable air of expectation in the foyer – it's quite clear many are here because they've heard the word; they know that this man is the last of a dying breed. It's ghoulish perhaps, but this may be their last opportunity to see him. As Michael Grade says, 'He is a throwback. He is eccentric, creative, original, funny. My wife is much younger than me and she always says, "I don't like that sort of thing," but I'd love to take her and sit her down and see whether he could get her to laugh. I'm determined to do that one day.'

In September 1990, Kate Saunders wrote a piece for the *Sunday Times* in which she declared that Dodd had suddenly, once again, become the darling of the trendies. She noted that at the charity preview of his Palladium show, *How Tickled I Am!* that 'there was a fair sprinkling of people with degrees and enormous Armani spectacles among the usual coach-party turnout of snotty kids and blue-haired old dears.' But Dodd had been around too long to be seduced by the mercurial blandishments of the nouvelle vague. 'People are celebrating comedy more than ever before,' he said, 'they argue about different kinds of comedians as if they were rival football teams.'

Doubtless he would be far more flattered by Victoria Wood's no-nonsense observation that, 'They go because he delivers.' She believes his appeal is timeless, and that his humour has escaped the ravages of time simply because it has always been so effective. 'I think Ken sort of stands out of time really. He's not old-fashioned and he's not modern. He's just really, really funny. He's very individual.'

Bill Tidy agrees: 'The image is of something that is old hat. But it's not. It's still new. And he keeps that image with the tremendous blast of power that he puts into it.'

In spite of his near octogenarian status, Dodd continues to collect admirers like trophies. In April 2004, for example, the *Daily Telegraph*'s Dominic Cavendish, a live Dodd virgin, eventually caught up with him at the Derngate Theatre in Northampton. He too was smitten by Dodd's exuberance and soon became a convert. 'There's an intense poignancy about Dodd's refusal to bow out at his allotted time, yet there's nothing desperate about his act,' he noted. 'This is no has-been clinging to past glories, but a comic who remains in full control of his considerable powers, firing gags out nineteen to the dozen. Most of them recycled, one suspects, but it's the way Dodd spins together his manic melange of random thoughts, "tattifilarious" nonsense and end-of-the-pier-show groaners that counts. Never one to get too topical, he does, nonetheless, get in a welcome dig at proud father Des O'Connor's expense: "He must get his pension and the baby's allowance at the same time." Then, with a wicked grin: "This time next year they'll both be waiting for their new teeth."'

Dodd's ability to appeal to a whole range of age groups is unquestionably another reason for his success. It's also something else that sets him apart. Peter Hepple is right when he says that unlike the modern generation of comedians who can only play to people the same age as themselves, Dodd can perform to any age group. 'He's very aware of various ages of audiences and children too.'

Professor Richard Wiseman thinks he can do this because he's created his own world – one that is completely divorced from reality and is therefore not tied to any age, sex or social group. It is also a world that we're keen to experience. We are more than willing to suspend our disbelief and meet Doddy halfway – we're complicit in the spell he's weaving. Thus we are perfectly happy to hear stories of his grandfather while being totally aware that this is an elderly man regaling us with such tales. 'Me Granddad,' he explains, 'stands with his back to the fire – we've had to have him swept. He goes to the Darby and Joan club. I don't know what he gets up to there, but he came home the other night with three notches on his walking stick.'

We're also open to the notion that this man knows our home patch as well as we do. In his act Dodd will often say that he was recently walking through 'the posh part of town' (in Watford's case, Cassiobury) and then ask an audience member where that is. After he has been told, he continues his story with: 'I was walking through Cassiobury yesterday, when . . .' Though his audience knows that he is simply making up the scenario for comic effect, such is the force of his personality that they are able to overlook this fact and join in with the deception.

According to Wiseman, by casting his net ever wider and embracing all types of material, Dodd has transcended the generation gap. 'Most comedians are talking about things in their lives which only appeal to a very limited circle. It's not even an age thing; it's a particular take on the world. Ken Dodd talks about certain things that aren't around quite so much nowadays, but a lot of it is just silly stories that have been around for a very long time. But the reason they have stood the test of time is because they work. They didn't just work in the 1950s, they work all the time.'

Unfortunately, television comedy producers don't see it that way. Perhaps due to the spending power of youth, the young is their target audience. Though older viewers may be thrown the odd *Last of the Summer Wine* series, generally speaking they are forced to leave the house and spend some money to get their fix of laughter. However, where Dodd is concerned, at least they're guaranteed a higher class of comedy. 'All I can see is a sea of white tops,' he tells them. 'I'm performing to 1,800 people waiting for a hip operation. Are you all from the same residential home? You'll be glad you spent your heating allowance on tonight's performance, I can tell you.'

Roy Hudd says, 'Comedy should appeal to everybody, but what they're trying to do now is make comedy appeal just to young people. So you've got someone like Ken who goes out there and does it all every bloody night somewhere. And if you look at his audience he does get young people – of course he does, because anybody who cares about seeing someone who is a master of their craft will go and see Doddy – but the majority of his audience are older. So the press don't think that is of interest to people. It is a sad comment.

'I go to Jongleurs in Battersea which has a lot of the new-style comics. Some of them are terrible and some of them are great. The thing is they all keep insisting, "We're different," but they're all alike! Someone like Ken has created this fantastic image, and there's no one like Ken Dodd any more. He's a throwback in that he goes out there, rolls up his sleeves, pulls up his knickers and boxes on.'

Dodd has always claimed that 'when you come out of a laughter show you should feel as if you've been through the wringer.' Professor Wiseman picks up on that and notes that the difference between seeing a 'normal' comedy set and a

Dodd show is that, with Dodd, you come out elated and buoyant. 'Most comedians attack the government or attack the situation in Iraq. Yes, it's funny: you come out of a comedy show and you feel good because you've laughed, but I wouldn't say you feel good about the world; you might feel worse about the world. Dodd is not like that: you come out feeling joyous.'

Despite his advancing years, the Liverpudlian funny man is still a sight to behold. Understandably less agile, and missing much of his formerly bountiful energy, he's still got the hair and more importantly, the eyes. But as Jimmy Perry says, he can no longer bend down. Arthritis has taken its toll; if he drops his tickling stick, there it stays. That said, he still gives younger rivals more than a run for their money. You're lucky if a modern comic's show lasts an hour these days – two hours into a Dodd performance and he has barely introduced himself to the front row.

Back in Watford, it was 8 p.m. as the band struck up 'Happiness', and a sober but familiar-suited Dodd made his first entrance; 11.30 p.m. marked the end of the first half. We finally bade tattybye to Dodd at 1.25 a.m. It's a long haul. And frankly, it's too long. Though the audience certainly can't complain about getting their money's worth, there are several rows of empty seats after the interval. Heaven alone knows how Dodd feels – we punters are cream crackered. But the duration of his show has now become a badge of honour. He continually taunts us. At 12.30 a.m. he'll say, 'Well, we've reached the halfway stage . . .' He reappears from the interval carrying a Thermos flask and a Tupperware box of sarnies – 'You mean you didn't bring any?' he'll tease.

It's undeniably funny for the most part, but one is left wishing that he had a strong director or producer who would rein him in, for there is an absolutely brilliant two-hour set in there. In a sense, by going on for so long (both in the show's duration and the number of years) he is, in many ways, devaluing what has gone before.

Part of the problem is the fact that Dodd is not as young as he was – despite his *Who's Who* entry, even he cannot hold back time indefinitely. Whereas he once exploded on stage, hitting the ground running and never relinquishing the pace, now he needs time to break off and recharge his batteries a little. Yet Dodd relies heavily on rhythm, pace and momentum. His is a high-energy act; a young man's act in fact. He can still work an audience up into a frenzy of hysteria, but when he breaks off to recover he now has to reboot them and start all over again.

'It's not like Oscar Wilde or Noël Coward. It's not rhetorical, genteel humour,' says Joe Riley. 'It's very physical . . . he could never be a sedentary act.'

But such is his asthma and emphysema that at first one has the distinct impression that he won't make the next hour, let alone the evening and early morning. But as he feeds off the faithful, his batteries are renewed, his stamina returns. Surely there is no better example of 'Dr Theatre' at work.

'The old-timers,' explains Denis Norden, 'used to call the stage "the green". I think maybe that's where the expression green room comes from. That was the slang word. And there was an expression called "Dr Green" which meant whatever ailment you had, this tremendous adrenalin charge that you get does wonders. One's known performers who stammer when they're not on stage, but immediately they go on their stammer disappears. There is definitely some kind of psychic interchange that takes place.'

It is therefore a quite remarkable sight to see Ken Dodd come alive before your very eyes. For most of the time you have to remind yourself that the man you are watching is on the brink of entering his ninth decade. Ironically, for a venue renowned for its acoustics – the music for both the *Star Wars* and *Lord of the Rings* trilogies was recorded at the Watford Colosseum – there is microphone trouble during this particular show, but Dodd takes it all in his stride.

It is also refreshing that he's not content to dwell on the past. He has a routine about TV commercials, but instead of trotting out gags about the Ovaltinies or the Oxo mum, he'll joke about being 'quoted happy', from a more recent advertising campaign.

'Doddy still talks about a world that doesn't exist any more or never did in quite that way,' says Barry Cryer. 'It's almost Dickensian, but cleverly injected with new stuff.'

'I think you have to keep changing the script every few years,' he told Alexandra Connor, 'otherwise you start to bore people. You have to keep changing and trying to stay ahead of the game.' That may be the case, but his is not exactly a brand new script. Michael Grade is nearer the mark when he remarks that Dodd 'refreshes his material; he sprinkles it with fresh stuff all the time, but essentially it's the same'.

In many ways, though, the Dodd show vintage 2004 is an amazingly old-fashioned evening. It has to be said that few could get away with offering such end-of-the-pier fare to younger audience members weaned on *Little Britain* and *Nighty Night*. The world has changed in fifty years and comedy has changed with it, except Dodd's unique brand. Many – Dodd included – mourn the passing of a simpler age. Although he is discreet about it, he is clearly no fan of what used to be called 'alternative comedy', and, as befits a man of a certain age, he has admitted to being a little unsure about the suitability of the type of humorous material favoured by some of the more modern comics. 'There was more "art" to comedy years ago,' he has said. 'Comics were masters of their craft. Today, there are precious few places to learn that craft and far too much emphasis on vulgar material. Sadly, swearing is being passed off as comedy. It has always been my belief that audiences expect to be entertained and relieved of their cares and worries for a few hours, and not insulted or embarrassed.'

Paradoxically, athough he never uses expletives in his act, Dodd is no stranger to swearing off-stage. The F-word emanating from the normally mild-mannered comedian has surprised many a journalist over the years. Equally, despite his predilection for McGill-like double entendres and phallic symbols, Dodd could almost be described as prudish in George Melly's view. When the two men were attending a boozy function for local Liverpool celebrities at the Grand National one year, Melly drunkenly retold a joke he had just heard to a gathering which included Dodd and Melly's stepdaughter. The gag ended with a deaf man misinterpreting the words 'Some country and western' as 'Some c**t from Preston', and though Melly had found it hilarious enough to repeat, Dodd was far less amused, suggesting it was rather inappropriate to mention in the presence of the former's stepdaughter. Thus Melly concedes that it was not a joke that Dodd was likely to tell. 'He's never dirty . . . just suggestive really.'

In the 1980s Dodd made his thoughts known on the state of comedy: 'Benny Hill's jokes are either denigrating about ugly women or put beautiful women in embarrassing situations. Then you've got the people whose material is sensational and vulgar, like Billy Connolly and Jim Davidson. I don't believe that's very clever either.' Despite this view, he did confess to John Stapleton that everyone laughs at what they're not supposed to, and he was happy to accept this as long as the humour doesn't cause offence, which he always aimed to avoid. 'Most of my jokes are based on the differences in life, incongruity, drollery; the stuff that comedians have laughed at for thousands of years. Slapstick humour. Animal humour. Whimsy. I love whimsy. My favourite book would be *The Wind in the Willows*. I love the Muppets.'

He's fully aware of the longevity of high-quality comedy.

'Fashions come and go, but good comedy is always good comedy,' he says. 'And laughter is the same thing it's always been. It's a noise that comes out of a hole in your head. Anywhere else and you know you're in trouble!'

Dodd's sentiments are echoed by David Nobbs. He too, misses the more subtle aspects of the comic art. 'When I saw Ken's act at Bournemouth there was one double entendre that stuck out, which to me illustrates how comedy has changed. He said: "An uncle of mine was a farmer. Well, only in a small way: he had a smallholding and a couple of acres." And they didn't roar with laughter instantly, they had to think about it. So he just looked at them while they thought about it until they laughed, then he almost nodded at them and thought, "We can proceed now."

'These days they don't *allude*; they *say*. It's all prick and balls now, and it's not as funny. There's no wit . . . and that was quite a witty piece of wordplay. We all had to think – that's the point. We all had to think together and then we laughed together. But that's live performance. I think that's a good example of what he did – involving the audience in the process.' It's that group experience again, which is simply impossible to achieve on the box.

Peter Hepple believes that Dodd is revered by many of the new generation of acts who were formerly known as alternative comics, because he does what they can't: 'He's a natural comedian and he's not actually preaching anything. I find that with most new comedians they have some sort of attitude. They work up an hour of material and go and perform it up at Edinburgh. And if they're successful there, their money will probably go up, but before long they're searching for other fields. I don't think Ken Dodd's ever searched for other fields.'

He's absolutely right: in an ever-changing world, Dodd has remained defiantly unchanged. Rather like his suit, he's been around long enough to become fashionable again.

Everything is cyclical: we appear to have bid a temporary farewell to politically-charged, message-heavy material and now thanks to the likes of Vic Reeves, Bob Mortimer and Harry Hill, silliness has become flavour of the month again. When they were on the lookout for new comedy writers, Steve Coogan and Henry Normal said that they were not looking for gag writers, but for people who created new worlds and new mythologies. Maybe it's time for those BBC Four documentary makers to take a closer look at Ken Dodd. Surely it's time to secure his place among the greats?

In the meantime, Dodd still tours the country, plying his unique trade. Punt thinks that seeing Dodd's act nowadays requires you to enter into the spirit of it. 'There's no point in going to see someone like Ken Dodd unless you're willing to be part of it.'

Griff Rhys Jones agrees. He picks up on Dodd's point about comedy having become a bit like a football team, 'where people take sides and take attitudes to it, and feel that things are important because they represent an ethos or they come from a tribe or something. I think Ken Dodd transcends all that, because he's so innocent. He's just there to be wildly funny, and if you're too sophisticated to find him funny then God help you!'

But Punt thinks Dodd has got himself into a position where he is now almost a one-man theme park. 'If I went to see Ken Dodd I would be going to see a sort of living example of variety theatre. He seems to have resigned himself to that about twenty years ago and thought, "This is what I do, this is what I like doing."'

And in essence, he's correct. 'My favourite place is on the theatre stage,' Dodd has often maintained. 'After fifty gloriously happy years I still enjoy the buzz of the live venue and a packed audience laughing their heads off. I'm lucky because I never tire of entertaining people. I think I've only ever had one day off in my entire career and that was suspected pneumonia. I was back on stage the next night with a mustard patch on my chest. The doctor insisted I wear it, but all the stage hands kept rubbing their ham sandwiches on it, so it had to go.'

Actress Alison Steadman recently revealed that seeing Dodd at the Liverpool Royal Court about twenty years ago was the best live event she'd ever attended. 'He had the worst cold ever and could hardly speak, but that didn't stop him. I thought I was going to die laughing that night.' Most performers, she says, would have done the show and got home as quickly as possible. 'Not Ken. He is so at home with his audience. I think too, performing in his home town, a place he loves so much, the audience feel safe and confident in his hands. Knowing that, they sit back and enjoy themselves. The howls of recognition from us that night were heart-warming.

'In Liverpool, the people have many phrases that are unique to the town. It creates a terrific bond between people when they are all laughing at themselves, but feeling a sense of belonging and camaraderie. One joke to illustrate: "There was this fella working down the docks . . . he was known as the crab – he got this name 'cos he was always going to the boss and saying, 'Can I go home early tonight, please – the nipper's bad.'" That joke in Ken's hands when an audience is really warmed up is great. The jokes, as you know, come thick and fast, and I remember feeling exhausted, but hoping he would just go on and on.'

When *Face to Face* interrogator John Freeman asked Tony Hancock why he continued to work when he'd got enough money to turn it all in, Hancock replied, 'Money is of no account in this. I do it because it absolutely fascinates me, because I love it and it's my entire life.' And the same – although not perhaps entirely agreeing with the financial sentiments – could be said of Dodd. 'We do it,' he once said rather cryptically, 'because that is what we do. We do it because that is what we are.'

Comedy is quite simply Dodd's life. Back in 1967, for example, with the surprising support of Prince Philip, he suggested launching the first British Laughter Week, to begin on 10 July. In defence of his notion he told *Morning Star* readers: 'Laughter and happiness are the greatest of all the tonics, and if a week of nonsense and fun can be organized on a national scale I'm sure that many lives could be brightened. After all, I believe that one of the best quotations I've ever heard is from Chamfort, which goes: "The most utterly lost of all days is that on which you have not once laughed."'

Certainly, he still loves the feeling that performing comedy to an eager audience gives him. 'It's this delicious fear that grips you,' Dodd told *Sunday Times* journalist Kate Saunders. 'Being up there alone makes you feel like a cross between a vicar and a gladiator. It's lovely.'

Joe Riley thinks that Ken Dodd gets his reward from hands clapping. 'The drug for him is the public response – that's why he can't stop working. He's a compulsive workaholic. Not because he needs the money . . . but because he needs the adrenalin and the love. That's his fix.'

Naturally, the word 'retirement' is anathema to Dodd. Perish the thought. As George Melly says: 'I think he'll retire as he falls backward into the grave.' But Mike Craig, for one, thinks that perhaps he should call it a day. 'I'd like to see him pack it in while he's at the top, but he won't.'

He's right. It's never going to happen. In fact Dodd seems highly suspicious of people who raise the subject of 'his' retirement, and has suggested that perhaps they're hinting at something. 'People retire when they stop doing the things they don't want to do and start doing the things they do want to do,' says Dodd. 'And I'm doing what I do want to do. I'm a gigster: I do one-night stands and I go around all the different theatres, and I draw up outside and people say, "Hello Ken." That's very nice. It's lovely to know that people remember you and want to be friendly to you.'

According to Joe Riley, Dodd can be quite conventional in private. 'Ken will have a normal time with you. He doesn't feel obliged in company to keep telling jokes. You do get comedians who can't stop being comedians. They think if they stop trying to be funny then the halo will slip. Ken Dodd will let the halo slip any time and just be Ken Dodd.'

Dodd, says Riley, remains a very private man to the extent that he walks around Liverpool city centre in disguise; generally 'with a big woolly hat on and his coat collar turned up hoping that nobody will recognize him'. On occasions when the two men have arranged to meet for a drink, on entering the bar Riley has to scan the room for the anonymously dressed comedian. 'I'll see a man in a corner wearing glasses and an overcoat and a tweed hat like you'd find on the pheasant-shooting moors. I'd know that under all that is Ken Dodd, but you'd never know if you were just going in. And then he'll shuffle off into a corner to have a drink with you – he doesn't hold court.'

It's true to say that the 'ordinariness' has never left Dodd. He seems untouched by the glitz of showbiz – he's still very much a bloke from Knotty Ash. 'He's a clean comedian on stage,' continues Riley, 'but he can eff and blind with the best of them off stage about a situation or a deal or a place or anything he doesn't approve of. In other words, the idea of him permanently being goofy with his teeth stuck out, his hair stuck up and just being sort of zany is wrong. It's also wrong to think, as is the case with many comedians I've met, that they're always funny and they're always happy. They tend to be among the more serious and depressed people I've ever known really.

'Ken Dodd has a very serious streak: he's very interested

in religion, philosophy and things, and is quite well read. He's certainly no fool and takes life seriously. A religious man, and a man who has great respect still for the memory of his parents, he regards the house he lives in and everything he does as being in stewardship of them. Every time he sees me he says, "There's nothing like your mum."'

While that might be an odd thing for a man of a mature age to say, Riley points out that it's because 'he hasn't got a family of his own.'

Riley has also seen another side of Dodd, a side he found enormously endearing – Dodd the starstruck fan. 'I remember once meeting with him a well-known classical musician of whom he was in awe. Normally with Ken Dodd everyone's going up to him and saying, "Oh Doddy! Oh Doddy!" He's the centre of attention. But if he met anyone who was the very best at what they did with something that he liked, then he was like a little boy himself. He suddenly became the fan and you saw the man who was always on the receiving end of other people's praise and adulation become the man in awe of the other artists for whom he has a great respect.'

While recognizing the paradoxes that make up Dodd's character, Riley admits that the comedian 'is somebody I respect immensely'.

Michael Billington had the luxury of ending his book by posing a question about what Dodd might do next. That was in the late 1970s, when Dodd was still a relatively young and healthy man. Now, however, it's difficult to imagine what he will do or where he will go . . . apart from continuing to do what he does now for as long as he possibly can. I'm sure the thought of what nasty surprises age might have up her sleeve fills his waking hours with worry. Working is, after all, his life, and in many ways his personal life was sacrificed on the altar of show-business success; indeed there was even 'no time' for him to marry.

Whether he could still manage that one-off Palladium appearance Michael Grade has been hoping for is open to conjecture. Peter Hepple, meanwhile, has always harboured a desire to see him play somewhere like Glyndebourne – 'Just because I think he would go as well there as he does anywhere else.' He also thinks he would also be quite at home at Shakespeare's Globe. I'd like to see him play the Glastonbury Festival.

As for television, Steve Punt sees him as perhaps finding a niche as a regular guest on a comedy programme in the same way that Ben Elton had Ronnie Corbett in a fixed slot on his stand-up show. The problem, Punt concedes, is Dodd's reputation for overrunning. A producer would say he doesn't know what five minutes means. That said, the *Daily Express* reported in early 2005 that Granada TV was keen to lure Dodd into appearing for a cameo in *Coronation Street*. 'We had Peter Kay last year,' a spokesman said, 'and we know Ken is a massive fan of the show. We're working out how we can work him in but, trust me, we will.'

On the subject of Dodd's continued longevity, Peter Hepple raises a terrifying prospect concerning the issue of potential memory loss, which has no doubt also crossed Dodd's mind in recent years. 'He has material for every occasion and what's more he has the ability to recollect it. I don't know what will happen when his memory goes . . .' Many of us fear the loss of our mental prowess as we get older, but Dodd must be more anxious about this possibility than most. Writing in *The Times* in January 2005, Giles Coren opined that he thought that there was nothing more depressing than a dead comedian. He went on to say that even worse was those who die on the stage only to have friends declare, "It's what he would have wanted."'

'Falling to your knees at sixty and gasping for air in front of 3,000 people you've never met, then rolling over and crapping the pants of your dinner suit while they all fall about laughing and the lights go dim – I can't see how anyone would want that.' When you put it like that he has a point, but without getting too morbid, it is likely that this really is the way Dodd would like to go. Far more horrific for him would be to spend his twilight years fading into obscurity.

It's hard to say what Dodd's legacy will be. The Great British Public may be loyal, but it has a notoriously short memory. For example, in a 2004 poll of favourite comedians for Channel Five and the 2005 comedians' comedian poll for Channel Four (in which Dodd came thirty-seventh), Frankie Howerd was conspicuous by his absence. Will Dodd suffer the same fate after his death? Will he end up a footnote in the history of comedy? It's monstrously unfair but unfortunately, due to his shortcomings in terms of his lack of television success, future audiences are likely to be mystified by Dodd's popularity. Theatre work is ephemeral and the human memory selective. Whereas the comic reputations of the Two Ronnies and Morecambe and Wise are safe, the same cannot be said of Dodd. No doubt future students of comedy will look at videotapes or DVDs of Ken Dodd's stand-up shows and, rather like a whole raft of TV viewers today, wonder what all the fuss was about.

There is, too, the perception held by many that somehow comedy is less important than tragedy. Woody Allen famously said that he wanted to eschew comedy in favour of drama so that he could 'eat at the adult table'. When Billington spoke of Dodd in the same breath as Laurence Olivier and Paul Scofield, he was not being fanciful. They each display the same professionalism, the same commitment, the same command of an audience, and in many ways the same acting skills – it's just that Dodd has the added pressure of having to be funny. Whereas there are many ways to interpret and appreciate a straight play, a comedian is obliged to deliver laughs. No matter how clever he is, how technically proficient, how dazzlingly brilliant, or even how lovable he is, if the audience doesn't laugh he must ultimately be deemed a failure. There are no grey areas in comedy, and audiences are less inclined to be generous. If a play doesn't quite hit the spot we may just shrug our shoulders, but if a comedian fails to make us laugh we feel almost personally affronted.

It is unlikely, however, that Dodd will worry about his legacy. Though we know how flattered he is to be the darling of the intelligentsia, generally he seems remarkably insouciant about such matters. 'He believes, like a lot of performers, that what he does out there should do the talking,' says Roy Hudd. 'Rather than people heaping praise on him, he'd rather get out there and do it.'

Hudd is also undoubtedly right when he says that he doesn't think Dodd is interested in books being written about him, but he is also perplexed by the lack of appreciation that comics in general receive. Like popular music-hall performers from days gone by, whose histories have been inadequately recorded, he feels that comedians are equally overlooked, and makes the valid point that it is only after they die that interest grows in their past lives and achievements. 'They tend to think that people are much more important once they've snuffed it, which is absolutely bloody ludicrous.'

It's true that many sneer at what is perceived as low comedy. The critics believe that it's easy; that anyone can do it. But how wrong they are. Good popular comics are – and always have been – as rare as hen's teeth. It's a remarkably specialized discipline. Many, for example, attempted to emulate the *Carry On* films because they thought the laughs were easy laughs, but no one succeeded. As anyone who has witnessed a really bad pantomime or a truly execrable sitcom can attest, there is great artistry in getting 'low comedy' right. In many ways there is as much skill in playing Widow Twankey as there is in playing King Lear. Like most things, making it look easy is not the same as it actually *being* easy. That's the skill. Indeed, if you get really, *really* good at it, therein lies true genius.

Sadly, a great deal of long-term eminence is down to television. In the same way that a brilliant politician will be sidelined because he lacks presence on the box, a brilliant comic can be ignored because he is not seen in his element, i.e., on stage. Television not only keeps a performer in the public eye, but crucially it brings him into the orbit of the younger generation. As Wiseman observes, you're only going to be a comedy great if the up-and-coming generation thinks you are. 'And although Ken Dodd is clearly a very intelligent man,' he says, 'I wonder whether his humour is viewed as being less sophisticated? If it works the same as magic it's not so much what you do as who you know, and I don't know how well integrated Ken Dodd is into the comedy scene.'

That said, Dodd's contribution to the comic cannon has not been completely overlooked. At the 1993 British Comedy Awards ceremony (made infamous following the unfortunate remark made by Julian Clary about the former Chancellor of the Exchequer, Norman Lamont), Dodd received the Top Variety Entertainer and Lifetime Achievement Awards, and keeping true to his comedy roots, he was presented with his esteemed prizes during a live performance on stage in Manchester.

In November 2003, at Croydon's Fairfield Halls, Dodd received the British Comedy Society's first Living Legend Award. In describing the recipient of the inaugural prize, the society's chairman, Gareth Hughes, remarked: 'The term "genius" is seriously overused, but in the case of Ken Dodd it is deserved.' The crystal award was presented by a fellow

Liverpudlian, Cilla Black, who said of him: 'I love him. He is one of those very rare people who you only have to look at to feel happy.'

Nonetheless his disappearance from our TV screens has made an impact. Steve Punt remembers that when he first saw Ken Dodd on television at the age of ten, the expansion of Dodd's profile was down to the impersonator Mike Yarwood, whose imitations had conveyed the comedian's unique characteristics to a much wider audience. 'Mike Yarwood would always be doing him long after Ken Dodd was actually on telly. It still happens: if you've got an impression that goes down well it can outlast the actual performer sometimes.'

It's this lack of exposure that is responsible for his being cheated of cult status among the younger generation, Punt thinks, as so few young people have ever seen him live. 'Ultimately you would have to be very into comedy and even then you'd only know him quoted as an influence because you would never have actually seen him. The other more technical reason is that he does a lot of puns, and puns seem very archaic now, unless you make them your whole speciality like Tim Vine. Harry Hill does a lot of puns, but he's the one person you might think of as slightly Dodd-like in a way. He's a kind of post-modern throwback – he's doing it knowingly.'

By Christmas 2004 it seemed that the years were finally catching up on Dodd. Indeed after seeing recent photos of the comedian, Joe Riley thought that he was seriously ill. 'He's a seventy-eight-year-old man who's not very well these days. If you look at him he looks terrible. There was a picture of him in the paper the other day, and he looked like he'd been in a concentration camp: the weight's fallen off him and he looked like a screaming skull. I've known him all these years and I can tell he doesn't look like he used to look.'

Despite Riley's observations, Dodd's tour dates have continued to fill his diary well into 2007. Although he had to cancel a few performances due to ill health in early 2005 his determination to press on remains undiminished. Rather like his show's duration, his obstinate ebullience is almost a point of principle now. The thing about Dodd is that he never gives in. It's us, the audience, who has to give in. When asked what he'd like his epitaph to be, Dodd answered: 'He made us laugh. He gave us a laugh. He did his best.' Few would argue with that.

However, it's probably best left to his friend Bob Monkhouse to sum up the emotional yet austere, confident yet insecure, mean yet generous, studious yet instinctive, private yet public, extraordinary yet ordinary paradox that is Ken Dodd. As Monkhouse told viewers of his two-part documentary series *Behind the Laughter*:

> I've talked about performers who really don't want to go on stage themselves, they will send a character on stage, a persona they've invented that they can project on stage – they'd rather hide behind that. Or they'll wear a disguise, a funny costume. What you can say of Ken Dodd is that his entire presentation is a bit of a disguise. So Doddy sends out a madman on the stage, a wonderful, organized, clever, spinning Dervish of a madman that he has invested with life. And he animates him and he keeps him alive as long as it gives him pleasure and the audience is laughing and he'll make them laugh longer than they ever expected. When he comes off I think he dies a little death and becomes once again the ordinary bloke that Kenneth Dodd is in real life. And he's not as exciting a person like the chap on stage, he's a quieter man – he's just as sweetly natured – but I think he's waiting to go back on. I think everything off stage is an interval.

This duality remains the most fascinating aspect of Dodd's personality. The difference between the Ken Dodd of Thomas

Lane – the contemplative man who watches satellite TV into the small hours and enjoys nothing more than a flutter on the gee-gees – is as far removed from the exotic, wild-haired loon that we know as Barry Humphries is from Dame Edna. Just because he works under his own name and addresses us directly we forget that that creation is as much a feat of acting as Olivier's Hamlet or June Brown's Dot Cotton. It seems to me that many comedians seek to create a character that represents what they yearn to be or weave a world that is a distortion of their ideal. The self-loathing Frankie Howerd, for example, created a leering, lascivious beacon of heterosexuality; a twinkle-eyed Benny Hill became the scourge of vacuous, mini-skirted dolly birds; and in his movies, Woody Allen is still the unlikely magnet for some of the most beautiful young women on the planet. Dodd, meanwhile, seems to have spent his professional life attempting to recapture those sepia-tinted, halcyon days of his youth.

It's difficult to pin down Dodd. Just as we form an opinion – either pro or anti – we learn something else that blasts that conception out of the water. We may know the incidents of his life and what some of his friends and colleagues think of him, but few – very few – people *really* know Ken Dodd. He's far too complex and secretive a man to show his hand to anyone – with a few still-rankling exceptions, we know what he wants us to know. The only person who really knows Dodd is Dodd himself.

Despite his strange attitude to money, power and relationships, what shines through is his humanity. Though he may have flaws and quirks of personality, ultimately I think he is a decent, honest man; paradoxically, a man of great generosity; a man who has given unfathomable pleasure to millions. I'm in full support of Michael Grade, whose summary of Ken Dodd is doubtless echoed by his legions of loyal fans:

'I really think he's a genius; a comic legend.'

Select Bibliography

Andrews, Nigel and others, *British Comedy Greats* (Cassell Illustrated, London, 2003)

Billington, Michael, *How Tickled I Am* (Elm Tree Books, London, 1977)

Brandwood, Neil, *Victoria Wood* (Virgin Books, London, 2003)

Davies, Russell (ed.), *The Kenneth Williams Diaries* (HarperCollins, London, 1994)

Double, Oliver, *Stand Up!* (Methuen, London, 1997)

Fisher, John, *A Funny Way to be a Hero* (Frederick Muller, London, 1973)

Hind, John, *The Comic Inquisition* (Virgin Books, London, 1991)

I'm Sorry I Haven't A Clue: The Official Limerick Collection (Orion, London, 1999)

Lewisohn, Mark, *Radio Times Guide to TV Comedy* (BBC Books, London, 2003)

Midwinter, Eric, *Make 'Em Laugh* (Allen & Unwin, London, 1979)

Smith, Gus, *Ken Dodd: Laughter and Tears* (W. H. Allen & Co., London, 1989)

Sykes, Eric, *Eric Sykes's Comedy Heroes* (Virgin Books, London, 2004)

Discography and Videos

1969 With You Beside Me / More Than Ever Now (*Come Prima*)
1969 Tears Won't Wash Away My Heartache / How Can I Say I'm Sorry?
1969 Sweet Memories / Don't Say A Word
1970 *Azzurro* (Blue Skies) / Time Slips Away
1970 Broken Hearted / Maybe Because Of You
1971 When Love Comes Round Again (*Arca Di Noe*) / One Thousand Nights
1971 This Is Our Dance / There Are Secrets
1972 Because Of You (*Il Tuo Sorriso*) / A Pink And Pleasant Land
1972 Those Golden Days / Just Out Of Reach (Of My Two Empty Arms)
1975 Think Of Me (Wherever You Are) / Togetherness
1976 All My Love / Homecoming
1976 I'll Never Forget You / Road To Happiness
1981 Hold My Hand / Where Did The Good Times Go?
1984 Little Words / In The Land Of My Dreams
1987 Tears / The River
1987 When A Child Is Born / Doddy's Diddy Party Medley: Doddy's Diddy Party

7-INCH EXTENDED-PLAY VINYLS

1960 ***Love Is Like A Violin*:** Love Is Like A Violin (*Mon Coeur Est Un Violon*); Dream That I Love You; Jealous Of You; Once In Every Lifetime; The Treasure In My Heart; Just For A While
1963 ***Beautiful Dreamer*:** Beautiful Dreamer; Romantica; Green Leaves Of Summer; I'm Always Chasing Rainbows
1964 ***Still*:** Still; Remember I Love You; Eight By Ten; Come To Me
1964 ***Happiness*:** Happiness; All My Life; Please Don't Talk About Me When I'm Gone; Fools Rush In
1965 ***Doddy And The Diddymen*:** Doddy And The Diddymen Make A Record; Old Macdonald Had A Farm; Wee Cooper O' Fife; Where's Me Shirt?; Tatty Bye
1967 ***Diddyness*:** The Ballad Of Knotty Ash; The Song Of The Diddymen; The Nikky-Nokky-Noo Song; Diddycombe Fair
1968 ***Doddy's Diddy Party*** (with the Diddymen): Doddy's Diddy Party; The Washboard King Of The Dixie Jazz Band; How'ya Diddling?; The Diddly-Doo Parade

Discography and Videos

1962   *Presenting Ken Dodd*: LP – I'm Always Chasing Rainbows;
You Brought A New Kind Of Love To Me; The Wonder Of
You; Thank Heaven For Little Girls (*Gigi*); Beautiful
Dreamer; Please Don't Talk About Me When I'm Gone; Fools
Rush In; Romantica; True Love; My Heart Tells Me; The
More I See You; Green Leaves Of Summer

1964   *16 Hit Singles*: LP and laser disc – Eight By Ten; Happiness;
Love Is Like A Violin (*Mon Coeur Est Un Violon*); Let Me
Cry On Your Shoulder; Wherever You Are; The River (*Le
Colline Sono In Fiore*); Tears; Tristesse; When Love Comes
Round Again (*Arca Di Noe*); Tears Won't Wash Away These
Heartaches; Still; *Un Fiore*; Just Out Of Reach (Of My Two
Empty Arms); Brokenhearted; Promises; So Deep Is The Night

1965   *Tears Of Happiness*: LP – I Don't Know Why I Love You (I
Just Do); More Than Ever (*Come Prima*); Say; With All My
Heart; My Thanks To You; The Very Thought Of You; My
Wonderful One; Younger Than Springtime (*South Pacific*);
The Story Of A Starry Night; This Year's Lovers; Tears Of
Happiness; I'll Be Seeing You

1966   *For Someone Special*: LP and cassette – For Someone Special;
I'd Do Anything; If I Had My Way; Happy Days And Lonely
Nights; I Can't Begin To Tell You; True; The Sum Of One;
Only You (And You Alone); It's A Funny Old World; If You
Love Me; A House With No Windows; Come Back My Love
(*Si Tu Reviens*); Can I Forget You; It's No Secret

1966   *Hits For Now And Always*: LP and cassette – Happiness; Still;
Remember I Love You; No One's Listening; One Rose;
Dreams; So Deep Is The Night; The River (*Le Colline Sono In
Fiore*); Eight By Ten; Someone Like You; Island Of Blue; Have
I Told You Lately That I Love You?; The One I Love Belongs
To Somebody Else; Now And Always

1967   *Ken Dodd & The Diddymen*: LP – Doddy And The Diddymen
Make A Record; Old Macdonald Had A Farm; Wee Cooper O'
Fife; Where's Me Shirt?; The Nikky-Nokky-Noo Song;
Diddycombe Fair; The Song Of The Diddymen; The Ballad Of
Knotty Ash; Doddy's Diddy Party; The Washboard King Of The
Dixie Jazz Band; How'ya Diddling?; The Diddly-Doo Parade

Ken Dodd

1967   *I'm Always Chasing Rainbows*: LP and cassette – I'm Always Chasing Rainbows; You Brought A New Kind Of Love To Me; I'd Do Anything (*Oliver*); Happy Days And Lonely Nights; Beautiful Dreamer; My Heart Tells Me; Only You (And You Alone); If You Love Me (I Won't Care); A House With No Windows; Come Back My Love (*Si Tu Reviens*); Can I Forget You?; It's No Secret

1967   *Somewhere My Love* (also issued as *I Wish You Love*): LP and cassette (later issued on CD) – You Were Meant For Me; What'll I Do; They Didn't Believe Me; When There Was You; As Time Goes By; Somewhere My Love; Time Goes Slowly; Among My Souvenirs; How Long Is Forever; Every Second, Every Minute; Let The Rest Of The World Go By; I Wish You Love

1968   *Don't Let Tonight Ever End*: LP and cassette – Don't Let Tonight Ever End; Back In Your Own Backyard; Every Little Tear; I'll Be Around; I Can't Hold Back My Tears; I Only Live To Love You; How Lucky You Are; Because I Love You; World Of Love; My Life; You Wanted Someone To Play With; Another Time, Another Place; Dancing With Tears In My Eyes

1970   *I'll Find A Way*: LP and cassette – Love Is Like A Violin (*Mon Coeur Est Un Violon*); What A Wonderful World; If I Should Lose; The Morning; Only A Rose (*The Vagabond King*); Only You (And You Alone); For Someone Special; I'll Find A Way; Last Mile Home; Moonlight *Clair De Lune*; How Wonderful To Know; Once In A While; Sweet Memories

1970   *Tears*: LP and cassette – Tears; Only A Rose (*The Vagabond King*); How Wonderful To Know; I'll Find A Way; Moonlight *Clair De Lune*; Only You (And You Alone); What A Wonderful World; Happy Days And Lonely Nights; For Someone Special; If I Should Lose; Sweet Memories; Last Mile Home

1971   *Brokenhearted*: LP and cassette – Once Upon A Time; It's Impossible; I Will Wait For You (*The Umbrellas Of Cherbourg*); Morning Please Don't Come; (They Long To Be) Close To You; I Have Dreamed (*The King And I*); If I Give My Heart To You; Meditation (*Meditaçao*); The Letter; Snowbird; A Pink And Pleasant Land; Brokenhearted

1971   *With Love In Mind*: LP and cassette – Five Minutes To Sadness; Try To Remember; It's All In The Game; The Long

And Winding Road; Mystifyin'; My Way Of Life; Nearest
Thing To Love; Who Can I Turn To? (*The Roar Of The
Greasepaint*); When I Fall In Love; Both Sides Now; Sunrise,
Sunset (*Fiddler On The Roof*)

1973 *Just Out Of Reach*: LP and cassette – Just Out Of Reach (Of
My Two Empty Arms); This Nearly Was Mine (*South Pacific*);
Love Is Like A Comedy; When Love Comes Round Again
(*Arca Di Noe*); Stars Will Remember; Broken Wings; And I
Love Her; There Are Secrets; Those Golden Days; This I Find
Is Beautiful; One Thousand Nights; Help Me Make It
Through The Night

1974 *The Very Best Of Ken Dodd*: LP and cassette – Happiness;
Love Is Like A Violin (*Mon Coeur Est Un Violon*);
Somewhere My Love (*Dr Zhivago*); The River (*Le Colline
Sono In Fiore*); There Are Secrets; Eight By Ten; Those
Golden Days; *Azzurro* (Blue Skies); Still; Brokenhearted; This
Is Our Dance; When Love Comes Round Again (*Arca Di
Noe*); A Pink And Pleasant Land; Tears

1976 *Love Together*: LP and cassette – May You Always; Because
You Know; Together; She; Until It's Time For You To Go;
Road To Happiness; Some Day (You'll Want Me To Want
You); *Plaisirs Demodes*; My Little Corner Of The World; *Y
Viva Espana*; *Quando Caliente El Sol*; For All We Know

1970s *The Ken Dodd Collection*: LP and cassette (CD issued in
2000) – Happiness; Promises; Tears; Eight By Ten; Still; So
Deep Is The Night; The River (*Le Colline Sono In Fiore*);
Love Is Like A Violin (*Mon Coeur Est Un Violon*); The Very
Thought Of You; Let Me Cry On Your Shoulder; She; The
Old Fashioned Way; Somewhere My Love; Tears Won't Wash
Away These Heartaches; Broken Hearted; When Love Comes
Around Again; Just Out Of Reach; (Think Of Me) Wherever
You Are; What A Wonderful World; As Time Goes By; I Wish
You Love; For All We Know

1970s *The Very Best Of Ken Dodd*: LP (undated) – Those Golden
Days; *Azzurro* (Blue Skies); Brokenhearted; Still; When Love
Comes Round Again (*Arca Di Noe*); Tears; A Pink And
Pleasant Land; The River (*Le Colline Sono In Fiore*); Eight
By Ten; This Is Our Dance; There Are Secrets; Lara's Theme
(*Dr Zhivago*); Love Is Like A Violin (*Mon Coeur Est Un
Violon*); Happiness

Ken Dodd

1980 **20 Golden Greats Of Ken Dodd**: LP – It Is No Secret; Matchstalk Men And Matchstalk Cats And Dogs; Brokenhearted; Just Out Of Reach (Of My Two Empty Arms); You're My Best Friend; Eight By Ten; Love Is Like A Violin (*Mon Coeur Est Un Violon*); Tristesse; Happiness; The River (*Le Colline Sono In Fiore*); Still (Geoff Love); Let Me Cry On Your Shoulder (Geoff Love); When Love Comes Round Again (*Arca Di Noe*); Wherever You Are; Pianissimo; Tears; Tears Won't Wash Away These Heartaches; More Than Love; Think Of Me; So Deep Is The Night

1981 **Ken Dodd**: Cassette (CD issued in 1991) – Brokenhearted; Eight By Ten; Try To Remember; Beautiful Dreamer; Love Is Like A Violin (*Mon Coeur Est Un Violon*); The Story Of A Starry Night; Love Me With All Your Heart; Happiness; Still; The Old Fashioned Way; Tears; Think Of Me; The River (*Le Colline Sono In Fiore*); She; Tears Won't Wash Away These Heartaches; Somewhere My Love; What A Wonderful World; So Deep Is The Night; When Love Comes Round Again (*Arca Di Noe*); Until It's Time For You To Go; The Very Thought Of You; Just Out Of Reach
CD bonus tracks: Only You (And You Alone); I Can't Begin To Tell You

1981 **More Than Ever**: LP and cassette – If I Had My Way; The River (*Le Colline Sono In Fiore*); Tristesse; Sunrise, Sunset (*Fiddler On The Roof*); I Wonder Who's Kissing Her Now; Someone Like You; I'll Be Seeing You; I Don't Know Why; Younger Than Springtime (*South Pacific*); Eight By Ten; Dancing With Tears In My Eye; The Story Of A Starry Night; She; The One I Love; The Very Thought Of You; More Than Ever (*Come Prima*); *Plaisirs Demodes*; Still; Try To Remember

1986 **His Greatest Hits**: Cassette and CD – I Wish You Love; Love Is Like A Violin (*Mon Coeur Est Un Violon*); Eight By Ten; They Didn't Believe Me; As Time Goes By; More Than Ever (*Come Prima*); So Deep Is The Night; Still; She; The Old Fashioned Way; For All We Know; What A Wonderful World; Happy Days And Lonely Nights; Just Out Of Reach (Of My Two Empty Arms); Let Me Cry On Your Shoulder; Promises
CD bonus tracks: Tears; Brokenhearted; Somewhere My Love; Happiness; The River (*Le Colline Sono In Fiore*)

Discography and Videos

1987   ***Ken Dodd's Palace Of Laughter***: Double cassette – Broadcasts
        which include the following items sung by Ken Dodd: Love Is
        Like A Violin (*Mon Coeur Est Un Violon*); Don't Dilly Dally
        On The Way; Sabre Dance; The Sound Of Music; *La
        Marseillaise*

1988   ***Greatest Hits***: Cassette and CD – Happiness; Love Is Like A
        Violin (*Mon Coeur Est Un Violon*); Somewhere My Love (*Dr
        Zhivago*); The River (*Le Colline Sono In Fiore*); Eight By Ten;
        They Didn't Believe Me; As Time Goes By; I Wish You Love;
        More Than Ever (*Come Prima*); So Deep Is The Night; Tears;
        Still; Broken Hearted; She; The Old Fashioned Way; For All
        We Know; What A Wonderful World; Happy Days And
        Lonely Nights; Just Out Of Reach (Of My Two Empty Arms);
        Let Me Cry On Your Shoulder; Promises

1989   ***Tears & Happiness***: LP, cassette and CD – Tears;
        Brokenhearted; Happiness; Eight By Ten; Beautiful Dreamer;
        Tears Won't Wash Away Your Heartache; So Deep Is The
        Night; The Very Thought Of You; Just Out Of Reach (Of My
        Two Empty Arms); More Than Love; The Story Of A Starry
        Night; Promises; Still; Think Of Me; When Love Comes
        Round Again (*Arca Di Noe*); The River (*Le Colline Sono In
        Fiore*); Love Is Like A Violin (*Mon Coeur Est Un Violon*); It's
        Love; Let Me Cry On Your Shoulder; *Come Prima*

1994   ***The Ken Dodd Show***: Cassette – Broadcasts of performances
        from various venues which include the following items sung
        by Ken Dodd: Love Is Like A Violin (*Mon Coeur Est Un
        Violon*); Leap Up And Down; *La Marseillaise*; Maigret;
        Morning Please Don't Come; Love Me With All Your Heart;
        Some Day (You'll Want Me To Want You)

1994   ***The Ken Dodd Show***: Cassette – Four vintage radio shows,
        from broadcasts on BBC Radio Two between 1972 and 1975

2000   ***The Very Best Of Ken Dodd Vol. 1***: CD and cassette – one live
        performance

2001   ***Presenting Ken Dodd / Hits For Now And Always***: CD –
        tracks as for the single LPs

2001   ***Happiness: The Very Best Of Ken Dodd***: CD and cassette –
        Happiness; Still; Eight By Ten; Tears; So Deep Is The Night;
        The River (*Le Colline Sono In Fiore*); Try To Remember;
        The Very Thought Of You; Promises; Until It's Time For
        You To Go; More Than Love; For All We Know; What A

Wonderful World; It's Love; Let Me Cry On Your Shoulder; Tears Won't Wash Away My Heartache; Only You (And You Alone); Somewhere My Love (*Dr Zhivago*); She; The Old Fashioned Way; Brokenhearted; When Love Comes Round Again (*Arca Di Noe*); Just Out Of Reach (Of My Two Empty Arms); Think Of Me (Wherever You Are)

2003   *The Very Best Of Ken Dodd Vol. 2:* CD and cassette – One live performance

VIDEO CASSETTES AND DVDs CHRONOLOGICALLY

1995   *An Audience With Ken Dodd:* VHS (DVD issued in 2001) – One live performance telling jokes and taking questions from celebrities

1999   *Ken Dodd – Live Laughter Tour:* VHS – One 100-minute live performance from his 1996 tour

2002   *Another Audience With Ken Dodd:* VHS and DVD – One live performance telling jokes and taking questions from celebrities

APPEARANCES IN COMPILATION VINYL AND CD ALBUMS CHRONOLOGICALLY

1965   *Hits For Now And Always:* LP – Eight By Ten; Happiness; Tristesse; No One's Listening; The River (*Le Colline Sono In Fiore*)

1966   *Stars Charity Fantasias:* LP – Happiness

1967   *20 All-Time Vocal Chartbusters:* LP – Happiness

1972   *20 Original Chart Hits:* LP – Just Out Of Reach

1976   *Hit Kaleidoscope:* LP – Tears; Think Of Me (Wherever You Are)

1970s   *20 Golden Weepies:* LP – Brokenhearted

1982   *The Million Sellers Collection:* LP – Tears

1984   *20 Golden Hits Of 1965:* LP, cassette and CD – Tears

1987   *Somebody Loves You:* LP, cassette and CD – Love Is Like A Violin (*Mon Coeur Est Un Violon*)

1989   *Great Stars Sing Their Greatest Songs:* CD – Love Is Like A Violin (*Mon Coeur Est Un Violon*)

1989   *Hits Of 1965:* CD – Tears

1989   *Hits Of 1966:* CD – Promises

Discography and Videos

1980s **Golden Songs From The Silver Screen:** LP – Sunrise, Sunset
1990 **Be My Love:** CD – Only You (And You Alone); I Can't Begin To Tell You
1990 **Hello Children Everywhere #3:** LP – Where's Me Shirt?
1990 **Music Of The '60s:** CD and cassette – Tears
1991 **Somebody Loves You: Classic Love Songs By The Stars:** CD – I Wish You Love; Love Is Like A Violin (*Mon Coeur Est Un Violon*)
1994 **Hits From The '60s:** CD – Happiness
1997 **Flaming June:** LP – Love Is Like A Violin (*Mon Coeur Est Un Violon*)
1997 **Greatest Singers, Greatest Songs:** CD – Still
1997 **Showstoppers:** CD – Sunrise, Sunset
1998 **Totally Groovy Hits Of The '60s (1963–1966):** CD – Tears
2000 **The Best Of The Sixties:** CD – Tears; Happiness
2003 **Sixties Number 1s:** CD – Tears Won't Wash Away These Heartaches
2005 **Memories Are Made Of This II:** CD – The River (*Le Colline Sono In Fiore*)

UNDATED
    20 Golden Vocal Chartbusters: LP – Happiness
UNDATED
    Music, Music, Music: LP – When I Fall In Love
UNDATED
    The Very Best Of The Very Best: LP – Tears

Index

Index

Index

Index

Index